Sicilian Epic and the
Marionette Theater

Sicilian Epic and the Marionette Theater

Michael Buonanno

McFarland & Company, Inc., Publishers
Jefferson, North Carolina

An earlier version of the Introduction appeared in *The World Observed: Reflections on the Fieldwork Process*, eds. Bruce Jackson and Edward Ives (Champaign/Urbana: University of Illinois Press, 1997), pp. 84–99.

LIBRARY OF CONGRESS CATALOGUING-IN-PUBLICATION DATA

Buonanno, Michael, 1954–
    Sicilian epic and the marionette theater / Michael Buonanno.
        p.   cm.
    Includes bibliographical references and index.

    ISBN 978-0-7864-7767-8 (softcover : acid free paper) ∞
    ISBN 978-1-4766-1500-4 (ebook)

    1. Marionettes—Italy—Sicily—History. 2. Puppet theater—Italy—Sicily—History. 3. Theater and society—Italy—Sicily—History. I. Title.
    PN1978.I8B755 2014
    791.5'309458—dc23   2014004129

BRITISH LIBRARY CATALOGUING DATA ARE AVAILABLE

© 2014 Michael Buonanno. All rights reserved

No part of this book may be reproduced or transmitted in any form or by any means, electronic or mechanical, including photocopying or recording, or by any information storage and retrieval system, without permission in writing from the publisher.

Front cover image: two knights (from the Collections of the Antonio Pasqualino Museo Internazionale delle Marionette); wood trim and background (© 2014 iStockphoto/Thinkstock)

Manufactured in the United States of America

McFarland & Company, Inc., Publishers
    Box 611, Jefferson, North Carolina 28640
    www.mcfarlandpub.com

Acknowledgments

My special thanks to the staff of the Antonio Pasqualino Museo Internazionale delle Marionette (International Museum of Marionettes), most particularly its founder, the late Antonio Pasqualino, and its past director, Janne Vibeak Pasqualino, for making their collections available to me for this study, as well as Anna Maria Brancatello for help in transcribing Sicilian portions of *The First Adventures of Rolandin*, Salvatore Palazzotto for help in transcribing difficult passages of *The Death of the Paladins*, Carmelo Cuticchio for explaining to me the operation of the stage apparatus and marionettes, and Teresa Brancatello-Pollina, Giacomo Cuticchio, Rita Gacioppo, and Enza Zito for many kindnesses throughout my stay in Palermo.

My special thanks as well to Dennis Tedlock, Diane Christian, and Bruno Arcudi, who advised me throughout my field project in Sicily and the writing of the dissertation upon which this study is based and particularly to Bruce Jackson who served as my dissertation advisor and permitted me to include a revised version of *The Genius of Palermo*—from *The World Observed: Reflections on the Fieldwork Process*, which he edited along with Edward Ives (University of Illinois Press, 1997)—in this volume.

Thanks to Mario Ferri for alerting me to the existence of epic at Palermo and for helping with the translation of *The Death of the Paladins* and Marcella Croce for directing me to the Antonio Pasqualino Museo Internazionale delle Marionette and aiding me in getting permissions for the photographs I took there. Thanks to Greg Hill for technical help with adjusting photograph parameters for publication, to Sabina Magliocco, Dorothy Noyes, and Luisa Del Giudice for suggestions on reworking this manuscript,

Acknowledgments

and to Anthony Tamburri and Harry Keyishian for help in placing this manuscript. Thanks to the current director of the Antonio Pasqualino Museo Internazionale delle Marionette, Rosario Perricone, as well as Maria Fasino, for finalizing permissions for the use of museum materials.

Table of Contents

Acknowledgments — v
Preface: A Storied Island — 1
Introduction: The Genius of Palermo — 5

One: The Cultural Context of Sicilian Epic — 27
Two: The Marionette Theater — 52
Three: Knights and Masques — 70
Four: Saints and Bandits — 88
Five: On Christian Soil — 109
Six: The Carolingian Cycle — 128
Seven: The Song of Roland in Sicily — 141
Eight: Social Order and the Fairy Tale — 153
Nine: City Legend and Secret Societies — 172

Conclusion: The Last Adventure — 183
Appendix: The Death of the Paladins — 199
Chapter Notes — 207
Bibliography — 217
Index — 221

Preface:
A Storied Island

Sicily—where the sea routes of Africa, Asia, and Europe converge—is a land which accrues legends and its landscape is as scoured and pocked by the exploits of its heroes as ever was Australia's by the peregrinations of its totems in the ancient times of the Dreaming. It was on Sicily's rugged coast that Odysseus, tired and hungry, incautiously entered the cave of the Cyclops Polyphemus. Luckily, he had the foresight to introduce himself to the cannibal not as Odysseus but rather as Oudeis: Nobody. Thus, when Odysseus and his men had tricked the Cyclops into tasting too much of their undiluted wine and blinded his single eye, Polyphemus, barricaded along with his intended victims in his cave, shouted out crazily to his fellow Cyclops that Nobody had poked out his eye and they ignored his mad ravings. Yet, upon escaping the treacherous monster, Odysseus couldn't resist taking credit for his trickery: "If anyone should ask who blinded you, Cyclops," he yelled as his ship set sail, "tell him it was Odysseus!" Thus, Polyphemus, bombarding Odysseus' ship with the jagged boulders that still jut out of the churning waters off Sicily's eastern coast to this day, was able to beg his father, Poseidon, to block Odysseus' passage home.

And, then, on the flower-strewn plain before Pergusa—a lake in the Sicilian interior, which because it is without a visible inlet or outlet is said to be the entrance to the underworld—Hades, burning with desire, swept down to abduct Persephone, wandering distractedly as she gathered the beautiful wildflowers. Zeus, at the urging of Persephone's mother, ordered his brother Hades, god of the Underworld, to release Persephone from his underground kingdom but Hades prevailed upon Persephone to eat but a single pomegranate seed before leaving his side, and upon tasting the rare fruit, Persephone was obliged to fulfill her wifely duty and remain with her husband and lord, Hades, for a third of each year. She issues forth from her husband's lair in the spring with the first of Sicily's preeminent crop, wheat, to spend the other two-thirds of the year with her mother, but, with the harvest over and the dreary winter settling upon the land, she retires once again to her husband's dusky kingdom.[1]

Then again, with Camelot in disarray and the knights of the Round Table dispersed, King Arthur, gravely wounded in mortal combat against his rebellious son, Mordred, was spirited by his sister, Morgan la Fey, to Sicily. The halcyon days of Camelot were there recreated in Avalon: Morgan's fairy kingdom at the foot of a belching Mount Etna. Yet, the fire and brimstone and the noxious flows of lava that the mountain daily emit are the constant reminders that this land of ghostly lords and ladies, of opulent palaces and marvelous gardens, is not Camelot but its pale counterfeit. Still, Morgan did what she could to render her magic kingdom an abode more suitable to a Christian king such as Arthur. When the Norman Count Roger first contemplated the enterprise of wresting Sicily from its Muslim overlords, he balked at the sight of the perilous Strait of Messina—that same strait which the Greeks populated with the shipwrecking monsters Scylla and Charybdis. Yet Morgan overcame Roger's hesitancy by placing a mirage in the shimmering waters between Italy and Sicily, a mirage of a city—replete with palaces, monasteries, fortifications, great gates, and sumptuous gardens—so close that one could almost touch it. The mirage—which appears in the strait to this day, and was well known

Roland (from the collections of the Antonio Pasqualino Museo Internazionale delle Marionette, Palermo). Originally published on the cover of *Journal of American Folklore*, 103, no. 409 (July-September 1990). Reprinted with permission from the American Folklore Society.

Preface: A Storied Island

enough in the nineteenth century to be mentioned by the seafarer Herman Melville in his novel *Moby Dick*—is called, after Morgan La Fey, *La Fata Morgana*. It convinced Roger to set sail in 1060 and create of Sicily a Norman kingdom. Now, in a crypt which Morgan prepared for her languishing brother in a mountain cleft, Arthur sleeps, his wounds slowly healing, until that day he awakens, rejuvenated, to reclaim his earthly kingdom. Yet, he has been seen now and again in his mountain hideaway, once in the time of the Norman King William II by a groom to the bishop of Catania who, chasing a runaway palfrey into a crevice of the mountain, was led by a "mysterious youth" to Arthur himself reclining on a sumptuous couch and displaying the wounds that open anew each year.[2]

And then there is Cola Pesce; cursed by his mother for spending all the hours of the day playing in the surf, he developed scales, gills, webbed feet and hands and was comfortable only in his beloved sea, gasping for air at those times that he had to venture onto dry land. One day Frederick II, King of Sicily and Emperor of the West, he whom the world applauds but whom Sicilian popular tradition holds a petulant tyrant, sent Cola Pesce to sound the perilous depths merely to satisfy his princely whims, throwing the half-fish, half-man baubles to retrieve when he demurred. How could Cola refuse Frederick's requests? He was a king, after all. And even if he could refuse, the glittering baubles sinking beneath the waves were more than he could bear. Nothing that Cola Pesce described—mountains and valleys beneath the waves, horrible monsters, even the fact that Sicily sat on three stone columns, one intact, another in ruins, and a third crumbling—satisfied the king, who kept sending Cola deeper and deeper until a trail of lentils streaming to the water's surface let the onlookers know that Cola Pesce had succumbed to the unknown perils of the depths, perhaps being caught in the vortex of Charybdis herself. Now, whenever the earth trembles, the people think of the third crumbling column which only Cola has seen and whose demise will spell the end of Sicily and all her inhabitants.

But, despite the continuous ebb and flow of legends which washed Sicily's shores, it was the Carolingian Cycle—the stories of Charlemagne and his hand-picked knights, the Paladins, preeminent among them Roland and his illustrious cousin, Renaud—which became, with time, the foremost folkloric expression of Sicilian culture. Since the days of the Norman conquest, Sicily's landscape has contained memories of these knights: the town of Capo d'Orlando (Cape Roland) and the promontory Monte Oliviero (Mount Oliver) commemorate the sojourn of these two Paladins who, legend has it, visited the island along with Charlemagne on their return from a crusade to Jerusalem.[3] And it was the Carolingian Cycle—particularly as it was rearticulated in Sicily's famed marionette theater—which completely revitalized the island's legendary history, offering it the singular focus which endures to this day.

Note: Throughout the text excerpts from folktales are italicized.

Introduction:
The Genius of Palermo

In the Midst of Things

On the Feast of the Immaculate Conception, I stepped out onto the street to be greeted by an extraordinary calm. I had come to Palermo to study epic but, as my fieldwork progressed, I came to find that epic—when current in a society's oral tradition—doesn't exist, and therefore can't be studied, in isolation. I found myself studying, instead, a compendium of many genres of Sicilian folklore, including not only epic but also farce, saints' lives, bandits' lives, Christian myth, fairy tales, and city legend, which commented upon, critiqued, informed, perhaps even negotiated the relations between the major classes that had historically typified Palermitan society: the aristocracy, the people, the clerical class, and the Mafia.

I had less than a month left in Palermo, and my work was reaching a feverish pitch. There was so much to do and so little time left in which to do it! But, now, the holiday seemed to offer some respite: a day off in which to simply enjoy rather than study the city. The route of that evening's procession had been laid out in arcs of incandescent lights suspended over the streets and the fitful rush of economic development, marked most notably in Palermo by an endless crunch of traffic, was momentarily halted. There are times when a low-lying blanket of wintry Mediterranean cloud—threatening to drench the city and turn its boulevards into torrents—enshrouds Palermo, when all movement is suspended, when all colors become saturated, when each detail of a particular landscape is indelibly impressed upon the memory. Such was that morning in Palermo.

Palermitans often view their city's history as a series of foreign

One of the four façades that make up the Quattro Canti, the heart of Palermo's Old City. Photograph by Urban, wikimedia.org.

occupations: Phoenician, Roman, Byzantine, Arabic, Norman, Swabian, French, Spanish, Bourbon, Italian, each leaving behind its indelible trace. And, indeed, that view made sense of what might have otherwise seemed a great jumble of architectural features as I wandered about the city that

Introduction: The Genius of Palermo

day. Palermo rises from the Conca d'Oro, the Golden Shell, an alluvial plain drenched in hot white sunshine and wedged between the sharp limestone peaks of Sicily's northern coast and the shimmering Tyrrhenian Sea. It is centered upon a low ridge that descends northward from the hills ringing the city to Palermo's harbor, La Cala.[1] Its historic center is divided into four somewhat irregular quarters by two boulevards: the Corso Vittorio Emanuele, running down the ridge from hill to harbor and presided over by the looming Cathedral, remnant of Palermo's most glorious Norman epoch, and the Via Maqueda which crosscuts the ridge just a short walk down Vittorio Emanuele from the cathedral.

Where the two intersect, demarcating the four adjacent quarters of the city's historic center, four ornate façades stand. These together form the famed Quattro Canti, or Four Corners, of Palermo. At ground level, four elegant fountains, caught in the façades' curving arcades and representative of the four rolling seasons, fill the Quattro Canti with the sound of splashing waters. Above the fountains, grand niches contain statues of four of Palermo's Spanish kings: Phillip I, II, and III, and the Emperor Charles V, under whose crown Palermo regained a slight glimmer of its old Norman grandeur. And above the kings, presiding over that square that Palermitans consider the very heart of their city, are the patron saints of the city's four adjacent—and original—quarters: Cristina, Agatha, Ninfa, and Olive. Scattered throughout this landscape are the numerous relics of a tumultuous past: here the scattered fragments of a Roman mosaic floor; there, the cracked casements of an Arabic keyhole arch; in one place, the heavily crenellated battlements of a Norman fortification; in another, the plateresque façades of Imperial Spain; throughout, the ponderous neoclassical monuments of a unified Italy.

Epic

On the morning of the procession, I took my coffee at a small café not far from my room, a place where I had stopped a few times before. The café was quiet, the day being a holiday, and the owner less harried than usual. He gave me a free coffee and asked what brought me to Palermo. "It's the only place where the Carolingian Cycle is still being told," I answered.

Introduction

As far as I know, Sicily is the only place where any of the great cycles of European legendary history—the Trojan, the Arthurian, the Carolingian—remain still in the oral tradition. Here, the stories of Charlemagne and his hand-picked knights, the Paladins, were available to me from four sources: (1) the Sicilian popular press of the nineteenth century, (2) the recitation of storytellers, today available mainly through ethnographic collections though the last remnants of this tradition were still extant while I was in the city, (3) the city's general populace, among which a wide knowledge of the Cycle is diffused and whose knowledge I only came with time to realize was invaluable to my project and, most importantly, (4) Sicily's famed marionette theater, which presents the Carolingian Cycle in some 270 hour-long episodes. It was undoubtedly the fact that the Carolingian Cycle became, over time, the preeminent matter of Sicilian puppetry[2] that epic still remained in the oral tradition where I was able to study it. Over and again, during my sojourn in Palermo, I would enter the marionette theater—its dim interior adorned with hand-painted posters depicting the scenes that were just then to be performed and presided over by the gaily painted and heavily festooned stage—amidst the maddening crash of the cylinder piano. And there I would—along with an ever-shrinking slice of the Palermitan populace and, ever more common today, a scattering of tourists—take my seat on one of the theater's spare benches. I was lucky enough to bear witness to a tradition which was rapidly giving way to, first, the cinema and, next, television and—probably as much as anything else—a reputation for being the entertainment of the masses without the veneer of glamour that contemporary products of a globalizing, consumer monoculture hold out.[3]

The café owner thought for a moment and said, "The Normans brought the Carolingian Cycle here, you know." He then added somewhat solemnly, "But they didn't take it back with them." He was intimating that the stories of Charlemagne and his Paladins somehow belonged to Palermo now, that they had somehow become Palermitan. And he looked hard at me to be sure that I had understood his meaning. "And what will you do with your studies?" he continued. "Are you writing your thesis?"

I told him that I was just then transcribing tape recordings of epic recitations from the marionette theater and translating the transcriptions into English. He was horrified: "But you'll ruin them by

Introduction: The Genius of Palermo

writing them down, in English no less. They're not meant to be read. They're meant to be heard." I explained that I would do everything in my power to translate these oral recitations to a literary medium, a process with which I am always in fact struggling, but he was only partially reassured. "Well, they might be beautiful," he said, "but not *truly* beautiful."

His proprietary concern for the stories suggested that it was not any version of the Carolingian Cycle that I was studying but the Palermitan version. He was moreover telling me that what differentiated the Palermitan version from the Old French, Franco-Venetian, and Italian versions before it was the fact that this version belonged to the city of Palermo.

A marionette from the Compagnia TeatroArte Cuticchio. Photograph by Andrea Matranga, www.andreamatranga.net/.

My task then was to understand how the Carolingian Cycle became Palermitan, how it became a legend which commented on Palermo itself. But it was only with time, and, to be honest, probably a little distance, that I learned that the Palermitanization of the Carolingian Cycle resulted most probably from the expectations and even demands of epic's predominate audience: the Palermitan working classes. This audience's ideas of a story worth hearing, a *meaningful* story, reshaped the cycle through (1) selecting the episodes which would be retold and omitting those which failed to intrigue or signify anything to the Palermitan people, (2) borrowing liberally from the rich tradition of Sicilian folk narrative (i.e., farce, saints' lives, bandits' lives, city legend, fairy tales and Christian myth) in order to reshape the retained episodes, (3) reconfiguring French knights as "types" recognizable on Palermo's streets, and, most importantly, (4) allowing those reconfigured knights to speak in real Palermitan voices. The voices which continuously intruded on the Carolingian Cycle were those of the nobility, the working poor (*il popolino*), clerics and Mafiosi, each refined and rendered more legible in a precedential folkloric genre—epic, farce, saints' lives, and bandits' lives—so that when these voices converged in the Carolingian Cycle a kind of rhetoric of Palermitan identity materialized. In fact, as I would eventually come to see, this rhetoric of identity—more than any of the admittedly stunning material dimensions of the marionette theater—was the crux of Palermitan epic, for, as puppeteers and their auditors alike continuously told me, "a marionette has no life until the puppeteer has given it voice." Thus, it was the puppeteers' voices, encapsulated in the Carolingian story itself, which would have to be the focus of my study.

Central to this immense story—as it emerged at Palermo—are the exploits of two heroes, Roland and Renaud. Roland is in essence the perfect knight, always maintaining fealty to his sovereign, Charlemagne, even when that sovereign's judgment has been clouded by the dissembling of that arch-traitor, Ganelon of Maiance. For his unwavering loyalty, Roland suffers death at the hands of the Saracens in a pass in the Pyrenean Mountains at Roncevaux, a death that has been prearranged by the traitor Ganelon with the Saracen king Marsilius. But Roland dies valiantly. He refuses to blow his oliphant and alert the main host of Charlemagne's army to the disastrous battle until he has broken the might of the Saracen host. When he finally blows the oliphant—ushering in the final apocalyptic battle between the forces of Christendom and Islam—the vein in his temple bursts. His cousin, the noble rebel, Renaud, having been banished from Charlemagne's court as a result of Ganelon's wicked machinations and resorted to banditry in order to survive, returns just in time to fight valiantly with the French at Roncevaux and hear the dying confession of his good cousin Roland:

> *Bishop Turpin, I repent having killed don Chiaro, a Christian. I repent having challenged my uncle, Charlemagne, with a glove. And lastly I repent having left my wife a virgin. Good Lord in heaven, I can barely see with my eyes! Where are you? Renaud? Ricciardetto? Bishop Turpin? I believe that I am dying. But at least I will die with my right hand towards Spain. Then, when my uncle Charlemagne finds me, he will know that I died as a hero and not as a coward!*[4]

Introduction: The Genius of Palermo

Renaud is the mirror image of Roland: a valiant knight but inverted. Instead of fealty, his troubled relationship with his sovereign is characterized by rebellion. And whereas Roland will quit the incessant battle against Saracen knights if he believes he can convert his erstwhile enemy to Christianity, Renaud inevitably fights to the bitter end. Roland's penchant for forgiveness—and, as we will see, its concomitant value, obedience—and Renaud's for vengeance—and, again, as we will see, its concomitant value, rebellion—speak to the most strikingly important difference of the two premier Paladins in the eyes of their Sicilian working-class audiences and point to the most significant feature of the Palermitanization of the Carolingian Cycle, a process to which we now turn.

Fieldwork is a funny sort of venture: one can be busily documenting a culture with little substantive result and then suddenly learn something essential while dawdling about the streets. Luckily, at some point during my stay in Palermo, I began to comprehend that some of my most important understandings of the significance of epic to the Palermitan people were to be had in some of my most casual conversations. Thus, I learned to toss my notebooks and tape recorder aside periodically and spend the day just hanging about and chatting with people. I learned, in fact, that hearing *about* the stories was just as important as *hearing* the stories. One of the first conversations I had about epic was with a shopkeeper on my street named Maria. She was probably well into her seventies and concerned herself with the welfare of everyone—particularly the young men whom elderly women in Palermo often simultaneously extol and keep in check—in the neighborhood. She insisted that I take milk with my coffee as it was winter.

"And have you had your coffee this morning?" she asked.

"Yes, Signora," I dutifully answered. "Just a moment ago."

"And did you take a little milk with your coffee?" she persisted.

"No, Signora."

"*Mio Dio*," she exclaimed to her daughter-in-law, who was just then taking inventory in the back of the shop, "here is a good boy who studies and studies, who never causes his mother any trouble; up and down the street he goes, always with his notebook in hand, and he can't even afford a little milk with his coffee. Rosaria, make the boy a cup of coffee; be sure to put a little milk in it."

Introduction

As I sipped my coffee, I explained to Maria that I was not a student at the university, but that I was in Palermo studying the Carolingian Cycle; she immediately told me whom I should like and whom I should disdain. "Don't pay any attention to Roland," she told me. "He's no good. There he had a perfectly good wife at home, Alda the Beautiful, and he ran around starting fights over Angelica, even with his own cousin, Renaud de Montauban. Renaud is the good one. Pay attention to him. He always acts honorably." Maria's privileging of Renaud over Roland is standard procedure in Palermo, where Roland is nicknamed Cross Eyes, and in fact is always depicted with eyes looking somewhat crossed and even a bit stunned, and Renaud—his eyes direct and perhaps a bit impenetrable—is nicknamed the Mafioso,[5] but what was most striking about Maria's comments to me was the fact that her interpretation of epic centered upon characters and their attributes; as a friend from a small, inland village who knew epic mainly from her village festival told me, "That's because these old people think those characters are real." A better way to explain this circumstance is to say that epic in the not-so-distant past was understood as history: history with marvelous elements added, but history nonetheless. We could probably call it *legendary* history.

An interpretive technique which centers on *legendary* history—that is, an interpretive technique which privileges characters and their attributes over, say, plot—has one special ability: allegory. Epic's characters are always literal, self-referential in their words and deeds, at one level, but they are always and equally allegorical, referring to various others through their words and deeds, on another. The penchant for allegory that characterizes epic in Palermo was pointed out to me by a friend who upon seeing a marionette of the infant Rolandin (diminutive for Roland) wrapped in swaddling clothes said, "See? The swaddling clothes! See? He's born in a cave," the cave being the traditional setting of Christ's birth in Sicilian nativities. "A shepherd is there! You understand? It's one of the puppeteers' tricks!"

Maria often commented on the adventures of Charlemagne, Roland, Renaud, Ganelon, and Angelica to me, and I once made the mistake, not having been long in Palermo and not yet knowing much about the traditional composition of epic's audiences, of asking her where she would go to see the plays. She was taken aback and said, "I've never been to one of those places!" I found out later that epic's audiences consisted exclu-

Introduction: The Genius of Palermo

Another marionette from the Compagnia TeatroArte Cuticchio. Photograph by Andrea Matranga, www.andreamatranga.net/.

sively of men and boys. Maria had learned all the stories from her brothers. And luckily, her offense at my inadvertent affront to her womanly modesty was momentarily shrugged off with the recognition that I was just another untutored, not to say dumb, foreigner.

Other conversations gave me further insights into the allegory that was elaborated in Palermitan epic. Roland was mainly disliked because he too often took the side of Charlemagne when the sovereign banished Renaud due to the various calumnies of that arch-traitor, Ganelon of Maiance. But Roland was not completely disliked. "When he's rescuing damsels or killing Saracens everyone cheers for him," one man told me. "It's just that Roland tends to be a little flat, too one-sided, always doing what he's supposed to. There are more sides to Renaud's nature." What was flat, then, was the perfect knight: a curious admixture of the loyal soldier, the martyr-saint, and, strangely enough, the Palermitan clergy. What was multi-faceted on the other hand was the knight who had the audacity to revolt. He was at once the rebellious baron of Old French epic, the bandit of Sicilian popular narrative, and the Mafioso of the Palermitan streets.

In fact, I was coming to learn that all epic's major protagonists were multi-faceted, being constructed from more than one genre of folklore, because epic existed as but one, albeit the pivotal, node in an entire folkloric repertoire. This repertoire also included farces derived from the Commedia dell' Arte: the seventeenth-century theater of improvisation which centered upon such masques—comedic characters—as Harlequin, Columbine and Punch and later, in Sicily, Nofrio and Virticchio, two vagabonds who, when it was available, took on the classic profession of Italian farces, that of the *vastone*, or porter.[6] Nofrio and Virticchio, as the comedic counterpart to that tragic pair, Roland and Renaud, will—as we will shortly see—regularly appear to comment upon, burlesque, even insert themselves into the epic arena. Thus, masque and knight will come to inhabit the same narrative space, epic themes and voices will play off their farcical counterparts, and the knight's significance will become a function of his relationship to the masque: he will become, in fact, a representative of the Palermitan aristocracy, because he fights, while the masque will become a representative of the Palermitan people because he works.

Knights and masques were soon to be joined by saints and bandits who bore with them the habitual themes and characteristic voices of their own particular genres of Sicilian popular narrative: the saint's life and the bandit's life. The saint was a permutation of the knight: noble but with a voice more aptly characterized by prayer and supplication

Introduction: The Genius of Palermo

than apostrophe and the challenge. He became epic's representative of the clerical class. Likewise, the bandit was a permutation of the masque: vulgar but with a voice better characterized by the boast and hyperbole than parody and the pun. He became epic's representative of the Mafioso.

Here is where Palermitan epic becomes interesting. The main protagonists of epic—the cousins Roland and Renaud, in particular—are not content to retain their allotted narrative function as knights. Rather, they range about their narrative space, incorporating the various characters that inhabit it and not only, chameleon-like, taking on these characters' various attributes but even adopting their mode of speaking. Thus, when the youthful Roland and Renaud find themselves banished from the court of Charlemagne and impoverished, they take on the attributes and adopt the voices of the masques who are their momentary companions, Nofrio and Virticchio. They become, through such a metamorphosis, one with the people. Palermitans seem to be thus suggesting that in order to rule justly the aristocracy must *become* Palermitan. This is especially meaningful when the aristocracy is almost—as we will see in our discussion of Palermitan history—invariably foreign. Then, when Roland in manhood puts on the mantle of the saint—converting Saracens, faring (by the way) rather badly in love, and finally sacrificing himself at the battle of Roncevaux for the sake of his uncle Charlemagne, he seems to be cut from the same cloth as the various functionaries of Palermo's clerical class. Palermitans seem to be offering in such depictions a critique of the clerical law of obedience and insinuating that the clergy acts too often as the strong arm of a sometimes oppressive aristocracy. And then again, when Renaud in manhood puts on the mantle of the bandit—robbing to earn his living, faring (by the way) much better than Roland in matters of love, and avenging his cousin's death at the battle of Roncevaux, he seems to be animated by all the swagger and bravado of the Palermitan Mafioso. In this, it seems as if Palermitans are suggesting that obedience is an untenable law leading to death and dissolution and offering an alternative law, one that allows a man to maintain his dignity in the midst of an often precarious existence: rebellion.

A secret, mythical correspondence between Roland and Renaud occurs as a result of the convergence of the various genres of folklore that are used to construct Sicilian epic: Roland, on the one hand, shares many of the attributes of Christ (and Christ surrogates): not the least of which is his self-sacrifice for the sake of his maternal uncle Charlemagne and his sounding of the horn of the apocalypse at Roncevaux. Renaud, on the other hand, shares many of the attributes of that progenitor of Christ, biblical King David: he is banned from the court of his sovereign under threat of death and takes to the mountains with a band of 600 (or 700, depending on who tells the story) brigands and he participates—as does biblical David in his youth—in comic thefts and impromptu partnerships. Together, the two heroes form a kind of double Christ for whom the laws of obedience and rebellion are not exactly opposites but rather two sides of the same coin.

What finally results from this peculiar convocation of knight, masque, saint, and bandit is epic that is at once multi-generic and dialogic: multi-generic because epic is now constructed not only in the themes of epic, but also in those of farce, saints' and bandits' lives; dialogic because knight, masque, saint, and bandit each speaks in his own particular voice, creating a kind of rhetorical cacophony that mirrors, comments on, and—from my perspective—even formulates the fabric of Palermitan society.

The multi-genericity, or construction of epic from various genres of folklore, is created from the admixture of themes, or formulaic episodes, out of which epic is constructed. Epic—whether spoken by storytellers or dramatized by puppeteers—is actually constructed in a limited set of themes,[7] most commonly oscillating between Council (the speech of the sovereign before his knights) and Battle (the facing off of opponents, quite often a Christian against a Saracen knight). But as the youthful Roland and Renaud descend among the people, they are temporarily caught in a simpler, farcical sequence of themes: Entrance (a masque aimlessly wandering upon the scene), Encounter (that masque literally bumping into another fellow), Brawl (a fight ensuing after some linguistic misunderstanding), and Exit (the two masques familiarly leaving the stage). The farcical closely mirrors the epic sequence. Then again, if a knight (most likely Roland) attempts to convert a dying pagan, certain themes from the Sicilian saints' lives such as Apparition (the appearance of an angel with orders from the Lord), Miracle (the appearance of baptismal water), and Glorification (the ascension of a soul to Heaven) will be borrowed. Likewise, if a knight (most likely Renaud) is found in revolt against the sovereign, certain themes from the Sicilian bandits' lives such as Theft (sometimes comic) and Abduction (always serious) will be borrowed. Dialogism enters epic almost automatically as a function of multi-genericity. If epic's knight temporarily takes on the role of a masque, he will speak as a masque; likewise, if he takes on the role of saint or bandit he will adopt as well their particular manner of speech. Thus, the youthful Roland and Renaud are often caught talking in the idiom of the masques: a familiar form of Sicilian rather than the knight's polite and refined Italian. And when Roland, in manhood, is caught in a saintly act he will inevitably speak in a particularly saintly prose, borrowing liberally from the cleric's liturgical repertoire. Likewise, Renaud in the perpetration of a theft will speak in a manner more consonant with the speech of a bandit, making recourse to the Mafioso's discursive use of sarcasm and the threat.

Dialogism in Action

I popped back up to my room for a moment where a singular tragedy was unfolding. Due to an inauspicious set of economic circumstances, I had taken a room in a set of one-room apartments rented out mainly to Tunisian immigrants to Palermo who were working for a while before returning home to perhaps buy a house or a shop or set up a business. One of the women was taking driving lessons so that she could start a taxi business upon returning to Tunis. I would sometimes see her gleefully barreling down the Corso Vittorio Emanuele in her conspicuously marked student-driver car, her driving instructor in the passenger seat, clutching the dashboard and white as a sheet. Her husband and son were both working as masons and would return home covered in the dust and sweat of their trade. Sometimes the Tunisians were not treated so well in Palermo, and I know our landlady was taking advantage of them. Yet, I remember one time when a Palermitan man was speaking poorly of Tunisians another stepped in to criticize him, saying, "No, the Tunisians are good people—so long as they assimilate to Sicilian society." I know that, mainly, the Tunisians managed to adapt enough to meet their goals but must have sometimes suffered terribly in a world where the word for barbarian is Turk,[8] a term resulting from the long

Introduction

years in which Sicily was the bulwark against the expansion of the Ottoman Empire and even served as the jumping-off point for the famed maritime battle of Lepanto between the forces of European Christendom and Ottoman Islam, but a word that as well seems to sometimes be used as a synonym for Muslim (just as Arab does, too often, in the United States today). I remember one night when a coup d'état was occurring in Tunisia (that very coup which brought the recently deposed Ben Ali to power) and we were watching the reports from Tunis coming fuzzily over the television (while taking turns holding the television antenna out the window), so near to Palermo is Africa. The events of the night inevitably led to discussions of the way things were back home in Tunisia and here in Sicily. Most of the Tunisians I lived with were fundamentalist Muslims and didn't empathize with the Tunisian government but one man did. He was sweeping the common area, not much more than a widened hallway, and he said he didn't care if Sicilians looked at him with disdain. "My shoes may be broken," he said, "but my pride is intact. Do you know what my pride is?" he asked. "No," I answered. "Wait a minute," he said and he went to his room and emerged with the Tunisian flag: the new moon and morning star on a field of red. He held it to the end of the broomstick and began waving it. "This is my pride," he proclaimed.

"You know what your pride is good for?" the woman taking the driving lessons asked. "Cleaning your broken shoes!" The man went to blustering that she wouldn't dare say that back home or she would have the constable (*maresciallo*) to answer to.

Beyond the Tunisians living in this set of rooms, there were me, an American, and Mohammed, a fellow from Togo. The Tunisians, Mohammed, and I shared one bath, with a toilet that could only be flushed by lugging in a bucket of water from the communal sink in the hallway and a tub that could only be supplied by a couple of buckets of water from the same sink heated by a gas plate, also in the hallway. There was no glass in the rooms' window casings but there were shutters which had to be closed in the daytime or one would come home to find that the cats who prowled the nearby rooftops had taken up temporary residency on his bed.

Mohammed, having the day off from work, had bought a chicken at the market, and, just as he was preparing to butcher it (in the same

Introduction: The Genius of Palermo

sink where I brushed my teeth, I was thinking, a bit disconcertedly), the bird flew out the window. "That stupid beast," Mohammed swore almost as soon as I had bounded up the stairs and into the hallway. "It has the mind of an animal." And, indeed, it looked pretty stupid standing out on the roof unaware that stray cats lived there and no doubt fed at times on incautious birds. Mohammed and I clambered out onto the roof of ancient and precariously slanted tile and began chasing the chicken. I was gaining more respect for this "stupid beast," which would let us come within inches of her and then flutter off, gobbling and clucking, to a point just beyond our reach. She was teasing us. As we hauled ourselves back into the window, I going first and having to catch all 270 pounds of Mohammed as he lunged headlong over the sink, Mohammed swore again, "That stupid beast! I was trying to save its life!" (In fact, he wanted to eat it.) The chicken clucked and strutted off, oblivious to the dangers that awaited her. As I was running back down the stairs, the Tunisian woman who was taking the driving lessons came in and, as her son and husband were still at work, she desperately needed someone to run to the market for her. She had learned all the possible complaints in Italian and decided to use them against me that day.

"Good morning, *Signora*," I said as I raced down the stairs.

"Oh, what a life full of misery. My stomach hurts and my tooth still aches. These Christians are so bad here. They take advantage of us and don't care if we live well or die. Only the French Christians are good. I wish we could go back there, or to Tunisia. Muslims are always good people. They take care of one another." As she was winding down, she asked me to go to the market and pick up some bread so I pocketed her proffered cash and hopped off to the Ballarò, one of Palermo's famed markets.

Is it fair to learn something from Mohammed and the Tunisians and apply it to Sicilian narrative? Does it break the rules of ethnographic verisimilitude?[9] Mohammed, the Tunisians, and I were—because of our various language skills—not always communicating through words alone but quite often through speech acts. Mohammed's speech act, I think, was syncretic, as much African as Palermitan, and I am unsure as to why he claimed to be saving the chicken's life, unless it was a means of reasoning with the chicken itself or perhaps the universe at large. The point is that this speech act was part of his attempt (unsuccessful as it was) to get the chicken back. The *Signora*'s speech act on the other hand was Palermitan, or, more properly, Mediterranean, and immediately recognizable to me; it was the lament, the spoken symbol of poverty not only in the streets but also in epic. I once heard Rolandin, in response to his mother's fearful warning that he should no longer beat up young nobles because "they can hurt us," cry: "But I am unable to accept their insults simply because I am poor; these rich men don't care if I live well or in misery."[10]

Perhaps due to my curious living arrangements, perhaps again due to the nature of fieldwork itself, I was coming to see that the voices of epic were varied through the translation of typical tones (a refined Italian, a familiar Sicilian, liturgical phraseology, sarcasm), specific speech acts (challenge, lament, prayer, boast), and various conventional figures of speech (apostrophe, pun, anaphora, hyperbole) from the streets and public squares of Palermo to the epic arena, and that when a knight, such as Roland or Renaud, changed his voice through an appropriate change in tones, speech acts, or figures of speech, he himself did not change but the thing to which he *allegorically* alluded. His knightly use of Italian, the challenge, and apostrophe alluded to the aristocracy. His masque-like use of Sicilian, the lament, and the pun alluded to the people. His saintly use of liturgical phraseology, prayer, and anaphora alluded to the clergy. And his bandit-like use of sarcasm, the boast, and hyperbole alluded to the Mafioso. It was in this marvelous cacophony of voices that the rhetoric of identity that so particularized epic to the Palermitan landscape was actualized. And it was in this rhetoric of identity that Palermitans discovered the mechanism by which they could covertly—and thus safely—explore the often fraught relationships that characterized their city's social order because once the real Palermitan voices of the aristocracy, the people, the priest and the Mafioso became embedded in epic, epic became a mirror held up to the Palermitan people where they could behold … themselves!

The Virgin and the Genius

I wandered here and there throughout the afternoon, just having a look around, until it was time for the procession. It began at the church

Introduction: The Genius of Palermo

of Saint Francis, home of the Immaculate Virgin, with a benediction, a release of white doves, and the ringing of bells. Bits of blue and yellow paper were dropped from the balconies above. They fluttered in a syncopated tumble, catching the light of the sun on each half turn, blanching and blushing as they fell. Hands stretched up to catch them for they were prayers; they read *Viva Maria Immacolata*! Long live Mary the Immaculate! A bell rang once. The penitents caught hold of the bier. It rang again. The bier was shouldered. It rang once more, and the penitents lumbered along the Via Paternoster; each locked one arm around the bier, another around the man ahead of him. Though the men beneath her stumbled and collapsed into one another, stopped to wipe the sweat from their brows, then moved haltingly along once again, the silver Virgin moved in a smooth, effortless progression, directing her gaze here and there about the adulatory crowd as a band of flutes and drums, trumpets and violins began to sound.

As she crossed the Corso Vittorio Emanuele, I ran ahead of the procession in order to arrive at the Church of Saint Dominick first and see the procession enter the square, but as I cut through the Vucciria, another of Palermo's famed markets, I caught my first glimpse of the oddest statue tucked into a niche of a wall. I thought it was a man being attacked by a serpent and I momentarily lost interest in the procession. I asked some other people cutting through the market what the statue depicted but they didn't know, so I trailed along to Saint Dominick's, where the procession stopped before a tall column supporting another Immaculate Virgin. Here, with the aid of a fire truck's hydraulic ladder, a bouquet of poinsettias was presented to the Virgin on the column, and I began to realize that this Virgin was the same as the one down on the square, Immaculate, and that it was not any Virgin who could be honored on this day, but only the Immaculate Virgin. In this case, Mary's attribute was not Intercession, Motherhood, or Pity, but only Immaculacy. Those other attributes belonged to other Marys and could only be addressed on other days, under different contexts. This circumstance is not limited to Palermo. Sabina Magliocco, for example, has noted that in Monteruju, Sardinia, the Feasts of the Assumption and the Nativity of the Virgin treat the two Madonnas as "having distinct personalities and attributes."[11] Yet, it seems to me sometimes more pronounced in Palermo, where whether in myth, legend, or folktale, a character could mean one thing in one story and then something completely different in another, and it made me think of the Greco-Roman gods who inhabited Sicily two millennia ago with their various attributes that changed from story to story. Like Mary, like Athena and Apollo, Roland and Renaud will display this uncanny, chameleonlike ability to adapt to their narratological surroundings and, in many instances, this adaptation itself will create the meaning of the story. If a young knight becomes a masque, the story involves the necessity of the aristocracy to become one with the people. If he becomes a knight again, the story involves the recognition of the poor boy's royal origins. If the knight in adulthood attempts like a saint to convert a dying pagan to Christianity, the story involves submission to God's authority, but if he resorts to banditry in order to survive, the story involves just rebellion.

The procession left Saint Dominick's and streamed into the Quattro Canti, there resting under the watchful eyes of the four quarters' patron saints. The night air was chill and the crowd hovered all the more closely about the Virgin, dark shadows flitting about the piazza, soft murmurs merging with the tumbling waters of the nearby fountains. It was here in this very same chill night air of the Quattro Canti during this same procession of the Immaculate Virgin that one of Palermo's most famous legends, that of the *Beati Paoli*, opens with an affront to a maiden's modesty.

The Beati Paoli

The innocent orphan Costanza, secretly married to the noble but penniless Corrado, is accosted by a certain Prospero, a vagrant who in the ensuing scuffle is wounded in the cheek by Corrado's sword. That evening as Corrado flies to Costanza's home disguised in the cape and beret of his manservant, he too is accosted. He gains the better of his assailant and chases him without the walls of the city. He finds himself in an open field where a group of men dressed, like himself, in capes and berets is gathering. He is herded along with the others into a secret chamber and thus by an accident of fate (and costume) finds himself in the midst of the Beati Paoli: A nocturnal convocation of men of the people whose sole intent is to avenge the injustices of the aristocracy and curb the excesses of the Inquisition. Among the petitions that Corrado witnesses that evening is one against a prince who is keeping the young son of a peasant locked up in his dungeon and administering daily beatings, another against a minister of the Inquisition who is attempting to ruin the reputation of a good family through pressing too insistently on a young daughter, and finally Prospero's petition against Corrado himself. The Beati Paoli grant Prospero his petition, the death of Corrado, but when the attempted execution is carried out, Costanza, hidden in the same cape and beret that had earlier allowed Corrado to be mistaken as a member of the Beati Paoli, is mistaken for Corrado and killed.[12]

It was as if the spirits of Constance, Corrado, and Prospero—to whose story we will later return in earnest—slipped silently among the crowd in the thick night air. The bells rang once, and the bier was shouldered; they rang once again, and the procession continued along the Corso Vittorio Emanuele. It culminated in a triumphal entrance into the Norman cathedral, massive, austere, darkening in the wintry skies, another benediction, and then (for me, as I lived just a few steps away) the vision of the procession moving steadily back to Saint Francis amidst the occasional stirrings of flutes and violins.

In the following days I tried to find out more about the statue I had seen, but the information I found was minimal. It dated to the Spanish occupation and was called the Genius of Palermo. More interesting was the fact that it was not a man being attacked by a serpent. Rather, it was a duke sitting serenely on his throne as the serpent fed at his breast. And, as it turned out, the sculptural theme was a popular one: there are at least five of these statues scattered about the city, one discovered the year I was there behind a decrepit wall. In at least one instance the Genius's throne rises from a scallop shell, the Conca d'Oro, the Golden Plain upon which the city rests, and in another a dog lies obediently at his feet. Giuseppe Pitrè, Palermo's illustrious folklorist, collected the following account of the Genius:

The Genius of Palermo

Our elders say that in ancient—oh, but very ancient—times there was a lord both rich and powerful who sailed here and there about the world simply for pleasure. One time it happened that a great tempest arose on the open sea and his ship was tossed from one side to the other. Miraculously, his ship wasn't overcome by the waves but after three days and three nights of terror—when he was next to death from fear and hunger—his ship was driven ashore on our land. He wandered here and there but found not one living soul—though the providence of God was everywhere. He fed on the fruits of our abundant plain until this lord—nearly half dead—was restored. And so he fell in love with this land—thinking it an earthly paradise—and because no one lived here and because he was very rich, he decided to here found a city. He gathered engineers and masons who constructed the city which was named, after the lord, Palermo.

Introduction

> *The same engineers and masons who built the city sculpted the marble statue of this rich lord, father and patron of the city, when he was already old. And this statue is the one found in the square of the Old Market.*[13]

Pitrè says of this story that it must surely be older than the statue and that seems likely: who would have commissioned such a statue (much less five of them) without some authorizing narrative behind it? But this story contains no mention of the serpent at the Genius' breast—much less the dog that, in one instance, lies at his feet—and thus is only a partial explanation of the statue's significance. I, at some point, became aware that the motif was characteristically commissioned by the Jurists' Guild, which apparently viewed it as a kind of emblem for its profession, but, still, that knowledge didn't lessen my quandary as to its meaning beyond offering me a vague sense that the statue had something to do with justice in some indecipherable way. But how?

I continued to nose around for some explanation of this curious symbol for the rest of my stay in Palermo: some people claimed that the statue represented the father and patron of the city; some people claimed that it somehow represented the classes of Palermitan society—but no one could say precisely how they came to their various conclusions. I was perplexed! The Genius in the Old Market is probably the most popular inasmuch as it was used to affix notes of protest during various insurrections. It was in fact thought to so much represent Palermitan rebelliousness that it was removed from the Old Market by the repressive Bourbon government—a government rendered almost paranoiac by the execution of the queen's sister—Marie Antoinette—in Paris. Only after the unification of Italy, 1860–1870, was it restored to the Market, a symbol of the people's victory over their Bourbon oppressors. The Genius that today stands before the city hall, not far from the Quattro Canti, admits a further explanation for it carries the following inscription: "Palermo, Golden Shell, you devour your own; you feed the foreigners." In effect, then, the serpent represents the foreigners who feed off the fruits of Palermo's abundant plain while Palermitans starve. But while such sentiments certainly must have existed, they could hardly have been patronized on five separate occasions through the commissioning of these statues.

This inscription is of the nature of the people's less durable protests attached to the Genius in the Old Market. Though interestingly, its

Introduction: The Genius of Palermo

oblique complaint seems to have given rise to speculation among the Palermitan populace that the Genius is the descendant of Saturn, the ancient Greco-Roman patron of Palermo, he who both gave birth to and devoured his own children. Perhaps it is this last speculation that has given rise to a little known belief, nearly lost in the murky depths of time, that the serpent which the duke, an emblem of the aristocracy, nurtures is his child, the Palermitan people (as is, almost unfathomably, the single dog that lies at his feet). What most fascinated me about this interpretation was not so much the reputed significance of the serpent but more the fact that an act of nurturance (inasmuch as the serpent's fangs are menacingly displayed) could so easily be reread as a venomous and deadly attack, as if representing the people's surreptitious warning to the aristocracy that the child, the Palermitan people, could—like Jupiter—turn on the threatening parent as well. Or, conversely, I suppose, the child could, if the father behaved according to the strict social contract which was adhered to at Palermo, lie—like a loyal dog—obediently at his master's feet.[14]

In this shadowy web of signification, I believe, lies a narrative that could have received the official patronage necessary to pay for the creation of these sculptures and their erection in prominent locales about the city for it propagated the necessity of the aristocracy in a manner consonant with the ideology of the people. The people feed off the aristocracy. If the aristocracy continues to provide the people with sustenance, the symbiosis is benign—as benign as the relationship between a man and his dog. But if the aristocracy oversteps the bounds of this social contract through tyranny, or simply fails to provide for the people through ineptitude, this benign suckling becomes a venomous sting: rebellion and retribution. This double-edged signification, it now seems to me, speaks directly to the manner in which Sicily's marionette theater has rescripted epic, shading the Carolingian Cycle with the deeper tints of a native sensibility. And it likewise speaks directly to the Palermitan people's habit of heaping abuse on that perfect knight, Roland, while covering that preeminent rebel, Renaud, in their unmitigated acclaim.

CHAPTER ONE

The Cultural Context of Sicilian Epic

The Early History

Central to understanding the pivotal place that the Carolingian Cycle holds in Palermitan folklore is a sense of the city's history—and the social order that emerges from that history—for, more than anything else, it is the inscription of Palermo's singular history in the Carolingian Cycle that makes the cycle Palermitan, that makes of the cycle—whether spoken forth by storytellers or performed by the marionette theater—a folkloric comment upon the city itself. This, I think, is the crux of the message that the café owner gave me on the morning of the Feast of the Immaculate Conception: that even if the Normans brought the cycle to Palermo, their failure to take it back with them when they receded from the stage of Palermitan history meant that it became the city's inheritance, the special legacy by which the city communicated its deep essence to itself. So let me take a moment here to chart Palermo's history, the effect of that history on the city and its inhabitants, and the infusion of the message of that history into the very fabric of the Carolingian Cycle.

The earliest occupants of Palermo have left scant remnants: Phoenicians, who founded the city along with a few other colonies on the northwestern coast of Sicily in the eighth century B.C., some vestiges of their once impressive fortifications; Greeks, who began colonizing Sicily shortly thereafter, but without ever dislodging Palermo's Phoenician inhabitants, a scattering of trade goods found among Phoenician artifacts. It was the Romans who finally chased the Phoenicians from their Sicilian stronghold. The Punic Wars, fought between Rome and Carthaginian Phoenicians, revolved largely around Sicily. Palermo was

The scant remains of Palermo's Phoenician origins; a stretch of the city's original fortifications incorporated into the wall of the Monastery of Santa Caterina. Photograph by SPQP, wikimedia.org.

taken by the Romans in the First Punic War (264–241 BC) and its inhabitants sold into slavery.[1] Greek Sicily, in the east, held out by means of an alliance with Rome but, when in the Second Punic War (218–201 BC) that alliance broke down, Greek Sicily fell too. Upon Roman entry, the majority of Sicilians, despite ethnic affiliation, were most likely speakers of Greek. Even culturally, Sicilians seemed to have participated more in Greek than Phoenician or Italic traditions: "Sacred heralds toured the island and summoned representatives to Delphi and other pan–Hellenic shrines; public buildings remained essentially Greek in style; and an occasional Sicilian ... turned up among the victors at the Olympic games."[2] And, in fact, it was the Greek name for Palermo, Panormus, or Great Harbor, rather than the Phoenician, Zis, which has endured to this day.

Of the Roman occupation, one finds a broken wall here and there, rising upon the base laid down by Rome's Phoenician predecessors and reworked by her Arabic and Norman successors, and sometimes among these scattered ruins one can find the remnants of mosaic floors, those at the Piazza Bonanno, on the Corso Vittorio Emanuele just above Palermo's cathedral, still largely intact. The Vandals and Ostrogoths who displaced the Romans in the late fifth and early sixth centuries occupied the city for too short an interval to leave any significant trace and even the Byzantines, who reestablished imperial rule—as well as Greek culture—from the early sixth to the early ninth centuries have left less than the Romans. This last occupation ended when the Byzantine admiral Euphemius invited the Aghlabid emir of Tunisia to aid him in his bid to become governor of Sicily, offering the island as an Arab tributary: "The response came immediately. An elite army of more than 10,000 men—Arabs, Berbers and Spanish Moslems—landed at Mazara, and another conquest of Sicily had begun."[3] The conquest lasted from 827 to 965, Palermo falling early on in 831.[4] Here a theme of Sicilian history made itself felt: "internal dissent [leading] to a foreign invader being invited in."[5] And as Christianity yielded to Islam and the Greek language of the Byzantine empire to Arabic, Palermo, now called Balerm, became the premier city of Sicily, and its court is said to have rivaled those of Cairo and Baghdad, but the monuments—including, by some counts, 300 mosques—of Arab Sicily in that city that were not destroyed in the succeeding Norman invasion[6] have been so heavily built over by subsequent generations that they are barely recognizable for what they were. Still, the stonework on the inner wall of the church of St. John of the Lepers is the original Arab construction of a fort seized by the Norman, Roger I, in his invasion of Palermo.[7] And Il Cassaro, the original name of the Old City's major thoroughfare, the Corso Vittorio Emanuele, is a cogent memorial to the Arabic fortification that stood at its head: Al Kasr.

The Norman Kingdom of Sicily

The Normans entered southern Italy around the year 1000, apparently as pilgrims without hostile intent, but, once there, they became caught up in the continuous squabbling of Lombard, Byzantine, and Muslim territories and gained a reputation as fearful mercenaries.

Robert Guiscard came south around 1046 or 1047. There, his half-brothers, William, Drogo, and Humphrey, were in successive control of Apulia. "His brothers gave him no welcome. He was left to make his own fortune, initially more or less as a brigand and horse-thief with a few followers in Calabria." And even as he wrested control of Apulia from his half-brothers' heirs, another of his brothers, Roger, launched his invasion of Sicily in 1060.[8] The Normans first entered Sicily in the same way as did the Arabs, by invitation.

> Moslem Sicily was at first a dependency of the Aghlabids, but early in the tenth century a civil war, complicated by the advance of the heretic Shiites, overturned this Tunisian dynasty. Their successors, the Fatimids, then moved eastwards and in 969 set up their capital in Egypt. Sicily was left much more independent, and by the 960s the Kalbid family had established themselves as the effective rulers of the island, binding the military nobility to them by ties of interest and patronage. Greater independence, though, was scarcely a gain. The move of the Khalif to Cairo was followed by the break-up of the North African civilization to which Sicily had belonged. The island was thus isolated, and Christian Europe at last had a chance to counterattack.
>
> An early sign of this was in the 1030s when the Kalbid Emir, confronted with rebellion, made a treaty with Byzantium. Local Moslem support was therefore forthcoming when George Maniaces, a Byzantine general, landed near Messina with a large force that included several hundred Norman mercenaries. These latter no doubt observed the richness of the country and propagated among their friends the idea of further piratical raids. Maniaces occupied much of eastern Sicily for several years and did much damage. But this was the last serious attempt by Byzantium to recover Sicily, and court intrigues at Constantinople soon forced Maniaces' recall. The Mediterranean balance of power had swung against both Constantinople and Cairo. Western Christendom was now on the offensive, and when Roger the Norman landed near Messina in 1060, the days of Moslem Sicily were numbered.[9]

By 1093, the Normans had conquered the entire island and retained Palermo, captured in 1072, as their capital.[10] The reign of the Norman rulers, including Roger I (1061–1101), Roger II (1101–1154), William I (1154–1166), and William II (1166–1189), enduring for 130 years, is considered by historians and Palermitans alike as Sicily's golden age,[11] and it is Palermo's Norman architecture that distinguishes it from any other city of the world, perhaps because the Normans called upon the vibrant Byzantine and Arab traditions of Sicily not only to administer their realm but also to adorn their edifices. The Norman palace, a stark and jagged citadel built upon the remains of Al Kasr, presides over the upper

One: The Cultural Context of Sicilian Epic

The Norman palace, built upon the remnants of Al Kasr, creates a formidable barrier between the hills above and the city's historic center, situated on the Golden Shell, beneath its Battlements. Photographer not specified, wikimedia.org.

horizon of the old city, creating a formidable barrier between the hills above and the city below. Its massive stone walls and heavy crenellation are cracked with age but sound as a result of successive generations' repairs. Inside is hidden the pearl of Palermitan artistry, the Palatine Chapel, a sumptuous basilica of golden mosaics, delicate spiraling columns, and geometric stone inlays glimmering quietly in a diffuse and tranquil light.

Somewhat midway down the Corso Vittorio Emanuele, between the Norman palace and the Quattro Canti, is the Norman cathedral. Here, the massive walls and unyielding crenellations are softened with slender lancet arches and geometric inlays of colored stone. The original Norman structure has been heavily reworked by successive generations. Gothic porticoes and towers were added in the fourteenth and fifteenth centuries and a grand neoclassical cupola at the turn of the nineteenth. I once heard a Palermitan asking a foreigner what he thought of Palermo's cathedral. And the foreigner, predictably failing the Palermitan's test, gave the standard response, that the gothic and neoclassical additions spoiled the pristine Norman design. "Yes," the Palermitan sighed, "this is what all the foreigners say."

Even more stunning to me than the major monuments of Palermo's Norman epoch however are the Churches of Saint John of the Hermits, Saint John of the Lepers, and Saint Cataldo. Soaring above the heavy stone construction in each of these churches, clusters of magenta domes speak of the Arabic occupation which ended with the Norman invasion. In my mind, these Arabo-Norman domes signify Palermo, perhaps because of the inability to determine precisely whether they represent Greek, Arab, or Norman culture: "Norman-Arab art and architecture," M. I. Finley points out, "exist as a vivid cultural phenomenon for most of the twelfth century. Woodwork and mosaic, coins and vestments, sculpture and lettering, show how a heterogeneous admixture of styles could in effect constitute a style of its own. The same too goes for architecture. With its five red cupolas, St. John of the Hermits seems as much

Palermo's cathedral. Photograph by Bengt Nyman, wikipedia.org.

a mosque as a Christian shrine."[12] And this amalgam of styles extends—or so it seems from the reports of those who sojourned at Palermo in the period—to every aspect of twelfth century Palermitan culture: needlework, administration, cuisine, and law. The Arab voyager, Ibn Jubayr, for instance, pointed out the "contentment" of Palermo's "Muslim subjects," commenting "in particular on the hospitals and almshouses provided by Muslims and Christians alike; and he noted with interest that the Christian women of the island followed the fashions of Muslim women; they wore veils and abbas when they went out of doors, and never stopped talking."[13] And while "Arabs and Jews had to pay a special tax…, Norman charters, following Arab precedent, ensured that 'Latins, Greeks, Jews and Saracens [should] be judged each according to their own law' and by their own judges."[14] Moreover, Arabic, the dominant language of the Sicilian people at the onset of the Norman invasion,[15] endured as "the language of government" in Sicily "for over a century after the Norman conquest."[16]

The Sicilian Vespers

Yet, the Norman occupation, in the scheme of things, was not a long one. With the death of William II, there was no Norman heir to the throne of Sicily; thus, the crown passed to the Swabian Henry Hohenstaufen, son of the Western Emperor, Frederick Barbarossa, and Sicily's second Norman king's daughter, Constance, and from them to their son, Frederick II. Under Frederick II's rule, Palermo lost some of its prestige for, though Frederick grew up in the city, he was Western Emperor—ruling Germany and much of Italy—as well as king of Sicily, and thus Sicilian affairs (at least in the minds of Sicilians) suffered.[17] Though the court was still at Palermo, Frederick, who had grown up there and said he only felt at home in that city, was most often abroad.[18] And, then, with the death of Frederick, dynastic strife—once again—threw Sicily into turmoil. The pope, in an attempt to weaken the power of the Western Emperor, championed the French Charles of Anjou to keep Manfred, Frederick's illegitimate son and the last Hohenstaufen ruler of Sicily, off the Sicilian throne. This intrigue led to Sicily playing a pivotal role in the history of Europe—simultaneously crushing the short-lived but oppressive regime

Sicilian Epic and the Marionette Theater

Church of the Holy Spirit. Photograph by Enzian44, wikipedia.org.

of Charles in Sicily and ending the complicitous papacy's hope of establishing, through Charles' military might, a theocratic state in Europe.[19] The papal design was subverted through a rebellion that began just before the vesper service on Easter Sunday, 1282, and is celebrated in one of Palermo's most important city legends.

> *The Sicilian Vespers*
>
> In Palermo, the French governed and there was a master shoemaker who had a wife as beautiful as the sun. The king had her called before him on a pretext and afterwards he married her. The Palermitans mocked her, saying, "Prima cuncupina, e ora riggina; First a concubine, now a queen." The king was angered and to spite the houses of the Palermitans he decreed that every girl who married had to sleep with a soldier on the night of the wedding.
>
> Giovanni Procida had a daughter who was promised, but, on hearing the cast of this law, he was afraid to let her marry. There was a captain living with him, posted as an orderly for the neighborhood. Giovanni said, "How can I allow my daughter to marry when she will carry the stigma (along with all the others) of having a soldier the first night? I won't permit her to marry." But he did, and when she returned from the church, the captain wanted her. The girl

One: The Cultural Context of Sicilian Epic

> fled and, throwing herself from a window, was killed. Her father could bear no more and feigned madness. He went about murmuring through a deaf horn into the ears of everyone. To the Palermitans he was saying, "On the Feast of the Holy Spirit," and he told them what day that was, "we will kill the French." Before the French he feigned madness. And in this manner he traveled about all the towns and villages and the French left him alone. They mocked him believing he was truly mad.
>
> When the hour arrived, I don't know how the fighting began, but the slaughter broke out at the Church of the Holy Spirit and from there spread everywhere. Not one Frenchman survived. The terrible thing is that even the pregnant French women were massacred and that was unjust. In order to know if someone were French, he was told to say čiči [chick pea] and if he said çeçi he was killed because the French don't know how to say čiči.[20]

The legend provocatively transects history. On Easter Monday, AD 1282, before the vesper service at the Church of the Holy Spirit, Palermo, a French sergeant harassed a young Sicilian woman, and her husband killed him. When the sergeant's comrades attempted to avenge him, they were likewise slaughtered. The carnage spread throughout Palermo where "the rioters broke into the Dominican and Franciscan convents; and all the foreign friars were dragged out and told to pronounce the word čirčiri [chick pea],[21] whose sound the French tongue could never accurately reproduce. Anyone who failed the test was slain.... By the next morning some two thousand French men and women lay dead; and the rebels were in complete control of Palermo."[22]

The Sicilian Vespers is among the most important of Palermitan city legends and sets forth a theme to which we will repeatedly return: the antagonism between a foreign nobility and the native populace. Intriguing is the legend's retention of the name Giovanni Procida. Though it has never been definitively established to what extent it was he who fomented the discontent against the papal champion, Charles of Anjou, he was, as advisor to Queen Constance (the daughter of Manfred and wife to Peter of Aragon who, through her, would obtain the Sicilian throne) an integral member of the Aragonese government which took the reins of power in Sicily in the rebellion's aftermath.[23] Thus it was that Sicily began her long history under Iberian rule, first a tributary to Aragon and, then, with the union of Aragon and Castile in the personages of Ferdinand and Isabella, as a tributary to Spain. For the better part of the next five centuries, Sicily would be ruled by viceroys appointed by the Spanish crown and though the "term 'Viceroy' was at least an acknowledgement in theory that here was a distinct kingdom," of the "seventy-eight successive appointees, very few were Sicilians by origin, and none at all after the first fifty years.... When the first Viceroy was appointed, a group from Messina misread the situation and asked him to become an independent King of Sicily. He refused, and few such proposals were ever heard again."[24]

The Decline of Empire

With the death of Frederick II, Palermo's position as an imperial capital—enriched by the coffers of its Norman and Hohenstaufen overlords—diminished. Then, under Charles of Anjou, the government of Sicily, along with that of southern Italy, was consolidated at Naples, only—as a result of the Sicilian Vespers—to be transferred, yet again, to Aragon. Finally, with the unification of Spain, Sicilian governance emanated from Madrid. Still, to this day, working and middle class Palermitans describe their history in the context of the dynasties which ruled them and the presence, or lack thereof, of a court at Palermo. This concern with the aristocracy is underscored by the fact that Palermitans even have a word, *cortigghiu*, or "court gossip," for discussion of intrigues and happenings in high places.[25] Perhaps this concern with the aristocracy results from the manner in which historians treat history. Perhaps again it results from the fact that the history of the working people is so little known. But, whatever the cause, an abiding concern of the Palermitan people has been the presence and composition of their court; is it Palermitan or is it foreign? After the Norman period—though the Normans presided over a diverse population consisting not only of Normans but also Arabs, Byzantines, and Jews[26]—the local populace seemed to view the court to be less and less Palermitan,[27] and, worse still, more pronouncedly subsidiary to a foreign power. And as Palermo moved from the center to the peripheries of imperial authority, the city lost not only in prestige but probably economic security as well. After all, the city which hosts an important court is generally more prosperous for its inhabitants. As the old Italian proverb, reported by Antonio Gramsci, cynically states: "Where a horse shits a hundred sparrows feed."[28]

One: The Cultural Context of Sicilian Epic

Palermo's famed Porta Nuova (New Gate), erected to commemorate the campaigns of the Emperor Charles V over the Ottoman forces of Suleiman the Magnificent, flanks the Norman palace and stands not only as the ingress of the Corso Vittorio Emanuele into the heart of the city but also the egress of the road to Monreale. It is the only true gate left in what remains of the city's once extensive network of gates and fortified walls. Photograph by Bernhard J. Scheuvens, wikipedia.org.

Not only did Palermo suffer a diminution of its position in the movement from Norman through French to Spanish rule but so too did all Sicily. The island had already been "deprived of the stimulating connection with Greece and Africa which had almost seemed a condition of her past greatness,"[29] and now she was annexed to the far-flung Spanish empire. It almost seems that Sicily became an early experiment in Spanish colonialism with her productivity siphoned off to invest in Spanish fortunes. Finley suggests as much when he claims that "[e]ven though Sicily escaped the trade monopoly practiced in Spain's New World dominions, this was still colonial rule of a kind: commodities were exported raw, navigation was run by foreigners, and agriculture was made to serve imperial policy."[30] It seems likely that this early experiment in colonialism gave rise to some of the less savory mechanisms Sicily developed to deal with exploitation: various secret, and sometimes criminal, societies—which seemed to proliferate during the Spanish occupation—as well as occasional violent upheavals. One rebellion in particular, at Palermo in 1647, stands out, as a significant riot of the city's populace over the lack of bread. It may have been led by "the escaped convict and murderer, La Pilosa, who seems to have linked the Palermo underworld with that of the surrounding villages."[31] During this insurrection, the rebels marched on "the Senate Palace fully intending to burn it down. There the protesters were pacified by priests reminding them of the risks they were taking."[32] It should be here noted that priestly collusion with a foreign aristocracy—even to the point of threatening the people with hell's fire should they dare rebel—is another theme of Palermitan history, recalibrated in epic, to which we will return.

Yet priestly collusion aside, Spain—slowly, inexorably—began to lose its grip on Sicily, though it was not until the eighteenth century that Sicily's last links with Spain were finally broken. With the appointment of Charles III to the Spanish throne in 1759, "the rest of Europe," fearing his growing might, "would not let him keep Sicily and Naples as well; so he presented these two kingdoms to his son, who became Ferdinand IV of Naples and Ferdinand III of Sicily.... The new King Ferdinand was to call himself an *Infante* of Spain and at first took orders from Madrid; but during his long reign of sixty-six years Sicily more and more developed the links which bound her to Italy.[33] Thus began,

One: The Cultural Context of Sicilian Epic

in the mid-eighteenth century, the Spanish Bourbon rule of the Kingdom of the Two Sicilies with Naples as its capital. Yet, hatred of rule from Naples, soon outstripping that of rule from Madrid, reached a peak in that year of revolutions, 1848:

> The first days [of that year] were a time of exceptional unrest in Palermo. Rumours of a new constitution were in the air. An unsigned manifesto circulated that claimed to speak for a probably non-existent revolutionary committee. It announced that a revolt for Sicilian freedom would start under cover of the King's birthday festivities on 12 January. The ruse succeeded and, when the day arrived, a popular preacher in the Fieravecchia began an incendiary harangue which set off a riot. The streets in the richer residential districts quickly emptied, doors were barricaded, and the shutting of shops added to the general alarm by raising fears of a food shortage. By the evening, barricades were going up. Early on the 13th, squads of peasants and "mountaineers" had already arrived in Palermo. Money had been seized from a government courier returning from the interior. The revolt was off to a flying start.
>
> The small class of liberals suddenly discovered that political reforms might now be attainable, whether Sicilian autonomy, a liberal constitution, or possibly a federal Italy.... [Outside the city], the news from Palermo ... was a signal for all who had a grievance to rise and remedy it, and this gave the revolt an immense and unexpected force. In the villages and towns there were bread riots and attacks on the "clubs" where the *galantuomini* [gentlemen] used to meet. Sheep were killed, hayricks burned, and ... woodlands destroyed as land was seized and cleared for cultivation. Often the Town Hall was attacked and a bonfire made of the title deeds to property. Government ceased as officials fled for their lives. The tribal morality of a subject population was evidenced in a general assassination of policemen and suspected informers, sometimes with unbelievable cruelty.
>
> Another element in the rising was the sudden appearance of the armed squads, often brigand bands under the leadership of a local underworld figure. Some of these men had probably been, and went on being, Bourbon employees. Others were hired by the ex-barons or even the liberals as a private police force. Still others were anarchic characters who simply used the riots as an occasion to fish in troubled waters. A breakdown of government was an ideal situation for them, especially when they could expect payment from one side or both. Men of criminal propensity ... now seized effective power in their villages and marched their men into Palermo, where for several months they remained near the centre of power.[34]

A year later, the revolution was collapsing and as Bourbon troops reentered Palermo, the populace in a desperate bid to save the city, dug trenches "round the capital, and ministers, priests, titled ladies and peasants from twenty miles around all lent a hand."[35]

The Bourbon regime definitively ended in 1860 with another popular insurrection, the arrival of Garibaldi in Sicily and the unification of Italy. But even here disenchantment quickly set in. Soon after the 1860 rebellion, "the legend was allowed to develop that Sicily had initiated a patriotic revolution only to be ... annexed [by Italy] as a conquered colony."[36] Thus, the "same anti-government feeling which originally made possible Garibaldi's success against [the Bourbon government of] Naples was soon directed against Italy itself, and the first anniversary of the rebellion was celebrated with a riot."[37] Here again, the desire for independence or, at the very least, some degree of self governance emerges as a dominant feature of Sicilian history, but whereas the independence movement that eventually took root in Sicily after World War II seemed almost chimerical in nature (even postulating making Sicily a star on the American flag, so many Sicilians by then residing in the United States), autonomy, a more realistic goal, was finally granted to Sicily by the Italian government in 1946.

The Arabo-Norman architecture which so defines the city's grandeur to its inhabitants and guests alike gives way over the turbulent centuries to a number of Gothic styles that were patronized by the Normans' Swabian, French, and Aragonese successors. The clusters of magenta domes that seem almost to float over a languid city and the stark crenellations beneath them are methodically hidden by rose windows, slender colonnades, and delicate spires as the sumptuous Goto-Catalan style wraps the city in its ornate mantle. Next, under a newly unified Spain, the heavy Renaissance gates and palaces, tiered and varied through the use of Doric, Ionic, and Corinthian flourishes, transform the city but these give way in turn to the ornate baroque façades which define Imperial Spain. In the statuary of this period, angry prophets raise their fists at the city while the gentle patrons shed quiet tears over it. With a single blast of Gabriel's horn, plump cherubs fall from the clouds and angels supplicate the Immaculate Virgin with hands extended in mournful prayer. Here, Emperor Charles V strides into the city in the guise of a beggar, ferreting out corruption in Palermo's judiciary; there, he presides over the city in all his imperial majesty, the corrupt judges flayed and their skin upholstering the seats of the new judiciary. Baroque architecture continues through the Bourbon period, and finally the neoclassicism of a newly unified Italy fills out Palermo's architectural scheme with its grand theaters, stately palaces, and ornate kiosks.

Throughout this tumultuous history, the curious tension between the rulers and the ruled—as if the historical context forever impinges upon the present—remains a defining feature of Palermo's political landscape; it is a tension that Giuseppe di Lampedusa aptly inscribes in his memoir of the decline of the old aristocratic order and the emergence of modern Italy: "The rains had come, the rains had gone," he glibly intones, "and the sun was back on its throne like an absolute monarch kept off it for a week by his subjects' barricades, and now reigning once again, choleric but under constitutional restraint. The heat braced without burning, the light domineered but let colors live; from the soil cautiously sprouted clover and mint, and on faces appeared diffident hopes."[38]

Social Order

Aside from its architectural splendors, Palermo, at first blush, seems like any complex mercantile city, a bustling port frenetic with the labor of many classes of men and women, each going about its own particular act of production and feverishly trading one item for another. As in all mercantile societies, class structure is based on a hierarchy of occupational categories which, for most of the city's history, encompassed a continuum between urban, rural, and seafaring laborers too multifaceted to do more than outline. And while Palermo today is an industrialized city participating like much of the rest of the world, America included, in a global economy, its citizens—especially the elderly—well remember an existence characterized by *miseria* (misery): an existence without enough food, sufficient work, or decent housing, an existence characterized by an unending scramble to make a hard living.

At the simplest peasant level—now almost nonexistent—shepherds and farmers lived side by side with various tradesmen in the villages of Palermo's hinterland. Absolutely necessary to even the smaller hamlets were the miller, blacksmith, saddle maker, cartwright, carpenter, cask maker, tinsmith, cobbler, tanner, and sieve maker, whose product was "wooden rings of different sizes, like tambourines, on which meshes of wire or pierced metal or woven leather cords in varying textures were stretched taut to winnow and grade wheat, olives, beans, and other crops."[39] The farmer, his frame bent under the tiresome labor of working his fields with his short, stout hoe—a necessity in such hilly terrain where the plow was not always tenable and draft animals costly—might have at one time grown the Sicilian staple, wheat, and rented his land with a portion of his crop; the shepherd might have paid for his grazing rights with the ricotta that his wife daily boiled from his sheep's milk. As elsewhere in the Mediterranean, the farmer feared the shepherd's wandering ways and precarious economy, and the shepherd envied the farmer's very relative wealth and stability. The shepherd anxiously guarded his flocks from potential rustlers, and the farmer nervously eyed the rainbow to predict his too often insufficient harvest: would he take in enough grain to supply him with a year's worth of bread (more yellow), produce enough must—squeezed grapes—from which he would vint his wine (more red), or press enough olive oil to flavor the piece of bread that for days on end formed his sole meal (more green)?[40] Today, one would find these peasants for the most part replaced by families who own their land and houses and, most importantly, have, unlike their progenitors, enough to eat. But even they—who can invariably afford the luxury of a kitchen with the latest appliances—are as apt to reserve their modern kitchens for show and will often continue their productive activities in the old-fashioned kitchens of their peasant forebears.

Fishing, from what I was told—and my information here is sketchy—was always considered more of a trade than a subsistence strategy and was never as widespread as farming or shepherding. In the post-war period, upwards of two-thirds of Sicily's 4 million inhabitants were farmers or shepherds; fishing would never have realized those sorts of numbers—even when taking into consideration the tuna fisheries with their extravagant *Matanzas*.[41] For one thing, the tools of the trade, most notably the boat but also the nets, lines, traps, and tackle, presented expenses that not too many—in the past, at any rate—could easily afford. Thus, fishermen were most likely to be wage laborers or, perhaps, a *padrone* (boss) would be the provisor of these tools and the fisherman would pay him back with a portion of his take. In rare cases, a cooperative might form to purchase a boat and fishing gear collectively—or some entrepreneurial fisherman might be able to finance his business on his own or with the

One: The Cultural Context of Sicilian Epic

help of his family—and then the day's take could be sold directly to a merchant in one of Palermo's markets. But such ventures were fraught with difficulty—as the Luchino Visconti film, *La Terra Trema* (1948), aptly illustrated—and the liability to lose rather than make money was a real possibility. Further, it seems that the bigger fishing concerns could undersell small fishermen and thus cut them out of the market.

As one moves from village to city, the trades increase exponentially and the traditional artisans are more and more augmented by industrial workers and the providers of innumerable services—bankers, teachers, police, and a proliferation of civil servants—all participating in a globalizing consumer economy.[42] Still, during my stay, those trades involving the provision of food, shelter, and clothing, and the tools to process or outfit those three commodities, seemed to predominate the Sicilian economy—at least for those lucky enough to have work, unemployment then hovering—I was told by locals—at an unhealthy 50 percent. Some trades—at least to my senses—seemed to be more omnipresent and evocative of the culture than others. I was always enthralled to see the bakers bustle through the streets in their white shorts and T-shirts in the midst of winter, a tray of freshly baked loaves held aloft to escape the dangers of the jostling crowd, or the chestnut vendors who would take a small handful of steaming nuts from their roasters and press them upon a homeless beggar. One could peek into the open shop doorways to see cabinet and furniture makers hammering away at the fixtures and furnishings that would outfit the interiors of Palermitan apartments. The laundresses too could be seen at their work, the doors of their establishments always flung open to let out the heat of their irons and presses.

There seems to have historically been a sort of clustering of trades in certain neighborhoods and a tendency to marry within that trade and thus, necessarily, within that neighborhood: Palermitan marital patterns were then characterized by a certain degree of endogamy (marriage within the group). Danilo Dolci, in the years immediately following World War II, speaks to Ignazio, a forty-year-old rag picker from Cascino Alley, just "two hundred yards from the cathedral," not more than a few steps from my own neighborhood. Cascino Alley consisted of some 1,500 people living in one-room houses, with dirt floors, sometimes a dozen people to the house. There was no running water, and chamber pots were emptied onto the alley. Outbreaks of typhus occasionally quarantined the neighborhood. The men of Cascino Alley would rent carts from bosses (*padroni*) who also provided them with a small amount of cash to purchase "scrap metal, used goods, [and] rags." The women of Cascino Alley were characteristically laundresses: "There's the rag pickers and the washerwomen," Ignazio explained: "Others don't do a thing. A few make and sell little pennants with pictures of Saint Rosalia. Then there's the prostitutes, but they do their work in other sections of town. See, we all know everybody's business. Most of the kids never go to school. They just play in the alley in that stink. When the girls get to be twelve or thirteen, they hurry and try to get married. But it's like intermarriage in this alley. Rag pickers marry off washerwomen to rag pickers, and vice versa." [43]

Nowhere is the freneticism and intense productivity that so defines Palermo more apparent than in the city's major markets: the Vucciria, Ballarò and Il Capo. To me, the Vucciria epitomizes the Palermitan market. It takes its name from the French *boucherie*, the butcher's quarter, and is the oldest of the city's markets. Here, one finds a varied collection of booths bordered by shop fronts and presided over by long tables buckling under the weight of eels, squid, octopus, and sardines. Here too one can find that old fashioned favorite, *milsa*, cow spleen, chopped and simmered in a rich broth, ladled onto a roll, and covered in grated cheese. Palermo's shepherds provide mutton, pork, beef, and cheese to the market. Its fishermen provide all the various species that the Tyrrhenian Sea affords. Fruit from the orchards—Sicily has been a rich producer of citrus since Arabic times—and vegetables—squashes and legumes, tomatoes and innumerable greens—from the gardens of the small agricultural villages that surround the city are always plentiful, and it seemed that in Palermo one supped often enough on a plate of pasta smothered in whatever fresh vegetables the market had to offer that day topped off perhaps with a pan of grilled sardines. The merchants ply their wares feverishly, and though a modern market economy with weights and prices prominently displayed, generally chalked on small pieces of wood, prevails, each transaction is based on a number of variables: how much you shop at the booth, how much you are just then buying, what wares or services you might provide the merchant in turn, and, perhaps just as important, how much the merchant likes you.

My favorite shop was a little niche in a building too small to display

A glimpse down the street reveals a slight glimpse of the Vucciria. Photograph by the author.

the various dates, olives, and figs that the shop had to offer, so that the wares spilled out onto the square in barrels, crates, and sacks. What I liked most about the shop were its proprietors, a grandmotherly and grandfatherly couple who would make me taste any number of olives before permitting me to buy my small handful and then would always drop a couple figs in my bag. They smiled so effusively to me—and all their customers—as they proudly displayed their wares and forced free tidbits on each and every visitor alike. But when they came face to face, their smiles vanished and they scowled menacingly at one another until finally one or the other broke into a string of bitter invective. And then, having vented their spleens, they passed joyfully back to work. Palermitans sometimes wear their emotions on their sleeves; yet, at others, they seem so private, displaying an almost alarming modesty, especially the women. At one moment they express a frank openness but at another an obvious distrust and even fear of strangers and perhaps especially foreigners. The market seems to emphasize this polarity as well as that which sometimes obtains—there and elsewhere—between the working classes and the elite whose relationships are somewhat strained in Palermo, characterized by patronizing attitudes by the elite on the one hand, diffidence by the working classes on the other. Perhaps this is why Palermitans, like other Italians, say "putting it in the market" to mean what Americans mean when they say "airing their laundry."

In the Vuccria, as in the other markets of Palermo, imports and manufactured goods were ever present. Perhaps they are even more so today; the great freighters that transport them to and fro are only a short walk away in Palermo's industrial port. But during my stay in Palermo, the Vuccciria was predominantly a market of local produce, patronized by local artisans and workers: barbers, hoteliers, barkeeps; monks, priests, nuns; shoemakers and tailors; Mafiosi, bankers, and soldiers; civil servants, teachers, and police.

The Palermitanization of the Carolingian Cycle

What remains to be seen in this excursus on Palermitan history and social organization is the manner in which the Carolingian Cycle is rendered Palermitan: that is, the manner in which the Palermitan people effect the Palermitanization of epic, appropriate the Carolingian Cycle and make it their own, invest the cycle with the historical tapestry and social context just now outlined. In order to get a sense of that process, we have to look at the cycle as it was received by Palermo—not

One: The Cultural Context of Sicilian Epic

A sign advertising a marionette theater with a glimpse of a Palermitan Street behind. Note Charlemagne (Carlo Magno), top center, flanked on the left by Roland (Orlando), the right by Renaud (Rinaldo). Roland's eyes are notably crossed here; this is a common feature in Palermitan depictions of Roland but is not found in the Italian literary tradition from which the Palermitan version arises. Angelica is depicted, bottom center. Notice her feathered headdress. She is spoken of as an Indian princess of Cathay and the Native American headdress results from the Indian appellation. She is said to be a pagan, and in "The Battle of Roland and Agrican" (see chapter five) she swears by the gods, Magon and Trevigant, who—according to the tradition of the marionette theater's narratives—are, along with Mohammed, part of a Saracen trinity. Photograph by the author.

probably as my earlier interlocutor, the café owner, suggested, at the hands of Sicily's Norman conquerors but more likely as an inheritance from the Italian literary tradition—as well as the cycle as it was transformed by the city's artisans. In order to do so, I will here present a synopsis of the Carolingian Cycle, something which seems hardly different from its sources in the Italian literary tradition, and, in the following chapters, I will present five seminal episodes of the Palermitan version of the cycle. I will as well intersperse those five episodes with examples of indigenous Palermitan folk narrative, including farce, bandits' lives, saints' lives, Christian myth, fairy tales, and city legend.[44] As we progress through those episodes, and the folkloric repertoire of which epic forms the central facet, we will find that, first, by investing epic's characters with a set of standard narrative progressions—in essence, traditional plotlines—and, second, by giving those characters what puppeteers' maintain is the essence of their art, voice, the Palermitanization of epic is effected. First, the synopsis, which is offered with an eye to contextualizing the five seminal episodes that center this study:

The Carolingian Cycle: A Synopsis

(1) Charlemagne's Early Adventures: Upon the advice of their mother's brother, Grifon of Maiance, the two illegitimate sons of King Pepin, Lanfroi and Olderigi, poison their stepmother, Berta de la Gran Piè, and assassinate their father. They intend also to kill their young stepbrother, Charlemagne, but he witnesses the assassination of his father and flees the city of Paris. His adventures take him to Saragossa, where he falls in love with Galerana, sister to Saragossa's future king, Marsilius, and to Rome, where his prowess at arms ingratiates him to the pope. When he returns to Paris, a man and a valiant warrior, he avenges his father's death, claims the throne of France, and installs Galerana as his queen.

(2) Rolandin's Early Adventures: Shortly thereafter, Charlemagne's younger sister, Berta, falls in love with Milon, who, after a dispute with members of the treacherous House of Maiance, is banished from Paris by Charlemagne. Berta follows him into exile. Soon after they are married, Berta is abducted. She kills her abductor and bears Milon's son, Rolandin (diminutive of Roland), in a cave that she shares with an aged shepherd outside the Italian city of Sutri. Some years later, when Charlemagne is summoned to Rome to be crowned Holy Roman Emperor, he stops at Sutri, where Rolandin steals a cup from his table. The incident leads to the pardoning of Milon and Berta and their eventual reunion in Paris. As the cycle progresses, Milon is killed in the course of the battle of Aspremont. Roland, who has recently escaped from the seminary, is advised by an angel that his father's killer is about to kill his uncle, Charlemagne. Roland arrives just in time to avenge the death of his father and save his uncle, gaining in the process the famous sword, Durandal. Shortly thereafter, that arch-traitor, Ganelon of Maiance, marries Milon's widow, Berta, ominously becoming the stepfather of Roland. Finally, Roland marries Alda the Beautiful. However, he vows not to have conjugal relations with her until he has conquered Spain, a deed which he will, of course, never accomplish.

(3) Renaud's Early Adventures: Ginamo of Maiance has stolen the wedding ring of Beatrice, wife to Milon's brother, Aymon, and claims Aymon's son, Renaud, as his own. Beatrice and Renaud—like Berta and Rolandin before

them—find themselves banished and hiding in a cave where, through the tutelage of Malagigi (who learned the art of necromancy from the lingering spirit of Merlin), Renaud gains his faithful destrier, Bayard, and the marvelous sword, Fusbert. So armed, he slays Ginamo of Maiance, who, dying, confesses his treachery against Beatrice and Renaud. Aymon takes them back as wife and son but—despite the happy resolution of this intrigue—Renaud's history is marred by numerous altercations with his sovereign, Charlemagne. He is forced to abduct his future wife, Clarice, from Charlemagne's court and to take to the hills, becoming chief of a band of 600 (sometimes 700) outlaws terrorizing Charlemagne's kingdom from their base at the Castle Somme d'Or, before he—in humility—renders himself subject to Charlemagne's crown.

(4) Angelica: Various adventures intervene before the beautiful Indian princess, Angelica, arrives at the court of Charlemagne with her brother, Argalia. Almost immediately, fighting breaks out between Christians and Saracens alike over the beautiful princess. Not only does Marsilius' nephew, Ferraù, take up arms against Argalia in his suit for Angelica but also the cousins, Roland and Renaud, begin to fight one another over her. Ferraù kills Argalia but fails to win Angelica. Another Saracen, Agrican, has in the meantime laid siege to Angelica's castle, Albracca, and refuses to relent until Angelica accepts his proposal of marriage. Angelica seeks out Roland, who defeats Agrican's army single-handedly. Agrican, dying, converts to Christianity, but Angelica, thwarting Roland's devotion to her, marries the common foot soldier, Medoro, causing Roland to go mad. She flees with Medoro to her father's kingdom of Cathay. However, the hated Ferraù catches up with her and slays Medoro. As Astolphe flies the hippogriff to the moon in order to retrieve Roland's mind, Angelica commits suicide rather than permitting herself to fall into Ferraù's hands. Her spirit elects the now restored Roland to avenge her.

(5) The Battle of Roncevaux: During a siege at Saragossa, Roland kills Ferraù. Ferraù's uncle, Marsilius, vows to avenge the death of his nephew on Roland and all the Paladins, a vow which he succeeds in fulfilling, with the aid of the traitor Ganelon of Maiance, at the battle of Roncevaux. Yet in killing the Paladins, Marsilius has broken his own forces, paving the way for Charlemagne's eventual capture of Saragossa and consolidation of the Holy Roman Empire.

It sometimes seems unusual to outsiders that French knights are the heroes of Sicilian epic but not to Sicilians. In fact, these knights are considered the ancestors—or, perhaps better, the ancestral genii—of the Sicilian people. The tradition of the Carolingian heroes as Sicilian ancestors runs deep. On its basis the "papacy had developed a specious claim to feudal lordship over Sicily, basing this on the multiple fiction that first Constantine and later the Carolingian kings had owned the island and ... 'given' it to the Pope. As a result the Normans had to accept feudal investiture" for the island.⁴⁵ This meant that they ruled Sicily at the pope's behest and, at least in theory, had to answer to him, but at the same time this investiture gave the Normans ecclesiastical as well as political authority over Sicily, allowing them, for example, to endow cathedrals and monastic houses, to create dioceses and appoint bishops. The whole question of investiture would create friction between the papacy on the one hand and the Normans and their heirs—especially the Hohenstaufen—on the other and would eventually lead to the Sicilian Vespers. Yet, despite some of the turbulence that this tradition supported, it did set up a rough (albeit legendary) line of succession for Sicily running from the Roman empire (Constantine) through the Holy Roman Empire (Charlemagne and the other Carolingian rulers), and then again through the papacy to the Normans (among whose ranks is included Palermo's own patron, Santa Rosalia), and finally, through them, on to the modern Sicilians themselves. Thus, the Carolingian Cycle, in many ways, represents—to the Sicilian mind at least—the crux of Sicilian history—tying up all the loose ends between Arab, Norman, Papal and Imperial claims upon Sicily and her inhabitants.

In fact, the significance of Charlemagne and his Paladins, and especially the first among the Paladins, Roland, and his illustrious cousin, Renaud, to the Palermitan people cannot be overstated. The images of these heroes are ubiquitous enough to have even made their way into Mario Puzo's *Godfather* legendry. When Michael Corleone enters Palermo in *The Sicilian* they are among his first sights.

> [Corleone's] car dwarfed the other vehicles surrounding it, especially the mule-drawn peasant carts which carried in most of the fresh produce from the countryside. These carts were painted in gay, vivid colors, every inch of them down to the spokes of the wheels [and] the shafts that held the mules. On the sides of many carts were murals showing helmeted knights and crowned kings in dramatic scenes from the legends of Charlemagne and Roland, those ancient heroes of Sicilian folklore. But on some carts Michael saw scrawled, beneath the figure of a handsome youth in moleskin trousers and sleeveless white shirt, guns in his belt, guns slung over his shoulder, a legend of two lines which always ended with great red letters that spelled out the name Giuliano.⁴⁶

The manner in which Palermitans make Charlemagne, Roland, Renaud, and the other Carolingian heroes their own is the complex process to which we will now turn, but the significance of the famed bandit, Salvatore Giuliano, to the Carolingian heroes—something which Puzo and probably many Italian-Americans (myself included) quickly intuit—will have to wait till a later chapter.

Chapter Two

The Marionette Theater

The Early Adventures

In Palermo, the Carolingian Cycle opens with the early adventures of Charlemagne, Roland, and Renaud, the major epic heroes. Each of these nobles has, in youth, to lose the trappings of privilege and descend among the people before he can, his royal origins finally recognized, resume his rightful place at court. Here is a theme shared with much of the folk narrative of Europe, from fairy tales to Arthurian romance. However, a sense of immediacy is lent to its Sicilian variation by the Palermitan belief that the foreign nobility has to become one with the indigenous populace in order to rule justly. In two seminal tales—the first dealing with the early exploits of a young Charlemagne (here called Charles), the second dealing with the first adventures of the young Roland (here referred to by the diminutive Rolandin)—we will begin to explore this proposition in earnest. But before launching into the stories themselves, we must briefly explore their provenance.

Today, the best source for Sicilian epic is the marionette theater, the epic singers *(cantastorie)* having exchanged their ancient repertoire for more contemporary subject matter, police and accident reports from the local newspapers,[1] in the nineteenth century before fading into obscurity, the epic storytellers *(contastorie)* being eclipsed by television and the incipience of a globalizing economy in the aftermath of World War II. The puppeteers, whose repertoire was integrally related to that of the storytellers (so much so that some men participated in both trades), nearly suffered the same fate as their colleagues in the post-war period but, probably because of the visual aspect of their art, continued to find limited audiences. Still, one could make a precarious living at the trade at best, one puppeteer telling me he was continuously thinking of emigrating to Canada. The stories, always intended for men of the

Two: The Marionette Theater

This decaying sign once alerted passersby to the presence of a marionette theater. Photograph by author.

working classes, were now often performed for children. At times, puppeteers would be invited to perform at village festivals or special events in Palermo, and today groups of tourists fill out the need for a paying audience. It must be somewhat strange for the puppeteers and in fact one even told me as much, lamenting that the new audiences don't quite know how to react to the stories and have even laughed at inappropriate moments. Still, it is the puppeteers who have allowed these stories to survive even into the twenty-first century and thus it is their versions that form the basis of my transcriptions.

The history of my transcriptions—inasmuch as I became invested in the Palermitan appreciation of the stories and was reticent to risk making them seem (as I had been warned I would) less engrossing then they actually are—is a long and arduous one to recount. The basis of the main narratives, as I have said, is provided by the marionette theater, though I have consulted the versions of storytellers, when available in ethnographic collections, as well as those found in the Palermitan literary tradition. The raw transcriptions look like play scripts but are difficult to read inasmuch as they lack all the physical apparatus of the theater, something a bit more essential in popular narrative than, say, Shakespeare. What I have done, as a result, is to present these narratives in a short story format. While dialogue is for the most part translated verbatim, narrative moments outside the dialogue are provided by turning one character's narration to another into authorial narration to the reader. Further authorial narration is provided by the theatrical setting of the action, the puppeteers' rich intonation, puppeteer notebooks, and literary sources. At times, I leave the raw script as it is. This is especially effective during those moments that the Greeks would define as *stychomachia*, a sort of clipped verbal dueling. At others, I have abridged what would otherwise be too unwieldy or too unclear to present in its entirety. The short story format seems to me less jarring to the modern reader than the play script. Plus, it offers the added benefit of framing the script in explanatory material. All analysis, however, is based on the raw transcripts of these plays, a portion of which, *The Death of the Paladins*, is included in the appendix of this book. Also, I have translated those Carolingian names that have somewhat common English equivalents (usually the French form) in my transcriptions. The remainder, I have left in the Italian form. Again, it seemed too jarring to refer to Charlemagne, for example, as Carlo Magno, or Roland as Orlando.

In the two stories that follow, we will witness the young hero's descent among the working people, and in the second story, we will witness as well the recognition of the young hero's noble origins. *The Death of King Pepin*, which we will first consider, is the opening tale of the 270 odd episodes that comprise the Carolingian Cycle at Palermo. Thus, it attempts to function as a kind of exposition for the cycle as a whole, explicating the first rupture—dynastic in nature and pitting a lineage of traitors (the House of Maiance) against the champions of Christendom (the House of Clermont)—to descend upon the Carolingian court. At the same time, it opens the sequence of tales which detail the young knights' descent among the people and, thus, offers our first, albeit brief, encounter of the incursion of farce—through the construction of a plebian alter ego for the young Charlemagne—upon the epic stage.

Yet, before we turn to the tale itself, this brief backdrop: Upon learning that Berta de la Gran Piè is about to marry King Pepin, her constant companion, Elisetta of Maiance—who would be indistinguishable from Berta if it were not for the fact that Berta's right foot is slightly larger than the left—is convinced by her wicked brother, Grifon of Maiance, to disguise herself as Berta and take her place as Empress. The plot is rendered infallible when Berta, terrified at the sight of her new husband, a deformed hunchback, asks Elisetta to take her place in the emperor's nuptial bed. Berta—at the order of the duplicitous Grifon and with the full knowledge of her onetime confidant, Elisetta—is taken out to the forest to be killed but her executioners, abashed at being asked to perpetrate such a deed and ashamed by Berta's gentle pleadings, kill a dog instead, tie Berta naked to a tree, and drench her dress in the dog's blood—thus offering irrefutable proof of Berta's death to Grifon of Maiance. Elisetta, in the interim, bears King Pepin two sons: Lanfroi and Olderigi. Yet, Berta, having been taken in by a Forester, is eventually discovered by her betrothed and proves to be the true empress by displaying her right foot—a defect indeed but a minor one at that and a defect, moreover, that reveals Elisetta's betrayal. Elisetta is burned at the stake, an act which her sons Lanfroi and Olderigi vow to avenge, and King Pepin is reunited with his true wife, Berta, who bears him the future emperor, Charlemagne, as well as a daughter, named after her mother, Berta, she who will one day give birth to Roland. The fairy tale ambience that is so notable in this opening sequence will be subsumed in the epic construction of *The Death of King Pepin*, to which we now turn; yet—as we progress further into the cycle—it will resurface in various and unexpected ways.

The Death of King Pepin

"Long live Pepin, King of France, and Emperor of Rome," cried the councilors as Pepin entered the throne room of his palace and opened his triumphant council. "My beloved warriors, Morando of Riviera, Bernardo of Chiaramonte, Girardo, Duke Naimes of Bavaria; my dearest sons, Lanfroi, Olderigi, Charles, I am content that peace reigns in our land, after the many wars that we have withstood against these vile Saracens who wanted to conquer France, who wanted to aggrandize the false faith of Mohammed. We have destroyed them, causing them to repent having ever set foot on Christian soil. And now, I wish to sponsor a holiday here in Paris in a manner that will allow the city's poor to disport themselves. I wish also to sponsor a sumptuous banquet and so carry the holiday into my royal palace itself."

Yet even as he spoke, he was interrupted by his youngest son, Charles, who pleaded that—despite his young age—he be made a knight: "Oh my Father," Charles cried, "I would like a suit of armor; I would like," he persisted, "to be a knight!"

"Charles, my son," Pepin chastised, "you are not yet old enough to support the weight of arms! You have only this year attained your eighth birthday; you're a little boy yet, and you still have much need of instruction to better your swordplay. That which I recommend for you, beloved son, is that every day, you should continue to practice your fencing."

But, "My father," Charles pleaded, "I feel more than enough strength to support the weight of arms, more than enough strength to confront the most ferocious enemy!"

"These words fill my heart with much joy," Pepin said, "and I promise you that as soon as possible, I will give you a beautiful suit of armor."

Yet, even as Pepin sent Charles on his way, Charles' half brothers, Lanfroi and Olderigi, sequestered themselves in their chambers and plotted the death of their father: "My dear brother, Lanfroi," Olderigi grumbled, "how do you like the fact that our father, King Pepin, loves our brother Charles so much more than us? Do you know what I think? I think that our father would like one day to leave his crown to Charles even though the crown of France rightfully belongs to us!"

"Certainly, the governance of France, after the death of King Pepin, will not come to us, but instead to Charles," Lanfroi agreed. "Thus, while our mother's brother Grifon of Maiance[2] still promises us his protection, we need to kill our father, King Pepin, and also Charles! But first of all, we need to advise Count Grifon, for he will gather together those people who will offer us succor. With his aid, we will make ourselves the rulers of France!"

Lanfroi and Olderigi thus enlisted the aid of their maternal uncle, Count Grifon of Maiance, and even as he began to prepare to lay siege to the city of Paris, the patricides crept into their father's bedchamber. "My brother," Olderigi whispered, "here we are finally in the room of that coward, our father. And here he is, sleeping."

"But what's this?" Pepin, awakening, exclaimed. "I hear footsteps in my chamber!"

"Father," Olderigi shouted, "coward and nothing more, you who wanted to leave the crown of France to that bastard Charles, we have come armed with daggers, bearing your death."

"Assassins," Pepin cried. "What are you doing? Are killing your own father? Damn you, my sons!"[3]

Yet even as he died, his last thought was of his young heir: "Oh, Lord in heaven," he gasped with his dying breath, "I commend to your care my son Charles."

"Coward and nothing more," Olderigi rabidly persisted. "You commend your son Charles to God, while we instead will take ourselves to his room because he, too, will die!"

Two: The Marionette Theater

But death was not to be his fate for Charles, who had come to visit his father and hidden himself behind a curtain, witnessed the murder, and as Lanfroi and Olderigi left the room to seek out their young stepbrother, Charles ran to his father's bedside.

"Father!" he cried. "My vile brothers, Lanfroi and Olderigi, have had the malevolence to kill you. And they will want to kill me as well. Thus, I have to secure myself and take flight from this city. But I swear on the blood of my father that I will one day return here to Paris in order to avenge you!" And crying once again, "Oh my father," he fled the royal palace.

Yet even as he took flight, an angel descended and, retrieving the spirit of the king, sang:

> "King Pepin, King Pepin,
> This was your fate.
> Your pallid face,
> I return to serenity.
> And your wearied soul,
> I transport to its destiny!"

In the morning, Pepin's counselors, Bernardo of Chiaramonte, Girardo of la Frata, and Morando of Riviera found Pepin's bloodied body but even before they could sound an alarm, Paris was inundated with the treasonous knights of the wicked House of Maiance. And as Paris fell, Morando of Riviera set out in search of his godson, Charles.

In the meantime, Charles found himself in the trackless forests which surrounded the city of Paris: "Charles," he lamented, "I am tired from the long trek that I've made in order to distance myself from the city of Paris. High God in heaven, I thank you for bringing me to safety—for if I fell into the hands of my vile brothers, Lanfroi and Olderigi, they would certainly kill me. Still, one day I will return to Paris at the head of an army and avenge the death of my father." But just then, spotting someone alone in the forest, he said, "But, what's this I see! In the woods, there is a shepherd grazing his sheep. I will ask him to exchange his clothes for mine; in that way, no one will be able to recognize me as Charles, Prince of France."

And even as he approached, the shepherd lamented his lowly state: "And I do nothing more than graze my sheep in order to gain my livelihood. Each day, I come to this very place where my flock can find something to eat. But, what's this I see; a youth coming toward me in all haste and alerting me that I should attend him."

Charles, out of breath from his flight, called out to the shepherd, saying: "Kind shepherd, I need to ask of you, I need to ask of you, a favor."

"But what am I able to do for you?" the shepherd, dumbfounded, asked. "You're very well dressed. You're without a doubt the descendant of a great family while I'm nothing more than a poor shepherd. What can I possibly do for the likes of you?"

"Listen, friend," Charles said, "I need to exchange my clothing for yours so that no one will be able to recognize me. I beg you to accept my proposition. I need to quicken my pace and distance myself from this place. Also, I wish to ask you, continuing along this path, where will it take me?"

"Continuing along this path," the shepherd answered, "it will take you to the monastery of Saint Homer. But are you serious," he persisted, pleased at the thought of putting on Charlemagne's fine attire in place of his own, "about exchanging your clothing for mine?"

"Yes," Charles insisted, "I'm serious! I beg of you! I don't think that I have much time!"

"But this all seems a dream," the shepherd mused as he began to undress. "All right; come on; I'll exchange my clothing for yours."

And the two exchanged their clothing quickly.

"Now that we have exchanged our clothes," Charles said, "I want you to make me a promise; if anyone asks you where you found that suit, you must say that you found it under a tree. I beg of you; no one must know that I have taken the path to the monastery of Saint Homer."

"All right," the shepherd agreed, "I promise. You may rest assured."

"God bless you," Charles called as he continued on his way.

And, "You also," the shepherd returned, still admiring his new set of clothing.

And as Charles continued on his way, he made plans for his deliverance: "Charles," he said to himself, "I feel so tired. I no longer have the strength to continue. Thank God, I've finally arrived at the monastery of Saint Homer. Now I want to talk with the father of this monastery. But I must not tell him that I am Charles, son of Pepin. I must not tell him because I fear that if someone knows, he will warn Grifon of Maiance and perhaps my vile brothers as well. I must say that my name is Mainetto rather than Charles. I will not say that I am the son of King Pepin. I will say that I am the son of Millery Washerwoman. And that my mother killed her husband and his lover and wishing to kill me as well, I put myself to flight. And I beg sanctuary in this monastery."

Thus, he found himself standing before the monastery door.

"Hey! You of the monastery," he called as he knocked at the massive door. "I say, you of the monastery!"

"Who is knocking at the door of this monastery?" the Father Superior intoned from a window above.

"Father," Charles answered, "I'm a poor wretch who is asking sanctuary. Help me, Father! Come down so that I might recount to you my misadventures."

"Are you a Christian?" the father asked.

"Of course, I'm a Christian!" Charles exclaimed shrilly.[4]

"Well," the father said, "then I'm coming immediately." And as the Father Superior admitted Charles into the monastery, he asked, "My child, you come at this hour, knocking at the door of my monastery? Tell me, what is it you want?"

"Father," Charles lamented, "know that my name is Mainetto. I am a fugitive from my own home because my mother killed her husband and his lover, and wanting to kill me as well, I thought to bring myself to a safe place. I beg of you, let me enter this monastery, so that my life may be spared. And so that I might pray for the soul of my dead father!"

"Oh, my son," the father consoled him, "hearing these words breaks my heart. Who knows in which day He will arrive. The world is changing but not for the better. All right, come into my monastery where you might take refuge and where you might pray for the soul of your dead father."

"I thank you," Charles said, and followed the Father Superior into the monastery. Yet even as he did so, Morando of Riviera, who had fled a burning Paris, scoured the trackless forests for any sign of his godson, Charles.[5]

Palermitan Puppetry

The Death of King Pepin opens with a solemn council between the sovereign, King Pepin, and his most trusted advisors: Morando of Riviera, Bernardo of Chiaramonte, Girardo of la Frata, and Duke Naimes of Bavaria, and, since its source is the Sicilian marionette theater, it communicates as much by its performative context as it does by its story line. Thus, I will take a moment to describe the visual aspect of the marionette theater as well as interpret the narrative format of the tale as we proceed through the following analysis. But, first, a quick note with regard to the marionettes themselves.

The puppet theater, in Italy, is characterized by three types of puppets: the glove puppet, the classic marionette manipulated by strings, and—the subject of this study—the *pupo* (plural, *pupi*) which is a marionette maneuvered by rods as well as strings. It is likely that the "rod marionette" is an earlier form of the marionette than the classical string marionette. Its retention at Palermo (and other places where armed marionettes formed the mainstay of the marionette theater) was likely the result of necessity. While classic string marionettes moved more naturalistically, rod marionettes could withstand the vigor of armed combat—especially when special effects such as the beheading of an enemy might form the climax of a play. Though the Sicilian word for a rod marionette is *pupo*—clearly cognate with the English word puppet—the term puppet is more often used to describe glove puppets in English and, further complicating the issue, the word *pupo* in southern Italy is more closely related to the very large linguistic class of words which refer to dolls (to which marionettes and glove puppets are considered to pertain).[6] Thus, I have opted to use the phrase marionette theater to describe the theatrical tradition and the word marionette to describe the actual figures that grace the marionette theater's stage. Conversely, I use the term puppeteer (rather than the cumbersome marioneteer) to describe the artisan who manipulates the marionettes and—more importantly from the puppeteers' perspective—gives them voice. Likewise, I use the term puppetry—as no term based on the root marionette exists—to describe the art form as a whole.

In the very first council of the Carolingian Cycle (as in all others which occur between the sovereign and his retainers), each knight, in order of ascending rank, steps out from stage right, crosses the stage with a halting, rigid—that is to say, heroic—gait, turns to face the audience, then steps back to form a line-up. Each entrance is accompanied by the furiously paced music of a cylinder piano and the heraldic cries:

> I---è--- viva!
> I---è--- viva, Re Pipi—-no!
> Viva sua Maestà!
> I---è--- viva!
> I---è--- viva!
> Long live the king!
> Lo---ng li---ve King Pepi---n!
> Long live his Majesty!
> Long live the king!
> Long live the king!

These knights are suspended, one by one, from a pole which stretches across the top of the stage lengthwise, because the two puppeteers (the first situated in the wings, stage right; the second, in the wings, stage left) will be occupied with the manipulation of the new characters to enter the stage: in this instance, King Pepin and the young Charlemagne.

King Pepin enters with the proper response to the heraldic cries after which he proceeds to exhort his Paladins with a speech punctuated by all the noble moves and gestures (a measured gait, the raising of the right hand, the striking of the breast, the stroking of the beard) available to the sovereign. He thus announces to the Paladins the end of hostilities against the Saracens and his desire to sponsor a feast in celebration of Paris' newfound peace. In the following brief transcription, I have

Two: The Marionette Theater

Here is the stage used at the Antonio Pasqualino Museo Internazionale delle Marionette, Palermo. Note the small cylinder piano in front of the left-hand corner of the stage; its furiously paced music demarcates shifts from scene to scene and punctuates knights' battles. Behind the stage are posters which present the sequence of episodes to be performed in a number of panels. These alert potential customers to the place in the cycle that the puppeteer has reached. From the collections of the Antonio Pasqualino Museo Internazionale delle Marionette, photograph by author.

attempted to indicate a bit about the puppeteers' declamatory style: each line is followed by a slight pause; words marked with dashes are elongated; words in bold face are stressed.

>   Vi---va si gri---da
>   nel mio pala---zzo rea---le,
>   Pepino, Re di Fra---ncia
>   e Imperator' di **Ro---ma**!
>
>   The cry--- of long li---ve
>   rings through my ro---yal pa---lace,
>   For Pepin, King of Fra---nce
>   and Emperor of **Ro---me**!
>   *

*My beloved **wa---rriors**:*
***Mora---ndo** of Riviera,*
***Berna---rdo** of Chiaramonte,*
Gira------rdo,
Duke Naimes of Bavaria

*My dearest **so---ns**:*
Lanfroi, Olderigi,
Cha------rles,

I am content
that peace reigns
in our land
*after the many **wa---rs***
that we have withstood
*against these **vi---le** Saracens*
who wa---nted to conquer France,
*who **wa---nted to aggrandize***
the false faith of Mohammed.
We---
have destroyed them,
*causing them to **repe---nt***
having ever set foot
on Christian soil.

While Council sets the story up by providing the audience with the background necessary to understand the episode and acts in a sense as the story's exposition, it is nonetheless the nature of Council to be interrupted by various sub-themes, which generally function to introduce some complication, perhaps even the major conflict of the story, into the plot. A complete progression of these sub-themes runs from Announcement through Audience to Dispatch. Announcement entails the appearance of a foot soldier before the sovereign to announce the arrival of an ambassador or a letter. Audience is simply the appearance of another character before the sovereign, but it is quite often the representative of another character, such as an ambassador, which acts as the sovereign's interlocutor. Moreover, in a variation of Audience, the sovereign may simply read a letter which has been delivered to him by the foot soldier in the sub-theme Announcement. Dispatch, which is quite often the sovereign's first step at resolving a conflict announced during the Audience, involves the sovereign's summons of

Two: The Marionette Theater

A detail of the theater curtain depicting a female warrior, perhaps Rinaldo's sister Bradamante. From the collections of the Antonio Pasqualino Museo Internazionale delle Marionette, photograph by author.

a foot soldier to deliver a message or more often a letter to another court. In all this, a series of visual cues serves to demarcate the puppeteer's narrative.

The marionette theater's visual significance results from the interaction of the marionette with his environment, his moves and gestures resonating and playing off the structure of the stage. The marionette is tripartite in construction, consisting of the frame, the armor, and the means of manipulation. The frame, carved in wood and pinned together with strong but resilient wire, consists of ten pieces: the head, the torso, two legs, two knees, two feet and two hands.[7] The armor is constructed in brass or gleaming German silver with arabesques in red copper and consists of about sixty pieces for each knight.[8] Beyond two rods (the first, passing through the head to suspend the frame; the second, affixed to the right, fighting, hand), the means of maneuvering the marionette include four cords. The rod which suspends the marionette's frame, in conjunction with a half centimeter shortening of the right foot to facilitate the first step, allows the marionette to walk.[9] The second rod, affixed to the right hand, allows the marionette to punctuate his speech with various gestures and, in conjunction with a cord, to brandish a sword. The right hand is carved into a fist with enough space between the clenched fingers to accommodate the hilt of a sword. A cord passes from the hilt of the sword, through the clenched fist, and is tied to the rod which maneuvers the right hand. This allows the marionette to sheathe and unsheathe his sword and to keep a tight grip on it during battle. A second cord is affixed to the left hand, which is carved palm open to accommodate a shield. A third cord is attached to the left knee, which allows the Palermitan marionette (unlike its Neapolitan ancestors or Catanian contemporaries) a number of moves involving the bending of the knees (for example, rendering himself subject to his sovereign). The fourth cord is attached to the visor of the marionette's helmet, allowing it to be raised after and lowered in preparation for battle. The means of manipulation give to the marionette a repertoire of about 50 moves and gestures: kneeling, raising an arm, sheathing or unsheathing a sword, raising a visor or—menacingly—lowering it.[10] These moves and gestures, once linked together, form the archetypal themes of epic—Council and Battle—and provide a kind of behavioral (or gestural) rhetoric which continuously underscores, and at times offers a counterpoint to, the verbal rhetoric that is, from the puppeteers' perspective, the mainstay of the puppeteers' artistry.

In *The Death of King Pepin* the simplest sub-theme, Audience, is used to interject the main character of the episode, Charlemagne, into the scene. Inasmuch as this is the initial episode of the Carolingian Cycle, it is enough that the theme illustrates the fighting spirit of Charles at the tender age of eight as well as the preferential treatment that he receives at the hands of his father, King Pepin. The puppeteers illustrate both these themes through the elaboration of the episode's first dialogue:

> Yet even as he spoke, [King Pepin] was interrupted by his youngest son, Charles, who pleaded that—despite his young age—he be made a knight: "Oh my Father," Charles cried, "I would like a suit of armor; I would like," he persisted, "to be a knight!"
>
> "Charles, my son," Pepin chastised, "you are not yet old enough to support the weight of arms! You have only this year attained your eighth birthday;

you're a little boy yet, and you still have much need of instruction to better your swordplay. That which I recommend for you, beloved son, is that every day, you should continue to practice your fencing."

But, "My father," Charles pleaded, "I feel more than enough strength to support the weight of arms, more than enough strength to confront the most ferocious enemy!"

"These words fill my heart with much joy," Pepin said, "and I promise you that as soon as possible, I will give you a beautiful suit of armor."

With Charles' exit, the council is closed in an exact reversal of its opening by the exit of the king and Paladins in order of descending rank, once again to the accompaniment of the cylinder piano and the heraldic cries of "*Ié viva!*"

If conflict has not been introduced in the initial council, it will quite often be elaborated through a number of subsequent councils. This is precisely the case in *The Death of King Pepin*, where Lanfroi and Olderigi decide to kill their father, King Pepin, and to advise their maternal uncle, Count Grifon of Maiance, of their plans. We soon find Lanfroi and Olderigi in their father's bedroom, about to carry out their intended patricide. The scene is constructed on the basis of epic battle. As the brothers lift their daggers above their sleeping father, he awakens and struggles with them, and the resulting blows which they deliver take on the rhythmical quality that is generally reserved by the puppeteers for battle. Moreover, the puppeteers underscore the rhythm of the clashing daggers by stomping the stage's floorboards in a strategy also most appropriate to battle. Interestingly, the last active Palermitan storyteller (*contastoria*), don Peppino Celano, also used the rhythmical declamation that puppeteers reserved for battle to render his version of Pepin's assassination. The suggestion is that as the machinations of the nobility always participate in the nature of the council, so too do their fights always participate in the nature of the battle, even if these fights are ignoble assassinations. And it seems that this suggestion holds as much for the puppeteers as it did for the storytellers who preceded them. Another peculiarity of this episode is a variation to it by which Charlemagne, hidden in the wings of the stage, is witness to his stepbrothers' infamous crime. Thus, a modified battle becomes the instigation of Charlemagne's flight from the city of Paris.

Battle is the most stylized theme of the marionette theater, consisting of clear opening formulae and gestures, a sequence of several battle rhythms, and a variety of conventional closures. It is also the only theme that employs all the manipulatory mechanisms at the puppeteer's disposal. Battle is signaled by the voicing of various boasts and rejoinders but is only opened when the two knights lower their visors, unsheathe their swords, and assume the *en garde* position (with shield and sword raised). To the nearly frenetic music of the cylinder piano, the knights begin to clash swords. The rhythm of the battle is maintained by the movements of the knights and the stomping of the puppeteers on the floorboards of the stage. Antonio Pasqualino describes the two main rhythms, *squadrone* and *battaglia*, as follows:

> The *squadrone* is carried out to a rhythm of four stomps. The puppets, with raised shields, first move the right (sword) arm forward and to the right (during the first two stomps) and then upward to the left (on the third stomp) and lastly backward to the right (on the fourth stomp), making the swords clash twice. At the same time, the warriors' heads follow the rhythm by turning to the right when the sword is moved to the left, and to the left when the sword is moved to the right. The *battaglia* is carried out to a ternary rhythm that gradually becomes faster. The shield is always raised and the right arm swings the sword downward to the right (during the first two stomps), and then (on the third stomp) moves it upward to the left, where it clashes twice with the enemy's weapon, and finally (during the interval before the next stomps) downward to the right, that is to say, to the point of departure.[11]

If death is to be the result of this battle, it will be accomplished with a final lunge and thrust of the sword, which in especially spectacular battles beheads an adversary or even hews a traitor from the House of Maiance or a Saracen from the House of Saragossa down the middle.

The Vastasate: *Palermo's Answer to the Commedia dell'Arte*

Council and Battle are the central themes of the marionette theater, providing an ideal narrative structure (though one certainly subject to reversal) of conflict and resolution. They are also the most spectacular themes, exhibiting with best effect the gleaming armor and astute movements of the marionettes. But the various twists and turns of chivalric narrative necessitate a number of other themes, and these are best viewed as the marionette theater's inheritance from the other genres that have historically formed the backbone of its repertoire: farce, saints' lives, and bandits' lives. And it is the first of these genres, farce, which begins to intrude upon the second half of *The Death of King Pepin*.

Here, the classic configuration of epic is slightly altered. We find Charlemagne, alone and frightened, on a forest trail, where he encounters his first true representative of the people, a young shepherd, who agrees to an exchange of clothing and offers Charlemagne directions to a possible sanctuary, the monastery of Saint Homer. The two exchange clothing but, as well as the physical disguise, Charlemagne takes on a further attribute of the people by constructing for himself a new history with which to veil his royal origins. As he prepares to ask sanctuary at the monastery of Saint Homer, he declares:

> "Charles, I feel so tired. I no longer have the strength to continue. Thank God, I've finally arrived at the monastery of Saint Homer. Now I want to talk with the father of this monastery. But I must not tell him that I am Charles, son of Pepin. I must not tell him because I fear that if someone knows, he will warn Grifon of Maiance and perhaps my vile brothers as well. I must say that my name is Mainetto rather than Charles. I will not say that I am the son of King Pepin. I will say that I am the son of Millery Washerwoman. And that my mother killed her husband and his lover and wishing to kill me as well, I put myself to flight. And I beg sanctuary in this monastery."

With this disguise, Charlemagne is accepted into the monastery of Saint Homer and taken under the wing of the Father Superior: a character replete with liturgical phrases, including the infamous point of the catechism, "Are you a Christian," to which Charlemagne properly—if peevishly—responds, "Yes, I'm a Christian," an exchange every Palermitan boy knows all too well.

In the youthful Charlemagne's exchange of noble for plebian attributes, we find a first principle of the Palermitanization of the Carolingian Cycle at play: the prince, to become a king, must first become one of the people. Not only is the social order of Palermo at play in this dictum, but also Christian myth inasmuch as God, in order to obtain the patronage of humanity, must become a man. Yet, what becomes most intriguing in Sicilian epic is that the symbol for the people (and, by extension, mythical "Man") is the masque, or, as he is referred to in Palermo, the *vastone*, or porter. The term *masque* (or mask) refers to the variety of stock characters—Harlequin, Pulcinella, various urban laborers (particularly the ubiquitous porter), as well as an affluent foil (such as the Doctor)—that populated the sixteenth century Italian comic theater known as the Commedia dell'Arte.

The Commedia, specializing in farces, spread throughout Italy and beyond and, as it did so, became heavily localized, its characters—first actualized by live actors, later by puppets as well—speaking in the local dialect and hurling their political barbs at the various political and even ecclesiastical dignitaries that asserted their authority too persistently upon the daily lives of the Commedia's not uncommonly popular audiences. "The process that gave birth to the masked figures of the Commedia dell'Arte," John McCormick reports, "was an ongoing one. The term 'maschera' (mask) continued to be used to indicate a stock type even when not masked. Many new 'masks' were no more than local variations of existing stock types, but some emerged directly from the theater or popular writing."[12] Early examples of such masques were Harlequin (Arlecchino) and Brighella.

> Both emerged in the Bergamo area. Brighella was the trickster and generally presented as an urban figure, while Arlecchino, who emerged in the Val Brembana near Bergamo, was, at least initially, the simpleton and the countryman. This is the classic coupling of the clever and the stupid slaves of classic Roman comedy. Bergamo was Venetian territory and like many poor people, Arlecchino and Brighella went to Venice to find work as porters, servants or any other menial employment and rapidly adapted to that city. The [masques] belonged to an impoverished underclass and were always the first to be in need in times of hardship or famine. Arlecchino is constantly shown trying to satisfy the pangs of hunger. On the puppet stage, making him eat spaghetti was a favorite trick with the showman (the same was also true of Pulcinella in Naples). North of Rome Arlecchino was ubiquitous [and on the marionette stage] he detached himself from his erstwhile companions and, like Pulcinella, became the mouthpiece for the showman and also served as an announcer. He often retained a servant's role, becoming the comic hero and bridging the gap with the audience.[13]

The masque has a noble lineage in Palermo. The company of the *vastasate* was a theatrical troop of improvisational actors whose characters were more particularized to the Palermitan landscape than were the Commedia dell'Arte's Harlequin, Pulcinella (Punch), and Columbine. Its major characters were Nofrio, his wife Lisa, and the Baron.[14] The actual performances, or *vastasate*, took their name from Nofrio's profession; he was a *vastone*, or porter. His profession would have put him in contact with various members of the upper class (to wit, the Baron) and thus permitted many of the farces' comic opportunities. Giuseppe Pitrè, writing in 1889, complains that Nofrio—"the ancient genius of burlesque"—was quickly being replaced in Palermo by Peppinninu and Virticchio.[15] The complaint was ill-founded. As we shall shortly see, Nofrio was not displaced by, but rather augmented with, these other masques. Besides Nofrio, Lisa and the Baron, contemporary farces regularly include Virticchio, Peppinninu, and Russidda.[16] And in their burlesques of epic's continuous battle between Christians and Saracens, farces put characters such as the Turk or the Muslim, Mustafà (whom we will encounter a bit later), in mock combat with Nofrio or Virticchio.

In one of these burlesques, collected by Antonio Pasqualino, Virticchio, meandering along a road, is startled by a strange chattering and cautiously backs into its source, a gigantic Turk who wishes alternatively to convert Virticchio to Islam and to purchase his head (*capuzza*, in the Turk's jargon). Virticchio, thinking that the Turk wishes to buy a goat (*crapuzza*, in Virticchio's Sicilian dialect), agrees to the purchase but mistakes the Turk's proffered tender, twenty ducats (*ducati*), as twenty turds (*cacati*), and throttles the Turk. Discovering that the Turk actually has money to offer, Virticchio goes off to fetch—not to say steal—a goat (which at any rate belongs to somebody else), but the Turk stops him and clears up the misunderstanding. When Virticchio realizes he has just sold his head, he faints. The Turk has vowed never to kill anyone lying on the ground (notice the nobility in the Saracen's moral code), so Virticchio, refusing to get up, cries, "Look! Who is that coming along the road?" When the Turk turns to look, Virticchio jumps to his feet and runs to the house of Aunt Laria (notice the ignoble behavior of our indigenous hero), begging for a utensil with which to pierce a piece of *salamelicchi* (i.e., salami plus *salaam'alaykom*). Virticchio returns armed with a knife, actually a Paladin's sword, with which he does battle with the Turk who is hit twice before Virticchio beheads him and exits the stage to share a dinner with Uncle Antonio, an avowed pig.[17]

CHAPTER THREE

Knights and Masques

The Puppeteers' Intreccio

In *The Death of King Pepin* we saw how the puppeteer varies his themes to accommodate a number of narrative contexts. For example, the announcements and dispatches of Council were used to actualize Lanfroi and Olderigi's plot against their father, and the various rhythms and cadences of Battle were used to actualize their assassination of King Pepin. In fact, it is through this dramatic variation of his few themes that the puppeteer distills the Carolingian Cycle and creates his own particular narratives. Unity of action is not an ideal in the construction of these plots. Rather, a concept analogous to Ludovico Ariosto's[1] *intreccio*, or the artful interweaving of themes and episodes, is at play. Each theme carries a significant communication and the careful sequencing, intertwining, juxtaposition and paralleling of these themes create the story's plot.

Further, inasmuch as the themes are the products of the various genres that comprise the marionette theater's narrative repertoire, that is, epic, farce, saints' lives, and bandits' lives, it follows naturally that the plots which they actualize will be multigeneric in character. Nowhere is this circumstance more clearly evidenced than in *The First Adventures of Rolandin*, the episode to which we now turn, where Rolandin's antics suggest a budding young knight on the one hand, a bungling *vastone*, or masque, on the other. The oscillation is created through the interweaving of farcical matter into the very fabric of epic.

In fact, the insertion of farce into the epic arena, which we briefly witnessed in *The Death of King Pepin*, achieves full dramatic force in *The First Adventures of Rolandin*. Here, the youthful Roland actually joins forces with Palermo's preeminent masques, Nofrio and Virticchio, and goes into mock combat against his own royal cousin, Oliver, he who

Three: Knights and Masques

Roland battling a lion: Here one can clearly see the mechanism by which the puppeteer allows the marionette to wield the sword. Not only is the rod which suspends the marionette visible above Roland's head but also the rod which manipulates the fighting hand is in play. Note the sword's hilt held in place in the space between the clenched fingers through the use of a cord which—slightly visible in this photograph—runs alongside the second rod. Note also that Roland's crossed eyes are quite visible here. From the collections of the Antonio Pasqualino Museo Internazionale delle Marionette, photograph by author.

is destined to die at Roland's side at Roncevaux. Moreover, as Rolandin descends into the world of the masques, we will find him not only acting the part of his lowly companions through adopting their repertoire of moves and gestures but even taking upon himself their idiom: an easy and familiar form of Sicilian rather than the refined Italian characteristic of even youthful knights. In doing so, Roland will—like the other paramount heroes of the Carolingian Cycle, Charlemagne and Renaud—make himself more congenial—for the time being at least—to the popular classes that tenanted the marionette theater's Palermitan audiences.

The First Adventures of Rolandin

Emerging from the cave which had been her lodging throughout her exile, Berta began to lament: "My friend, Galisena, many years have passed since my husband, Milon, and I fled Paris, having been banished by my brother, Charlemagne. After we embarked upon a ship, the captain had his page assault my Milon. And I was abducted by the captain who, wanting to take advantage of me, transported me to this shore. And I, feigning to consign myself to the insane desire of that man, allowed him to embrace me. And when I saw him inebriated with joy, I killed him with a dagger which I kept hidden upon my person. An old shepherd who was camping nearby heard me scream for help, and, since the years augment pity, he approached, and as if I were his own daughter, he brought me here to this cave."

One day, upon hearing a lament arising in the forest, Berta and the aged shepherd stumbled upon Berta's friend, Galisena, who asked the shepherd to take her in as a second daughter. And now the two women, Berta and Galisena, the shepherd, and Berta's young son, Rolandin, lived together as a family within a lowly cave.

The shepherd had just then gone into the city of Sutri to sell cheese and had not yet returned. Berta was concerned that Rolandin had, once again, gone off as well: "What am I to do with my son, Rolandin, who is always slipping off from the cave?" *Berta lamented.*

Galisena attempted to console her friend, saying, "Why must you constantly worry, Berta. They'll be back before long. Rolandin is a very clever boy!"[2]

Just then the shepherd returned, saying, "My daughters, Berta and Galisena, I don't feel well today. In fact, I believe that my time has perhaps come."

"What are you saying, Old Man!" *Berta protested.*

"No, my daughter, Berta," *the shepherd continued,* "I no longer have the strength to stay on my feet. I only hope that Rolandin will be able to provide you with the sustenance you need."

And even as he spoke, the shepherd collapsed.

"Good Lord in Heaven," *Berta exclaimed,* "the old man is dead! And now, who will provide us with our sustenance?"

Just then, Rolandin, breathless, ran up calling, "Mama, Auntie Galisena, I've been out in the forest ... picking ... berries. But, what's this I see! The old man is sleeping!"

"My son, Rolandin," *Berta patiently explained,* "the old man is dead."

"Oh," *Rolandin responded pensively,* "the old man is dead." *But, then, impulsively, he blurted,* "And what does it mean, the old man is dead?"

"What! You don't know what it means to be dead," *Berta replied weakly.* "It means that the old man will walk no more and eat no more."

"Whoa!" *Rolandin exclaimed.* "If the old man will eat no more, then I'll go ahead and eat his food myself!"

Berta: "What are you saying, Rolandin! Take the old man and bury him."

Three: Knights and Masques

Rolandin: "Oh, all right. Hey, Old Man, get up so that we can go bury you!"
Berta: "Rolandin! He can't hear you! You have to pick him up and carry him away!"
And as Rolandin picked up the shepherd and carted him off, he cursed his luck, saying, "Damnation! Every little task falls always to me."
Yet, he had only gone a few steps before he came running back to the cave, shouting, "Mama, Mama, know that I carried the old man over there by that mountain. And I said to him, 'Hey, Old Man, stand right here while I prepare the hole!' But no sooner than I had turned my back, the old man threw himself down the mountain!"
"What?" Berta feebly asked, "You threw the old man down the mountain?"
"No, Mama," Rolandin whined, "it was he who fell!"
Berta: "Oh, Good Lord in Heaven. It's late. Let's go to bed. Tomorrow, we can go out in search of food."
The next morning, Rolandin arose before his mother Berta and his Aunt Galisena and went off to the forest in search of food, saying to himself, "Rolandin, here I am in the forest, as is my habit. In the morning, as soon as the sun rises, I slip off from the cave. Now, however, I must go in search of small game to bring home to my Mama Berta, as well as my Auntie Galisena. But just now, in this forest, there is nothing to be found."
Yet even as he was speaking, he heard a howl arising deep within the forest and he was almost instantly set upon by a dragon. "But, what's this I see," Rolandin exclaimed as the dragon rushed against him, "a fat, fat serpent! I think I'll go ahead and kill it!" He, thereupon, threw himself upon the dragon, throttling it with his club and, when he had killed it, he exclaimed, "This cowardly serpent really made me sweat. Now, I'm going to take it back to the cave, so that we can cook it and eat it!"
And even as Berta worried about Rolandin's disappearance, he came running back to the cave, shouting: "Mama! Mama! Look what I've brought you! A fat dragon for our dinner!"
Berta: "What! Rolandin, one doesn't eat dragons!"
Rolandin: "What's this I hear! Are you telling me that I accomplished this task for nothing! Damn my rotten luck!"
Berta: "My son, Rolandin, listen to me. If we eat this dragon, we will die of its venom. Therefore, take the dragon, and throw it down the mountain."
Rolandin: "Oh, all right, even this task falls to me."
And as Berta and Galisena began to scour the forest for something to eat, Rolandin wandered into town where the news of his slaying the dragon was already spreading among the poor boys, one of whom, Nofrio, announced: "Cumpari Virticchio,[3] how does it strike you that yesterday, this little fellow, with the body of a vastone, killed a dragon nearly twelve meters long!"
Virticchio answered, "Cumpari, this young fellow, with the strength that he has, would do well to participate in the joust, taking the part of the poor boys."

Sicilian Epic and the Marionette Theater

And even as they discussed him, Rolandin passed by calling, "Alms! Alms! Please, spare me some alms!"

"Give me a moment," Nofrio said to Virticchio, "so that I might speak with this boy, Cumpari."

And, as Nofrio approached him, Rolandin blurted out, "Give me some alms or I'll cut your face!"

"Whoa," Nofrio exclaimed. "Listen, boy, do you want to participate in the joust of the rich boys against the poor that every year is organized here in Sutri? If you win the joust, you will receive an abundance of food every day as well as a beautiful suit of armor."[4]

Rolandin, pleased with the proposition, said, "You wish to give me a beautiful suit of armor as well as food! All right, I swear to you and promise you that I will participate in this joust with the hope of winning the tournament!"

"Bravo," Nofrio exclaimed, "Long live ... Hey, wait a minute! What's your name, little fellow?"

"My name is Rolandin, and I live in a cave in the forest nearby together with my Mama, Berta, and my Auntie Galisena."

"Good, Cumpari," Nofrio said, and then, looking toward Virticchio, he added, "but now you must go a round with this little fellow in order to test your strength against his."

"All right, Cumpari, but I warn you that I feel the strength of a bull this morning."

Virticchio stepped forward. "Rolandin, now you must go a round with me, in order to test your strength against mine! Are you ready?"

"Yes, I'm ready," said Rolandin and he fell upon the little vagabond, knocking him to the ground.

But then Nofrio stepped forward: "Rolandin, you have shown your mettle against Virticchio but now you must go a round with me! Are you ready?"

Rolandin: "I'm ready!"

Nofrio: "En garde!"

And in the fury of Rolandin's assault, Nofrio as well was beaten to the ground.

"Cumpari, do you want to go another round?" Rolandin called.

"No, what are you saying, Cumpari!" Nofrio said as he wiped the dirt from his pantaloons.

Just then, Oliver, son of Renier, governor of Sutri, entered the arena. As Renier paced his royal apartment, pondering Charlemagne's banishment of Berta and Milon and their subsequent disappearance, Oliver challenged the poor boys. "Hey, Jousters," he shouted, "Who wants to go a round with me? Let him step forward!"

"Oliver," Virticchio offered, "I would be pleased to go a round with you. For I, with the strength of a bull, will knock you off your feet!"

"This we shall see, Virticchio!" Oliver rejoined, "En garde!"

Within moments, Oliver knocked Virticchio to the ground.

"Damnation," Virticchio whined, "I have been felled!"

But before he could even gather himself up, Oliver imperiously shouted, "Virticchio, you have been beaten. Withdraw!"

Then Nofrio entered the fray in order to safeguard the reputation of the poor boys: "Listen, earthworm," he chided, "now you must go a round with me. Know that I am Nofrio and I will make you understand the stuff that I'm made of!"

Oliver: "This we shall see, Nofrio. En garde!"

But Nofrio likewise was knocked to the ground.

"Oh," he cried, "how shameful! Oliver, do you believe that you felled me?"

"Of course, how could it be other than that I have felled you?" Oliver countered.

"Well, you must know," Nofrio defended, "that while you believed you were oppressing a pebble beneath your feet, I slipped and fell."

"Fine, Nofrio," Oliver disdained. "Withdraw!"

Then, turning his attention to Rolandin, Oliver said, "Listen, boy. Who are you? I have never seen you here in the city of Sutri."

"Oliver," Rolandin answered, "Know that I am Rolandin. And you will no longer play the cock in the midst of hens!"

Oliver, dumbstruck, said, "What's this I hear!"

Rolandin: "Are you ready?"

Oliver: "I'm ready, Rolandin!"

Rolandin: "All right, en garde!"

And with the strength of his arm, Rolandin knocked Oliver to the ground.

"Damnation," Oliver moaned, "I was the champion but this boy has felled me. Listen, Rolandin, I want to go another round with you."

"I, not wishing to offend you," Rolandin responded, "refuse to accept your challenge. You were the loser. Withdraw!"

"What's this I hear," Oliver blustered. "You refuse me, you coward?"

"Coward," Rolandin protested. "You have dared offer me that unforgivable insult! Now you will pay double, you coward!" And with that he set upon Oliver, beating him to a pulp.

Meanwhile, back at the cave, Berta worried aloud about the whereabouts of Rolandin: "My friend, Galisena. The hour is late. And still my son, Rolandin, has not returned from Sutri. I hope nothing has happened to him during the course of the joust."

Galisena: "But why must you constantly worry, Berta? Rolandin is a very clever boy and he knows how to handle himself in any situation. Look! Here he comes now."

Rolandin: "Mama! Mama! Know that I won the joust! But when Oliver, the son of Governor Renier, was felled, he wanted to go another round. Then I refused, and that coward gave me a terrible insult. Then I let him feel the weight of my hands!"

Berta: "What's this I hear! Rolandin! You were too insolent. You must know that the sons of great men ought to be respected because they can harm us!"[5]

Rolandin: "But I am unable to accept their insults simply because I am poor. These rich men don't care if I live well or in misery."

"You're just like your father, Milon," Berta sighed. "Very well, Rolandin. Come along. Let's go have our dinner."

In the meantime, Governor Renier sent a soldier to arrest Rolandin and the soldier, upon returning to the palace, sought an audience with Renier.

Soldier: "Permission."
Renier: "Come forward, Soldier."
Soldier: "Governor, I advise you that we have arrested, Rolandin."
Renier: "Well done, soldier. Bring him into my presence."
Soldier: "Yes, sir, immediately."
Renier: "Tell me, boy, I wish to know why you, like a madman, felled my son, for you have gravely injured him."
Rolandin: "I gave him what he deserved."
Renier: "What's this I hear! What's your name?"
Rolandin: "And you! What's your name?"
Renier: "My name is Renier."
Rolandin: "And my name is Rolandin and I live in a cave in the woods."
Renier: "What's this I hear! Do you live in that cave alone?"
Rolandin: "And you! With whom do you live?"
Renier: "What's this I hear! I live with my wife and my children."
Rolandin: "And I cannot tell you that I live with my Mama Berta, and my Auntie Galisena."
Renier: "What! What's your mother's name?"
Rolandin: "I'm not telling you that her name is Berta."
Renier: "Tell me something; your father, what's his name?"
Rolandin: "And your father! What's his name?"
Renier: "My father is Girard of Vienna."
Rolandin: "And my father … is named … Milon."
Renier: "What! You're the son of Berta and Milon! Fine, Rolandin; let me call my son, Oliver, so we might judge who is in the right between the two of you."

Thereupon, Governor Renier ordered a soldier to summon his son to the throne room, and Oliver, upon entering into the presence of his father, said, "My father, you have called. Command me."

Renier: "Listen, Oliver, I want to know how things fell out in the square between you and Rolandin."
Rolandin: "I would never have abused your son, if he had not offended me, giving me that terrible insult. Therefore, I gave him what he deserved."
Renier: "What's this I hear! Oliver, did you offer an insult to Rolandin?"
Oliver: "Yes, my father, I offered him an insult because he felled me and I wanted to go another round with him but he refused."
Renier: "What's this I hear! Oliver, withdraw!"

Then, turning to Rolandin, the governor said, "All right, boy; I want to see *justice done. My son, Oliver, being in the wrong, the promised prize is yours. To the winner of the joust goes food from my own larder for three months. Beyond that, I will give food to your mother, Berta, and to your aunt, Galisena."*

Governor Renier ordered a soldier to accompany Rolandin to the royal pantry where he was provisioned. And as Rolandin collected food for himself, his mother, and his aunt, Renier worried aloud about how he might rescue Berta without incurring the wrath of Charlemagne.[6]

The Intrusion of Farce Upon the Epic Stage

The First Adventure of Rolandin's opening, while not containing any of the formal pageantry apparent in the opening of *The Death of King Pepin*, conforms, nonetheless, to the thematic elements of epic. It consists of a council between Berta and Galisena in which Galisena is the passive recipient of a brief summary of past events. Once again, this part of Council acts as the exposition to the narrative, offering an introduction to the dramatis personae and defining their initial predicament. It is offered in the noble diction of Berta and is nearly devoid of any real dialogue. The council is interrupted by two audiences (that between Berta and the shepherd and, fast upon its heels, that between Berta and Rolandin). As previously mentioned, the epic sequence, Announcement, Audience and Dispatch, usually involves the introduction of a conflict, as well as some initial step toward resolving it, into the narrative and such is the case with these two audiences. The first conflict involves the loss of the shepherd: the only member of Berta's family who knows how to work for a living. The second involves the inability of Rolandin to fill the shepherd's shoes.

It is the second audience, that between Berta and Rolandin, which begins to erode the epic base of this story with farce. Rolandin can only comprehend the shepherd's death as a tedious task and a means to get more food. His hunger and laziness, his exuberant speech (something unobtainable in the transcription/translation process), and his inability to comprehend his predicament bring him more into coincidence with Virticchio than the young Charlemagne. There is a turning away from the more noble acts and patterns of speech characteristic of epic in this audience, a turning away which will become further accentuated as the story progresses.

Rolandin makes a first, bumbling attempt to resolve the conflict by slaying a dragon. In this, Rolandin's first chivalric act, we are struck by his prowess at arms—even if his weapon is the lowly club—at such a young age and jettisoned into the world of chivalry, and, in fact, the dragon slaying is depicted in the classic features of epic battle. Yet when Rolandin speaks of taking the dragon back to the cave so that he can eat it, we are instantly reminded of the masque who has just dropped the shepherd down the mountain and thus tossed back into the world of farce. Hunger, tired resignation to labor, and buffoonery are its earmarks.

As if to underscore the significance of farce to this episode, we almost immediately encounter the masques, Nofrio and Virticchio, inserting themselves into chivalric narrative and discussing Rolandin's recent adventure as they ready for Sutri's annual joust between the rich boys and the poor boys, a popular subject with epic's working-class audience. Rolandin interrupts them in one more attempt at providing for Berta and Galisena, this time through begging. That we are firmly entrenched in the world of farce is enforced by the masques' extensive use of Sicilian dialect in juxtaposition to the knight's (or in this case, young prince's) use of Italian. More importantly, as Rolandin falls under the tutelage of Nofrio and Virticchio, he will himself adopt certain words and phrases more characteristic to the masques, most notably the use of the word *Cumpari* (Friend) to address his new companions:

> *Nofrio: Cumpari Virticchio, chi vi ni pare ca ajeri un picciriddu con un corpo di vastone ammazzo un serpiente ri qual chi rurrici mitri!*
> *Virticchio: Cumpari, stu picciriddu cu sta fuerza chi havi fosse buono ffar participare na giostra nella parte dei poveri.*
> *Rolandin: Ehi! Fatemi elemosina!*
> *Nofrio: Aspetta un minuto, che ci parliamo, Cumpari.*
> *Rolandin: Ehi! Fatemi elemosina o ti prometto che ti taglia la faccia.*
>
> [Nofrio asked his companion Virticchio], "Cumpari Virticchio, how does it strike you that yesterday, this little fellow, with the body of a vastone, killed a dragon nearly twelve meters long!"
> Virticchio answered, "Cumpari, this young fellow, with the strength that he has, would do well to participate in the joust, taking the part of the poor boys."
> And even as they discussed him, Rolandin passed by calling, "Alms! Alms! Please, spare me some alms!"
> "Give me a moment," Nofrio said to Virticchio, "so that I might speak with this boy, Cumpari."
> And, as Nofrio approached him, Rolandin blurted out, "Give me some alms or I'll cut your face!"

Three: Knights and Masques

At this point, mock epic battle of the sort at least as old as the medieval English poem, *Tourney at Tottingham*, occurs. But such battle quickly deteriorates into the classic brawl of masques, or their real sociological analogues, poor boys. A definitive move away from epic and toward farce has occurred. For example, the usual sequence of themes characteristic of epic—Council (open), Announcement, Audience, Dispatch, Council (close), Battle—has been here modified by the simpler, farcical sequence of Entrance, Encounter, Brawl (with, in this case, a veneer of epic battle), and Exit. Just this sequence occurs over and over again in Palermitan farces: Virticchio is found meandering along the road, perhaps singing a plaintive song, and stops to address the audience or sometimes just to wonder aloud. As he continues along his way, he encounters a stranger, quite often a Saracen, or another masque, perhaps his *Cumpari*, Nofrio. They begin to discourse but inevitably some sort of confusion arises; Virticchio misunderstands the words of his interlocutor or vice versa and a fight ensues. Whether Virticchio vanquishes his enemy or the misunderstanding is somehow cleared up and an armistice declared, Virticchio leaves the way he came: aimless and singing his plaint. A general air of vagrancy and camaraderie pervades the farce (except in those instances where the farce explicitly burlesques epic battle); alliances are easily formed and the occasional fisticuffs which intrude upon them are always temporary and quickly forgotten.

As well as multigenericity, dialogism, its natural function, becomes a more prominent feature of *The First Adventures of Rolandin*. Beyond the usual alternation between Italian and Sicilian, which denotes the encounter between the young knight and the masque (i.e., the nobility and the people), Rolandin commits a specifically noble speech act, the oath (rendered more noble through the use of anaphora: the repetition of a word at the beginning of successive clauses), when he declares "I swear and I promise that I will participate in this joust." Yet he also has recourse to the vulgar threat "I'll cut your face!" as well as the familiar address implied through the use of the term *Cumpari*: a term which (like Friend or Brother in some English tales) acknowledges equality among speakers. It is thus through multigenericity, the interweaving of themes from different genres of Sicilian popular narrative, and dialogism, the borrowing of characters' voices from these various genres, that farce intrudes so persistently upon *The First Adventures of Rolandin*.

Nowhere is the interweaving of epic and farcical matter more apparent than in the varied use of the epic theme Battle in this tale. First, Battle is used to actualize Rolandin's slaying of the dragon and practice jousts with Virticchio and Nofrio. Next, it is used to actualize the jousts between a rich boy and a poor boy: that is, Oliver and Rolandin. But in each of these cases, Battle, an ostensibly chivalric act, is transformed by Rolandin's erratic behavior and exuberant speech into farce's characteristic fisticuffs. While Rolandin is perfectly capable of slaying a dragon, he does so only to eat. And while he excels at the joust, he is just as comfortable with the common brawl. More importantly, Battle, in this narrative, parodies some of the knight's most abiding concerns: the slaying of dragons, the joust itself, and, most notably, the accusation of cowardice: this last a concern we will not leave until the aftermath of the Battle of Roncevaux.

Toward the conclusion of the story, we find Berta, as usual, worrying aloud to her confidante, Galisena. And Rolandin does little to allay her fears when he returns from the day's adventures and relates to her how he beat up a noble. Berta's worries, in this case, are well founded, for Rolandin soon finds himself under arrest—a condition fraught with historical significance given the nature of the relationship between Palermitans and their foreign rulers—and in the hands of Governor Renier. But as luck would have it, Rolandin, in classic epic (and fairy tale) fashion, inadvertently reveals his royal origins during his audience with Renier. During that interview, Rolandin's character manifests a subtle shift in speech. As his royal origins are revealed, Rolandin switches his form of address from the familiar *tu* (you, second person, singular), characteristic of the working classes, to the polite *voi* (you, second person, plural), characteristic of more regal address. While the distinction between *tu* and *voi* suggests little more than conventional deference in everyday speech, it suggests in its narrative context the shift from masque to knight.

In Rolandin's exchange with Renier, a number of figures and speech acts interact to color Rolandin's character. While his desire to withhold information is probably noble and allies him to the young knight, his inability to do so is comic and expresses the masque's near imperative to enter into dialogue. He hesitates (short pauses) and occasionally refuses to speak (long pauses). He evades answering by responding to questions with further questions: a classic instance of linguistic subterfuge. Yet at times he spews out more information than the question calls for ("My name is Rolandin and I live in a cave near the forest") and at others he gives information under the pretext of not telling (paralipsis): "And I cannot tell you that I live with my Mama Berta and my Auntie Galisena" and, "I'm not telling you that her name is Berta!"

Once Renier has ascertained Rolandin's royal origins, he questions him further on the incident in the square, and Rolandin makes it clear that he throttled Oliver only because the latter had offered him the most humiliating insult possible to a knight: the accusation of cowardice. It is notable at this point that Rolandin's act of beating up Oliver as a result of the accusation of cowardice is deemed evidence of this apparent masque's true (read noble) character. Renier summons his son, who admits that he did indeed offer such insult, whereupon, Renier summarily dismisses his son with the same deprecatory command that Oliver had used during the tournament: "Withdraw!" Rolandin, in the eyes and ears of epic's audience, has been vindicated at that moment, and the Palermitan belief that a ruler can be just as well as demanding, something that is cryptically revealed by the Genius of Palermo, has—with that simple word—been ably reinforced.

Plebian Disguises and Royal Origins

It seems then that *The First Adventures of Rolandin* consists of a bifurcated plot which can be stated as follows: Rolandin goes hunting and fails to bring home edible food to Berta and Galisena after which he jousts and brings home food befitting Berta and Galisena's royal upbringing. In other words, subsistence acts (i.e., gathering berries, hunting small game, begging alms) are the proper province of the masque, whereas chivalric acts (slaying beasts, jousting) are the proper province of the young knight. Rolandin fails at the former simply because he is not truly a masque; conversely, he is successful at the latter because he is in actuality a young knight.

To a certain extent we are dealing with a common enough tale: the royal origins of an apparent peasant boy or street urchin are finally recognized. What nonetheless becomes remarkable about this particular rendition of that tale type is the care with which the "poor boy" is delineated; he has an insatiable appetite, a tired resignation to having to work for a living, a tendency to wander, and a familiar manner of speech as well as social communion. He is, in a word, a masque. He is moreover that character who uses Sicilian dialect, who is the direct descendant of one of the more notable Palermitan laborers (the porter, *vastone*), and who is the most privileged (if freedom in action and the ability to evoke laughter are any indication of such privilege) in epic. He is, in fact, epic's representative of the Palermitan people. He is that character which most completely mirrors (and, perforce, satirizes) his very audience.

The knight, rather than work, fights. It is his privilege to bear arms. He rarely goes hungry, and he does not have the prerogative to wander at will. His oath of fealty to the sovereign prevents that. His speech is noble and inherently encumbered with obligation; it reflects the complex network of deference that is his social environment. His language is Italian (i.e., foreign) and the mirror that he therefore presents can reflect (and at times satirize) nothing more than the Palermitan aristocracy.

The simple equation, work is to masque as battle is to knight, is enough to let us see that the masque represents the Palermitan people and the knight represents the Palermitan aristocracy, for the juxtaposition of work with battle is the primary economic justification of a people that has historically defined itself in relationship to its court: its simultaneous destruction and well-being. The curiosity, however, in *The First Adventures of Rolandin*, is that the young prince takes on the characteristics of the masque, becomes, through that peculiar circumstance, one of the people. This is not an unprecedented circumstance in Palermitan epic. In fact, the young Charlemagne undergoes a similar transformation in the very first episode of the Carolingian Cycle. When he encounters the shepherd during his flight from Paris, he begins to envelop himself in the habit of the masque, and his brutal tale of Millery Washerwoman is just the initial suggestion of that habit. Later in the Cycle, as the young Renaud finds himself in similar straits to those of Rolandin, he will also adopt the mannerisms and peculiarities of speech characteristic to the masques. In this, a first general principle of epic comes into focus: prince becomes masque so that he might become knight.

This principle is historically meaningful to Palermitans who, as we have previously seen, view their history as a series of occupations by foreign courts. Palermitans shrug off the aspect of occupation as inevitable but there is a caveat in their resignation. The court must at least attempt to become Sicilian in order to be accepted by the people. The failure to have done so on the part of the Angevin King Charles may have led to that seminal event in Palermitan (and European) history, the Sicilian Vespers.

> It was [Charles'] practice in each of his dominions as far as possible to employ officials drawn from some other of his dominions. But he took no account of the resentment that such a policy might cause. He seems to have thought that, as in France, the element dangerous to the monarchy was the nobility, and the lesser folk would automatically rally to the king. In his Italian lands he diminished the power of the local nobility and relied upon imported French nobles and knights, to whom he never allowed too much territorial power. He failed to see either that these imported noblemen did not at once become efficient and incorruptible functionaries, just because they were divorced from their ancient hereditary territories, or that a local population might dislike foreign officials even if they were efficient.[7]

And in the early stages of the Spanish occupation which followed the Angevin, Sicily, as we have seen, invited the viceroy to become the king of Sicily, an invitation which he summarily rejected. We will return to this principle of prince-become-masque and its political ramifications as this essay progresses. For now, we may simply reiterate that the device which, in fact, effects such a transformation is dialogism: "the interaction of several consciousnesses" expressed through the juxtaposition of distinctive dramatic voices.[8] But what is singular about dialogism in Palermo is the fact that not only do different categories of characters, say knight and masque, represent their distinctive consciousnesses through distinctive voices, but a single category of character, say knight, transforms his social persona—reconfiguring himself as, say, a masque—through the transformation of his voice.

Dialogism Revisited

As we have thus far seen, epic's dialogism is obtained through a variation of the puppeteer's diction, a variation primarily effected by a change in the figures of speech which are used to connect and control the formulas (or repertoire of stock phrases) out of which the puppeteer composes his narrative even as he performs it. A figure of speech is a verbal construction that expresses something through its form (i.e., particular syntax) as well as its content (i.e., particular choice of words). In epic, figures are often those explicitly recognized in rhetorical theory, a metaphor for example, but they are just as often created by modifying a speech with a specifying word or phrase—thus, creating a speech act—or by allusion to various patterns of speech—tones for instance—to be found on the streets and public squares of Palermo.

Traditional figures which we have already encountered are apostrophe, the pun, and paralipsis. Apostrophe is specifically an address to an inanimate object but more generally a redefinition of the speaker's audience, moving the address away from another character and toward the actual audience or even one's self through a stylization of one's speech. It is this aspect of stylized address to a redefined audience which renders apostrophe noble and most pertinent to the knight. Council is in fact primarily defined by such stylization. Not only is there a heavy use of the vocative throughout but the entire theme is biased toward allocution (i.e., the hortatory address to passive listeners) rather than the true dialogism which characterizes the masques' encounters. Apostrophe nonetheless extends well beyond the confines of Council. For example, the knight will often address himself in the third person. It might be countered that he does this simply to make himself known to the audience, but such an artificed speech act is not common to the masque (unless he is parodying a knight) who rather—as Nofrio does time and again—steps onto the stage with the Sicilian salutation, "*Sabbenerica a tutti*" (God bless you all), offered directly to the audience, "*ed a me cumpari Virticchio*" (and to my good friend Virticchio), offered directly to his companion. The knight's stylized self address, based in apostrophe and expanded through allocution, reaches a pitch of nobility (read, perhaps, tragedy) in the soliloquy, which intrudes upon the momentous moments of epic and which, again, befits only the tongue of the knight.

Apostrophe is then that figure which colors the knight's speech throughout epic and sets it off from the masque's more natural speech patterns. But it would be improper to simply define the masque's speech as natural for it too, as we have just witnessed, is figuratively constructed. Among the various figures at the masque's disposal are the pun—which hinges on the variable meaning of a single word (that is, a homonym) or the different meanings of similar sounding words—and paralipsis: the telling under the pretext of not telling. Such figures in conjunction with various techniques for withholding information (brute silence, answering questions with questions, long pauses) define the masque's speech as a system of linguistic subterfuge. It is such definition that most clearly allies the masque with the various tricksters who populate the world's folk narrative.

Despite the rich use of traditional rhetorical figures in epic, a figure is often created simply by placing a word or phrase before a typical speech and creating thereby a specific speech act. For example, by placing "know that" before "I am" a formulaic introduction becomes a formulaic challenge: "Listen, Agrican, know that I am Roland, First Paladin of France, nephew of Charlemagne!" This figure, which we will encounter in a coming episode and which may be termed Challenge, clearly demarcates the speaker as a knight. Epic's dialogism is most often actualized, however, through allusion to specific speech acts and typical speech patterns (genres of discourse) that are to be found in the very streets of Palermo. An example already discussed is the differentiation of speakers through their use of the polite or familiar forms of address. While on the streets and in the public squares this variation emplaces a social continuum that differentiates relations familiar and egalitarian on the one hand from relations characterized by deference and respect on the other, in epic this variation serves to demarcate various characters' generic affiliation. The use of the familiar *tu* demarcates the masque while the use of the polite *voi* demarcates the knight.

The variable use of Italian and Sicilian is in effect an extension of this concept. The masque speaks Sicilian while the knight speaks Italian. Perhaps more than any other variation of speech pattern, the differential use of Italian and Sicilian suggests differential class affiliation, so much so that such signification was carried from Sicilian into Italian-American culture. Jerre Mangione, in his memoir of life in the Italian-American community in Rochester, New York, relates the following:

> My Uncle Nino claimed that Italian was "feminine" and Sicilian "masculine." He also said that the only reason Sicilians ever addressed each other in proper Italian was to show off their schooling and prove to each other that they were not peasants. He probably was right, for I noticed that the osten-

tation of speaking proper Italian was dropped as soon as two Sicilians had known each other for an evening and showed any desire to be friends. Anyone who persisted in speaking Italian after that was considered a prig or, at least, a socialist.[9]

This distinction between the "feminine" Italian and the "masculine" Sicilian (or southern manner of pronouncing Italian) is common. I have heard it from southern Italians, both Neapolitans and Sicilians, and Italian-Americans alike. Usually the speaker will take great pains to imitate an effeminate northern Italian accent, mincing all the way through his speech, and then practically growl out his Sicilian, Neapolitan, or southern Italian example, very masculine indeed!

Other examples of speech patterns that are borrowed from the Palermitan streets are the prayers and supplications which center the voice of the saint (we hear them at mass or during the processions on various feast days) and the boasts and bouts of irony which center the voice of the bandit. I heard them when I was trying to convince another foreigner that the men robbing the storeroom in her apartment building were not robbing the storeroom and that it would be best to just continue upstairs (as everyone else was doing) rather than engage the "new men" (who admittedly used metal clippers rather than keys to get into the storeroom) in conversation as they seemed quite busy.

Within this context, we are able to see how the choice of figure with which to describe and construct a similar incident can change the very nature of that incident. For example, when Rolandin, upon killing his first dragon, says, "This cowardly serpent made me sweat! Now I want to take him to the cave so that we can eat him," we hear the voice of the masque who just dropped the shepherd down the mountain. But when in manhood, Roland slays a dragon, his voice is clearly that of a knight: "Ugly, venomous serpent, do you know how much anguish you have caused during your life? So long has your hide endured that not even my sword, Durandal, was able to cut it through." What differentiates the voices in these two instances is the choice of figures in which to embed epic's formulae. Rolandin's voice is naturalistic and couched in the terms of direct address. The masque is always involved in dialogue, whether with another masque, the audience, or himself. Roland's voice on the other hand is stylized, in this case by the traditional use of apostrophe.

A change in diction—defined as a variation of the figures, speech acts, and tones used to construct and control a speech—is enough to change our perception of that speech and perforce the character who speaks it. In the two preceding narratives we find various examples of the transformation of a character through a transformation of his voice. After Charlemagne encounters the shepherd, he fabricates the story of Millery Washerwoman. When Rolandin encounters the masques, Nofrio and Virticchio, he not only borrows their manner of speech but even intersperses his own with words and phrases in their Sicilian dialect. The same sort of transformation occurs, as well, with the youthful Renaud. Perhaps one-sixth of the 270 odd episodes that comprise the Palermitan version of the Carolingian Cycle are involved with this early history of Charlemagne, Rolandin, and Renaud and thus, necessarily, with their alter egos: the masques. Dialogism, of the same sort that effects the transformation of these youthful knights into masques, creates within the Carolingian Cycle a kind of rhetoric of identity—that is, a mode of communication that simultaneously establishes networks of affiliation and demarcates moments of enmity—which, as we will shortly see, inscribes within Palermitan epic its historical specificity as well as its sociological implications.

Chapter Four

Saints and Bandits

The Rhetoric of Identity

Marcel Danesi suggests that metaphor, perhaps the central figure of speech in the arsenal of rhetorical strategies, confirms, to some extent, the Sapir-Whorf hypothesis, linguistically shaping our sense of reality "because it springs," in a very immediate way, "from our experience of reality." Here Danesi is underlining a major function of rhetoric. "Consider the expression," Danesi continues, "John is a monkey."

> The topic in this case is a person named John and the vehicle the animal known as a monkey. Portraying John as a monkey forces us to imagine a human person in simian terms. If one were to call John a snake, a pig, or a puppy, then our image of John would change in kind with each new vehicle—he would become serpentine, swine-like, and puppy-like to our mind's eye. Like Franz Kafka's ... horrifying short story *Metamorphosis*, where the main character awakes one morning from a troubled dream to find himself changed to some kind of monstrous vermin, our perception of people (and of ourselves) is altered (probably permanently) the instant we paint a picture of their personality in animal terms. Like the spell put on people by shamans, people become what our metaphors say they are.[1]

Metaphor, then, is not simply a rhetorical flourish in Danesi's reading. It is as well a mechanism for constructing cultural reality. But metaphor is just one tiny nodule of rhetoric. What of the other units of rhetorical analysis? There are any number of tropes beyond metaphor: metonymy (referring to something by an attribute), synecdoche (referring to something by one of its parts), antonomasia (referring to something by an epithet rather than a name), and—one of my favorites—cryptonymy, a trope which, like the Genius of Palermo, seeks to reveal through concealment.[2] There are also innumerable speech acts: hyperbole (overstatement), litotes (understatement), and apostrophe (exclamatory address),

Four: Saints and Bandits

just to name a few. And then there are tones—essentially genres of speech—to consider: sarcasm, irony, consolation, threat.

Whether dealing with tropes, speech acts, or tones, rhetoric entails the mobilization or redeployment of linguistic formulas in order to imply something more than the mere denotative value of an utterance. Phonetics can be used to suggest different class affiliation: in the early history of the Massachusetts Bay Colony, for instance, omitting the final *r* in words allowed colonists to emulate the privileged accent of the home country. The artful use of morphemes can offer an utterance various suggestive qualities: for instance, the morphological form *-er* can be added to the name of a political group in order to suggest a degree of fringe ideology (John Bircher, Teabagger, Birther) or the Spanish suffix *-ero* can be added to the ethnic term Maya in order to rhetorically transform an ethnic label into an occupational label (i.e., *Mayero*, or Yucatecan agricultural worker).[3] Altering the intonation pattern of a word can insinuate a different meaning of the term than generally intended: for instance, in a justly famous example, Indian cafeteria workers offering gravy to British mechanics at an English airport lowered rather than raised their intonation pattern when they spoke the word gravy suggesting to their British patrons that rather than offering gravy they were, more or less, saying, "We have gravy; take it or leave it." Not surprisingly, unnecessary friction was the result.[4] Similarly, altering the grammatical environment of a word can give that word a connotative rather than denotative value: "I see the light," for instance, rather than "Turn on the light." There can even be gestural cues or specific social settings that might alter the normative understanding of a communication: think about the significance of the statement, "You look gorgeous in that outfit," if the speaker rolls his or her eyes while saying it.

When language—and, importantly, the nonverbal communication that surrounds it—is explored rhetorically, analysis moves beyond that which is merely informative to that which is culturally charged. Rhetorical analysis considers language that serves not simply to communicate cultural realities, but as Danesi suggests, construct such realities and in doing so, I would add, establish identity. In fact, I think dissecting the rhetorical strategies of various cultural products—such as folklore—in order to chart the effects of such strategies on identity is essential, because it draws attention to the contested nature of cultural products:

to the fact that cultural products exist only in their negotiation and renegotiation by actual flesh-and-blood members of a society. And it is through this negotiation, I would contend, that cultural identity—the actual locus, or place, where culture is situated—emerges. The reason that rhetoric is the crux, even the crucible, of identity—at least in my reading—is this: identity must be learned and then displayed through communication. Thus, rhetoric—viewed as the deployment of verbal, behavioral, and even material symbols—becomes the filter through which communication renders identity legible.

Roger Abrahams seems to have assigned such a role to rhetoric in folkloric production: "As the rhetorical approach considers techniques or argument," he maintained, "it assumes that all expression is designed to influence, and that we must simply discover the design. Folklore, being traditional activity, argues traditionally." It thereby attempts, in Abrahams' reading, to inculcate normative cultural values in the individual members of society, for instance through sprinkling one's speech with adages.[5] More recently, the work of rhetoricians such as Kent Ono and John Sloop and folklorists such as Robert Glenn Howard and Elliott Oring have elucidated the role that rhetoric might play in cultural studies in general and folkloric studies specifically. Ono and Sloop, in particular, have alluded to the aspect of rhetoric that I wish to explore here when they claim that vernacular discourse, speech that is characteristic of a defined community, "does not exist only as counter-hegemonic, but also as affirmative, *articulating a sense of community* that does not function solely as oppositional to dominant ideologies [emphasis added]." In other words, rhetoric—at least in the realm of vernacular discourse—constitutes community with all its attendant concerns and agendas.[6] Howard, exploring web-based versions of *The Sinner's Prayer*—a prayer which in evangelical Protestant tradition invites non-Christians to repent their sins and accept Jesus into their lives—notes that inasmuch as the readers of Christian-based web pages have already accepted Jesus into their lives, the rhetorical function of *The Sinner's Prayer* here becomes epideictic—"articulat[ing] values already accepted by [the sites'] audience in order to indicate group identity."[7] Oring brings some badly needed structure to the often unwieldy rhetorical analysis of folkloric material through constructing an outline of traditional tropes that function to offer legend its truth value. For instance, he suggests, that

Four: Saints and Bandits

tropes (defined as narratological techniques) such as distancing, affirming, or managing expectations—deftly managed by the storyteller—offer legend its veneer of historical validity and, thus, its persuasive authority within a community of auditors.[8] In essence then (and this is where identity enters Oring's analysis), rhetoric not only establishes the storyteller as a reliable narrator but also allows his or her listeners to establish a sense of (following Kenneth Burke's terminology) identification with the storyteller as well as his or her characters.

Ono and Sloop, like most rhetoricians, approach their subject matter—as does anthropologist Clifford Geertz—as cultural texts: that is, texts that can be deciphered for their underlying symbolic structures or, to maintain fidelity to the Geertzian terminology used in our analysis of the Genius of Palermo, to disentangle the web of signification that lies deep within the cultural text. Howard and Oring, like most folklorists who wade into the analysis of rhetoric, tend to defer to the rhetorical project as set forth by Abrahams, firmly grounding their analyses—as most folklorists do—in the performative context. But whether approaching their subject from a Geertzian or performative perspective, each of the preceding analysts has not simply attempted to dissect cultural artifacts through rhetorical theory; embedded in each of the actual analyses is the suggestion that rhetoric not only shapes, focuses, refines and—in the final analysis—communicates information but that it also, in one way or another, establishes identity: both intergroup and—more importantly in the context of the Sicilian marionette theater—intragroup identity.

In doing so, each analyst participates in the rhetorical project as set forth by Kenneth Burke, who viewed rhetoric not merely as the art of persuasion but also, and equally, as the mechanism of identification: "Burke's refinement of Aristotle," Robert Brooke and Charlotte Hogg contend in their analysis of ethnographic voice, "suggests that the relationship between the writer and reader," as well as that between speaker and auditor, "is more than just a textual feature contributing to persuasion."

> For Burke, identification between persons is the fundamental act in rhetoric, at both foundational and persuasive levels. Foundationally, we make the effort to listen or read, Burke says, only when we already believe the speaker or writer is engaged with us in a common project of some sort.... We are

> persuaded when we come to believe that the speaker or writer speaks for us in some way. Hence, identification, or the means by which two dissimilar persons come to be identified as "with" each other in some significant sense, is the fundamental rhetorical act.[9]

Perhaps the clearest indication of the use of rhetorical analysis toward the end here suggested is offered by Dexter B. Gordon, who asserts that while rhetoric was mobilized in the project of justifying—and thereby preserving—the enslavement of African peoples in America, it likewise and simultaneously allowed for the oppositional Black Nationalist movement: "It is as blacks respond to ... rhetorical efforts to define them and delimit their lives," Gordon maintains, "that we see an open rhetorical contestation of histories and futures, of epistemologies and ontologies. Perhaps more significant, *we see how rhetoric functions materially to shape identities* [emphasis added]."[10]

One point more: whether embedded in cultural movements, vernacular discourse, or folkloric texts, rhetoric—it would seem—not only shapes identity for society at large but, perhaps even more importantly in the context of our discussion, for an audience's interpretation of the various characters that populate its stories as well—and this fact is especially essential to understanding the stories that emerge from the Sicilian marionette theater. Just as rhetoric is the mechanism through which the members of the aristocracy, the people, the clerical class, and the Mafia express their group affiliation "on the ground," that is, in real Palermitan time, it is also the mechanism through which the knight, the masque, the saint, and the bandit are actualized in epic—for, as we have seen, Palermitan puppeteers borrow the style of speech of the aristocracy, the people, priests, and Mafiosi to express the nature of the knight, the masque, the saint, and the bandit respectively.

But here's the problem with applying rhetorical theory to the sort of cultural analyses such as folklorists undertake and exploring, in turn, the relationship of culture and identity: Rhetoric—as a discipline—has historically been so unwieldy! What exactly are the metaphors—or symbolic equivalencies—that rhetoric isolates? Where is the list of them? And where the definitions? Shakespeare, apparently perturbed at the limitations that the jumbled nature of rhetorical theory placed on him, resolved his dilemma (characteristically, one might add) by making up his own figures, two of which—declension (the postulation of a set of paradigmatic relations) and derivation (the postulation of a sequence of causal relations)—he regularly employed to construct his dramatic voices—including those of Hamlet, Horatio, and Polonius. I cannot pretend to completely answer the questions raised by the seemingly haphazard nature of rhetorical theory or to offer a systematic treatment of the rhetorical devices that emerge in Palermitan epic, and I remain unsure as to whether a completely systematic treatment is called for or even possible, but what I have attempted to do is organize my observations about the rhetoric of identity with recourse to three major subsets of rhetorical devices that seem to regularly recur in Sicilian epic and seem, as well, to effect a translation of Sicilian social order to the epic arena: (1) tropes, in which one thing—through a number of technical operations—stands for or symbolizes something else, (2) speech acts, in which the grammatical organization of an utterance serves to imply something more (that which Deborah Tannen describes as a "metamessage")[11] than is explicitly stated, and (3) tones, in which everyday speech patterns (genres of speech) serve to mobilize an emotive response to an utterance.

I think that to get at the effect of culture—and, especially, the more deeply contested arenas of culture—on identity, one must explore the dialogue that culture, especially when viewed as a Geertzian text, provides. And this dialogue, I think, is expressed in the tools that rhetoric—that is, tropes, speech acts, and tones—provides. Thus, rhetoric, in my reading, provides the key to the web of signification—and its ramifications on identity—to which Geertz has significantly directed our attention. Interestingly, Robert Glenn Howard, in his article "A Theory of Vernacular Rhetoric," points out that Geertz's cultural analysis, while explicitly relying on the sociological work of Max Weber, implicitly relies as well on the rhetorical analyses of Kenneth Burke, even drawing attention to the fact that Burke uses language that we have come to associate almost exclusively with Geertz: "Our presence in a room is immediate, but the room's relation to our country as a nation, and beyond that, to international relations and cosmic relations, dissolves into a web of ideas and images that reach through our senses only in so far as the symbol systems that report on them are heard or seen."[12] Thus, it seems reasonable to argue that Geertz's analysis—probably the richest approach to unraveling the complexities of cultural contestation—is firmly situated in the rhetorical and particularly well placed to address the effect of culture on identity.

In a way, it seems to me, culture—whether manifested in a folktale, in the serial output of the popular press, or even, today, in a Web site—works very much like in a wiki: everyone in the society has an editorial role, an ability to participate in the dialogue that is ultimately culture, but the dialogue itself—the culture proper—resides in no one. It is supraindividual; at the same time, however, it informs the individual at least in the context of establishing identity, for it gives voice to what would otherwise be inchoate information and allows it to express not simply *itself* but also *the self*. In essence, we might say that rhetoric effects the assimilative function of culture: Inasmuch as there can be no "corporate" entity—that is, an entity which exists for a group as a whole—such as culture without an assimilative function, there can be no "corporate" entity such as culture without rhetoric. Put another way, we could say that culture is not something which resides in a society or, for that matter, in any individual member of a society. Rather, culture should be viewed as a process of communication—certainly verbal but also behavioral and even material—which allows members of a group to "speak" or, better, to represent themselves to one another as well as outsiders. Culture, then, is a thing that is—very literally—spoken, performed, and crafted. Viewed in this way, one cannot honestly say when speaking of Sicilian culture that Sicilians do this or that. Rightly speaking, nothing can be truly predictable about a Sicilian simply on the basis of the fact that he or she is a member of Sicilian society. Rather, one can say that a Sicilian who wishes to manifest affiliation with a Mafia style subculture—a subculture that has, for Sicilians at least, historically been denoted by a manner of speech, behavior, and dress more extensively than group affiliation—may do so through the affectation of a recognizable rhetorical repertoire that includes a number of verbal, behavioral, and material cues that collectively speak to his toughness. And, more to the point of this study, his rhetorical strategies—that is, his speech, behavior, and dress—have the uncanny ability to worm their way, somewhat surreptitiously, into the world of Sicilian epic.

In folklore, then, rhetoric—and this is particularly notable in Palermitan epic—serves to introject identity (read as the recognition and communication of group affiliation) directly into the narrative arena.

Four: Saints and Bandits

On the one hand, it defines Palermitan affiliation—and this is significant in a society where the term Christian is synonymous with human being and the term Turk is synonymous with barbarian—*as a whole*. On the other, it defines class affiliation *within* Palermitan society: in other words, rhetoric functions as a kind of communicative "grouping up," a linguistic mechanism for picking one's team. Here is how it works:

As the Carolingian Cycle progresses away from the early adventures of its preeminent heroes—Charlemagne, Roland, and Renaud—and the dichotomy of knight and masque that actualizes them, a new juxtaposition emerges: that between saint and bandit. The saint, as we will see, is a permutation of the knight: noble in speech, obedient to the point of subservience, and tragic in character; the bandit, on the other hand, is a permutation of the masque: his speech is preeminently familiar, his demeanor rebellious, and he often presents the opportunity for comic relief. Just as the dichotomy of knight and masque actualizes the early adventures of the Carolingian heroes, the dichotomy of knight and saint on the one hand, knight and bandit on the other, actualizes an entire sequence of adventures intervening between the heroes' coming of age and their inexorable destinies at Roncevaux.

Themes from the lives of bandits, most notably Abduction and Theft, pass into epic in a more haphazard manner than do those from farce. Yet they leave their indelible imprint on such narrative, creating of it something other than it was before. When a knight resorts to abduction or theft, he is enshrouding himself in a different character, a character no longer representative of fealty to the sovereign but representative instead of rebellion. These knights, the "courtly" bandits of Palermitan epic, are heirs to the medieval tradition of rebellious barons in Old French epics, or Chansons de Geste—a tradition which apparently grew out of the real threat that barons presented to their sovereign in the decentralized feudal state—and include among their ranks Renaud de Montauban. But, as we will see, these courtly bandits are heirs as well to the thieves who populate the Sicilian bandits' lives. In *Renaud Abducts the Beautiful Clarice*, we begin to witness the earliest moments of the recasting of Renaud in the role of the traditional Sicilian bandit.

> *Renaud Abducts the Beautiful Clarice*
> One day, Charlemagne's queen, Galerana, while walking along the beach with Roland's beloved Alda the Beautiful and Renaud's beloved Clarice, espied

a knight hastening toward them threateningly: "Take heed, my friends," she warned, "a knight is approaching us with his visor lowered, signaling to us that we might attend him."

"High Queen, pardon me, if Love makes of me such a villain," the knight, with his visor still lowered, declared when he had ridden up to Galerana, "but without the woman I love, I can never be happy."

"Clarice," Galerana commanded under her breath, "Come along with me! I wish to take you away from here!"

But scarcely had the words left the queen's lips than the knight swept Clarice up and went galloping away with her.

"My God," Alda cried, "that knight has abducted Clarice! He is no doubt some sort of villain who will take her to market and sell her as a slave."

"My friend, Alda the Beautiful," Galerana summarily bid her companion, "come along with me! I shall recount everything to my husband, Charlemagne!"

But when the knight had achieved a safe distance from the palace, he dismounted and spoke soothingly to Clarice, saying, "Princess Clarice, please don't cry. I understand your sadness. But I would appreciate knowing why you direct all your grief toward me. Calm yourself, I beg of you! I took you away for your own good and not at all to do you any harm. Therefore dry your tears and cease your lamenting. I did not conduct you away to ravage you because I would prefer death over perpetrating such a vile act. With me you are secure because I maintain for you a great love. And my desire rests completely on you. I only want you to understand that I am neither an idiot nor out of my senses in abducting you. My own prudence has caused me to do so inasmuch as I know that a Saracen named Francardo has asked Charlemagne for your hand. Clarice! I am your Renaud!" *the knight declared, raising his visor for the first time.* "Look at me! Tell me if you still love me, Clarice, or if you prefer to marry a Saracen?"

Clarice: "What's this I see! Renaud, it's you? Oh, my Renaud, I feel growing in my heart the ardent flame of desire!"

Renaud: "How beautiful you are, Clarice! And the more I look at you, the more beautiful you become! Kiss me, my love."

Clarice: "Of course, Renaud."

And as he kissed her, he said, "And now, Clarice, I finally see your face serene and, seeing that, I leave aside my torment. But, now, we must find some habitation."

Yet, even as he sought to transport her to safety, a knight approached him threateningly.

"Don't worry, my love," Renaud spoke soothingly to his beloved Clarice. "Put yourself out of harm's way because if this knight has any evil intentions, I will give him that which he deserves."

And as the knight approached, he spoke menacingly to Renaud, saying, "Where are you going, foolish knight? You're not worthy of this noble beauty whom you have wrongly acquired. Leave her to me now unless you wish to see how well my sword wounds the flesh."

Four: Saints and Bandits

Thereupon Renaud exclaimed, "What's this I hear? Cowardly knight, I will make you repent all that you have said."

Yet almost as soon as Renaud set upon him, the knight took flight. And worse yet, as Renaud was distracted by the first knight, a second appeared, as if from nowhere, and abducted Clarice. And as Renaud raced off to rescue his beloved, he heard a lone cry for help emanating from the impenetrable forest: "What's this I hear, Renaud! A voice crying for help! Perhaps it will be my Clarice invoking my aid! I will therefore hurry my steps so that I might rescue her!" Yet when Renaud discovered the source of the cry, he was shocked to find that it was no damsel in distress, much less Clarice, but it was rather a young shepherd invoking his aid. "Tell me, young man," Renaud exclaimed, "why are you so forlorn?"

"Knight," the shepherd began. "Know that I am of Numizia, where I was born under an iniquitous star. My father was the richest man there was in that land, and I, whom you now see in the lowly guise of a shepherd, am called Florindo. Know that in Numizia one finds a marvelous temple which our elders dedicated to the goddess, Venus, into which on the first day of May come knights of every kind. And entrance is not prohibited even to shepherds and to kindly damsels. Rather with equal honor are they all received by the priests. And everyone presents gracious gifts to the goddess. This ancient custom still lives on despite that among us is worshipped the great god, Mohammed.

"On this day there are many games such as archery and jousting. And moreover, he who best demonstrates his valor in these contests comes into the honor of the Goddess. Later, the women of the lower classes lose the day in dancing while the ladies of noble blood kiss the one and then the other. And she who is the most kissed is known as the most desirable of all women. The festival is celebrated for two months and I attended only to increase my anguish because, in the midst of all those happy damsels, was one whose beauty compared to the stars and the moon and this one is called Olinda. She is the daughter of our king. I, by her, was cruelly wounded for the first day that I saw her, I lost my peace. I have never found an infirmity equal to Love for, even though I knew I could never have the beautiful Olinda, princess that she is, Love carried me to that festival.

"And when the time came to wrestle, so much virtue did the Love that I carried within give me that I proved myself the strongest for I won and was reputed to be the strongest of all the contenders. And Olinda, being the daughter of a king, had to award those who were winners. And I, when she gave me my gift, squeezed her hand and her face turned red. Then came the time for the damsels to frolic together. And I seeing that many women were kissing my beautiful Olinda was taken with jealousy and thought to create a fraud so that even I might kiss that damsel whom I adored. So, with strategy and art, feigning a fall, I threw myself upon her beautiful breast, which I not only kissed but also held closely to my beating heart.

"Now, however, see to what end Love induced me! I bided my time and *waited for the following year. When the day of the great festival returned and everyone went to the temple, I disguised myself as a damsel. I robbed the clothes from a lady who found herself in that festival. And then I took myself to the place where the ladies dance and where they play the game of kisses. This was easy for me to do because my beard had not yet appeared. And so I went to the temple and, there, giving myself out to be a damsel, I readied myself for the games with the other ladies. And when the moment came that I was obliged to kiss my Olinda, knight, my lips would not detach themselves from hers.*

"And she recognized me. And she said that I must distance myself from the court because, if her father came to know what had happened, he would have me put to death. Now I find myself in these parts because I must discover the Temple of Love where the future is predicted but, as of yet, I have found no sign of its whereabouts."

Renaud, dumbfounded, exclaimed, "What's this I hear! Young shepherd, know that while I carried off my beloved Clarice, a knight came and wanted at any cost to compete with me. But, when the battle began and I put that cowardly knight to flight, another Saracen carried off my Clarice. Listen, I want to ask you something. Might I go along with you to this temple and ask what destiny Love intends for me?"

Florindo answered, "Knight, you may travel at my side. And when we arrive at the temple, we will speak to Cupid's Simulacrum so that we might learn the fate of our two damsels. Come! Let us search out this temple together!"

After two days of travel, Renaud and Florindo had not yet found the Temple of Love. But they saw an old man bent under the weight of his years. "Stop," Renaud begged of him. "Tell me, good man, might you indicate to me where one finds the Temple of Love which enshrines the speaking Simulacrum?"

And the old man answered, "Knight, the temple is not far from this place. But if you want to enter you must know the customs which are to be observed there. In front of the great god, one does not speak if he does not faithfully adore him with gifts. Know that the magician Merlin, in his florid age, desired that in front of the Simulacrum of the graceful Cupid every lover must bow. And, upon bended knee, he must ask what he wishes to know. But all those who don't know the custom, going to the temple, find their entrance impeded with an ardent flame."

Renaud thanked the man courteously, saying, "I thank you, good man, for that information. I however have not brought a gift. But, with a resolute spirit, I tell you that, if the son of Venus wishes to show his benevolence at my appearance, I will offer him my lance." And the old man wished him well, saying, "Fine, knight, try your luck. Who knows? Perhaps the Simulacrum will speak to you."

Just then Florindo noticed a flame on the horizon. "My friend, Renaud," he said. "Look! Over upon that mountain I see a shining and resplendent temple. But, I see also a flame in the path which leads to its great portal. Perhaps it is the flame of Vulcan. Yet, I believe that that flame is insignificant when com-

pared to the passion that burns inside my heart. I despise any danger! I will run with assurance through that flame in order to reach the Temple of Love!" And he dashed ahead of Renaud, who exclaimed, "Renaud, I am ashamed at seeing the courage of my friend, Florindo. Especially because he is a simple shepherd and I am a knight. Therefore, I also will find the valor of Florindo and I take myself as well to this temple in order to know my future!"

And so the two friends, Renaud and Florindo, braved the flame and entered the Temple of Love, where they were greeted by Cupid's priest: "Gentlemen, you are welcome. I desire that you enter with true faith and pray with all your strength. On your knees! Now I offer to this god these turtledoves and sacrifice them as a gift to the temple. Therefore, Lord Cupid, we fervently pray that you respond to the desires of these two young men."

Renaud: "Priest? How is it that the god does not respond?"

Priest: "Knight, we of the temple believe that to the fervent prayers delivered by myself he will respond. Yet, you must know that the enchanter, Merlin, after he formed this temple, imposed on the Simulacrum an order of silence if first a gift was not offered him by anyone in love who dares to know his fortune."

Renaud: "Priest, know that I am in possession of a lance and I will offer it to the Simulacrum."

Priest: "Very well, good knight, now let us pray in silence."

And while they prayed, Cupid descended into the Simulacrum with an explosion and spoke to the two sojourners: "Follow, Renaud, your first desire and you will soon have reason to boast of your arms. Clarice will be your wife and you will live with her contentedly. He who abducted her was no Saracen but an enchanter, a sorcerer named Malagigi, whom you will know before long. And he it was that sent the first knight to distract you. As for you, Florindo, take up arms and abandon the trade of the shepherd. And because you don't know it and are, as yet, unaware, I advise you that your love for the princess Olinda is not in vain. You are the son of a king and you will one day embrace your true parents. This is the future which I make known to you!"

And even as Cupid ascended, Renaud and Florindo raced from the Temple of Love, causing the priest to exclaim, "But look at these cowards! They present themselves to the Simulacrum without so much as bending a knee or making a reverence and run off without a scrap of remorse or piety!"[13]

The Courtly Bandit

Once again, our narrative opens with a modified council, this between Galerana, wife to Charlemagne, Alda the Beautiful, Roland's beloved, and Clarice, beloved of Renaud. The three have absented themselves from the castle to walk along a beach where they are accosted by a strange knight. The act of abduction, which the knight undertakes, is in itself an act of banditry for which Renaud announces himself to be behaving like a villain and—in a rhetorical cue hovering between the behavioral and the material—the act of leaving his visor lowered (when not involved in combat) signifies this fact. Thus, Galerana, upon exclaiming that a knight is approaching them with his visor lowered, accents the word "lowered" at Renaud's approach. Renaud's bandit voice is detailed by two speech acts in this passage: first, the apology ("High Queen, pardon me if love makes of me such a villain"), which excuses an act of just villainy, and, second, justification ("But without the woman I love, I shall never be happy"), which explains the motivation behind his nefarious behavior. Both speech acts, apology and justification, are necessary to the bandit whose villainy is—in Sicilian bandits' lives, at any rate—always in the service of honor. That is to say, the bandit is a bandit because he has been wronged, and his acts of banditry will be launched against those who have wronged him.

Shortly after the abduction, Renaud declares the honorable nature of his deed to his beloved, and, in this, the voice of the bandit becomes more apparent.

> *Princess Clarice, please don't cry. I understand your sadness. But I would appreciate knowing why you direct all your grief toward me. Calm yourself, I beg of you! I took you away for your own good and not at all to do you any harm. Therefore dry your tears and cease your lamenting. I did not conduct you away to ravage you because I would prefer death over perpetrating such a vile act. With me you are secure because I maintain for you a great love. And my desire rests completely on you. I only want you to understand that I am neither an idiot nor out of my senses in abducting you. My own prudence has caused me to do so inasmuch as I know that a Saracen named Francardo has asked Charlemagne for your hand. Clarice! I am your Renaud! Look at me! Tell me if you still love me, Clarice, or if you prefer to marry a Saracen?*

Here, Renaud continues his use of justification ("I took you away for your own good"), but augments it with a heavy use of the imperative ("Dry your tears and cease your lamenting"), a touch of irony ("But I would appreciate knowing why you direct all your grief toward me!"), a slight boast ("My own prudence has caused me to do as much") and a heavy use of hyperbole ("I am neither an idiot nor out of my senses!"). These are precisely those twists of everyday speech patterns by which the bandit most efficiently maintains his reputation for toughness and thereby the respect of his peers.

Four: Saints and Bandits

Also, two figures of synonymy (repetition of the same idea through two successive but differently phrased lines) are at play in this passage. Perhaps these are simply examples of the parallelism, two successive lines illustrating a single concept, that often embellishes epic and offers it much of its poetic tenor, but they seem here somewhat particularized to the voice of the bandit. In the first figure, antithetical synonymy, Renaud says: "I took you away for your own good and not at all to do you harm," and in the second, complementary synonymy, he says: "Therefore, dry your tears and cease your lamenting." What is curious about the bandit's use of parallelism is that synonymy permits the movement away from a neutral statement to one either implying a veiled threat (harm) or an emphatic imperative (cease). I am not suggesting that Renaud is bullying Clarice but that implied threats and decisive imperatives are part of the bandit's repertoire of figures and that synonymy seems an apt vehicle for such speech acts.

Throughout the Cycle, Renaud's voice is etched with bravado, sarcasm, and even, at times, a certain frigid cruelty. But it is, at the same time, lent gravity through its regular recourse to assertions of righteous indignation. And it is not only in the marionette theater that this sort of verbal ferocity—tempered always with warm declarations of honor—is on full display. In Giusto Lodico's *History of the French Paladins*, the author (probably as much the result of the influence of Palermitan storytellers as that of the literary antecedents to his publication) constructs Renaud's lament at the death of his comrade Roland in terms which are in keeping with Palermitan puppeteers' declamatory art.

> Renaud threw himself over the cold body of his cousin and, lamenting piteously, he cried, "How, dear brother, can you go to your happiness without bringing Renaud along with you? I was always companion to your perils and, now, when I have put my life on the line for you, you go to your reward without offering me, your dear brother Renaud, a single word of comfort!"[14]

Then, again, in a justly famous passage of the marionette theater's version of the Cycle, when that arch-villain Ganelon attempts to shame Renaud, who is poor, by boasting of what he can offer to enrich—and thus safeguard—Charlemagne's court and then invites Renaud to do the same, Renaud ends an entire string of boasts over his martial exploits with the oath that he will cut Ganelon's face, a oath which leads Charlemagne to banish Renaud from his court for such an insolent display.[15]

Taken together, Renaud's linguistic maneuvers are probably native to tough guys everywhere. But the voice of the Mafioso—of which Renaud's is the marionette theater's preeminent exemplar—is particularly characterized by linguistic features that collectively speak to a particular—simultaneously threatened as well as threatening—brand of fierceness—hard, urban, and brutally cool. Antonino Uccello sees the voice as springing from that place which expresses, "in essence, those moods, concerns, thoughts and feelings that typify the Mafioso and can be expressed in the threat, the code of silence [omertà], revenge, loyalty, hatred for the police and any manner of betrayal, contempt for the law and [a commitment] to obtain justice through force." Its most profound expression, according to Uccello, may be found in the especially well-formulated and particularly chilling stanza of a Sicilian prison song:

> I am an herb that poisons everyone,
> He who picks me cannot eat me,
> He who puts me in his mouth cannot swallow me,
> But if he somehow manages to swallow me,
> I'll choke him to death.[16]

With the loss of Clarice, whom we will later learn was not abducted by an unknown knight but rather by the necromancer Malagigi, who is intent to embark upon Renaud's education in the bearing of arms, the voice of the bandit momentarily gives way to that of the forlorn lover. Renaud falls into an impromptu partnership with Florindo, and the remainder of the episode is taken up with Florindo's lament to unrequited love as well as the two errant knights' pilgrimage to the Temple of Love. It is peculiar that Renaud first mistakes Florindo's lament for that of a damsel in distress and the audience of this particular episode giggled sheepishly when Renaud, slightly confused, found the author of that lament to be a man. And then Florindo's tale of transvestism seems to carry on the theme set forth by Renaud's misapprehension. While transvestism certainly fits into the scheme of epic—and indeed the story of Florindo's stormy love is found in the literary sources of Palermitan epic—it may be that this notion of transvestism is particularly appropriate to the realm of the bandit's life which deals with reversals, disguises, and men living at the interstices of society—and it underscores a peculiar affinity that exists for both the bandit and the saint, each of whom tenants an all-male society. For the time being, however, we will be privy only to the voice of the lover of medieval romance and we will leave the realm of banditry and just retribution entirely aside.

Bandits' Lives

Yet, despite the brief sojourn into the world of courtly love, much of what occurs in *Renaud Abducts the Beautiful Clarice* is informed by Sicilian Bandits' Lives, among which is found *The Life and Death of Antonio Di Blasi, alias Testalonga*. Antonino Uccello reports that the bandit, Testalonga, "was born at Pietraperzia and led a life rich in adventure. With his band he scoured all of Sicily, spreading terror, until in September 1766, he was arrested with his faithful lieutenant, Antonino Romano, near Pergusa Lake and conducted to Mussomeli, where he suffered the gallows along with his lieutenant."[17] And Denis Mack Smith, in his history of Sicily, states that "like many brigands before, the famous Testalonga was caught in the 1760's only by disaffection and treachery inside his own gang. This bandit was making travel and commerce hazardous for anyone who did not buy a safe conduct from him, and the fact was having a seriously restrictive effect on agriculture. The Prince of Trabia was therefore charged to raise a posse of irregulars against him, but the criminal was brought to book only when printed notices reached his accomplices offering them rewards and a free pardon in return for his capture."[18]

The following text originates from an unedited notebook play script (*copione*) belonging to the puppeteer don Gaspare Canino and published by Uccello. Beyond illustrating the major features of a classic Sicilian bandit's life, it is interesting to ponder that this bare outline of a plot will become a richly dialogic hour-long narrative in the hands of a storyteller or puppeteer:

> *The Life and Death of Antonio Di Blasi, alias Testalonga*
>
> The landlord kicks Antonio di Blasi's aged mother out of her house, throwing her to the ground. Antonio arrives and kills the landlord. Antonio finds his friend, Antonino Romano, and narrates the event. Romano curses the landlord saying that that man has been the cause of his own misfortune as well. The two, searching for some way to feed themselves, decide to seek refuge at a nearby stock pen. Antonio and Romano present themselves to the herdsmen

pleading for refuge but the herdsmen refuse them. They return to the stock pen armed and knock open the door. A boss comes out and Antonio unloads his carbine. Some of the herdsmen flee but two of them kneel down before the bandits, offering them sustenance.

A bandit hits old Simone. His daughter faints and the bandit carries her off. Antonio arrives and interrogates the wounded old man, then goes off in search of the assassin. The woman comes to and, seeing the bandit's intention to dishonor her, flees. The thief shoots a round of ammunition, putting Antonio on the right track. Antonio saves the woman just as her father arrives drenched in blood. Crying, the daughter recounts her ordeal. Antonio calls his bandits. The woman recognizes the malefactor, and Antonio kills him in retribution.

Antonio receives Giacomo, who has escaped the Viceroy's prison in Palermo. Giving proof of his valor, Giacomo is admitted to the number of the bandits. Then soldiers arrive. Antonio attacks, taking the helmet of the captain.

The Prince of Trabia thought to obtain jewelry for the princess on the occasion of a festival and it was robbed. Trabia ordered Testalonga [Antonio] to be arrested. His soldiers attack Antonio, who flees rather than be inculpated in the theft. But he also swears vengeance against the Prince. Trabia hears noise in the garden. He prepares his pistols and advances on Antonio who, declaring his innocence, brings forth a box containing the jewelry and the ears of the thief who robbed it. Word goes through the castle that a waiter was found with his ears cut off.

Antonio receives a letter. His companion, Don Girolamo of Palazzo Adriano, was ready to pay back a sum of money to him that evening in the Garden of Oranges. Antonio departs to recover the sum. The captain arranges an ambush by his soldiers who wait for Antonio at the garden. Antonio arrives and, with his horse, catches a round of fire. Wounded, he falls from his horse. The soldiers follow the horse. Antonio is saved by the old man whose daughter he had liberated. An old lady comforts the daughter, Teresa. They hear a knock at the door. They admit Antonio. He goes to bed. The soldiers arrive. The captain, drenched through, sets aside his cloak. Antonio hears the noise, steals the cloak, and leaves the house as a captain. A round of fire announces the theft to the soldiers.

A man cries that he cannot bury his wife because the parson desires money. Antonio gives a silver coin to the unfortunate man. The parson receives his payment but Antonio climbs through his window and takes back the coin.

Old Tomasso (a member of Antonio's band) is taken through treachery. Antonio and Romano, hiding out in a cave, discuss the string of arrests that have afflicted their companions; some were hanged, others sent to the Viceroy's prison. They receive Tomasso who speaks of the restrictions on his movements. A soldier, urinating in a fissure of the cave, is spotted by Antonio who fires upon him, alerting the other soldiers. They give battle. The bandits run out of ammunition, commend their souls to God, and are killed by the soldiers. The captain obtains victory, carrying away the bodies of the brigands.[19]

Four: Saints and Bandits

What becomes apparent upon reading Canino's notebook is the contiguousness of the bandit with the knight on the one hand and the masque on the other. There are even points of continuity with the saint, as we will shortly see. While the bandit's actions are for the most part noble (or, more appropriately, honorable), he occasionally lapses into the comic: for example, when he steals the captain's helmet and cloak and again when he climbs through the parson's window to retrieve his silver coin. The bandit is then epic's serio-comical character who stands somewhat midway between the masque and the knight. His noble battles and, at times, comic thefts ally him with the King David of Hebraic legend who as a youth must also take to the hills and caves, resort to banditry in order to survive, lead a rebellion of (at one point) 600 outlaws and exiles against the unjust authority of Saul, and resort to comic (and ironically fitting) thefts. In one episode which may offer the ur-text for the urinating soldier in *The Life and Death of Antonio Di Blasi*, David cuts off a segment of Saul's robe—apparently as the king relieves himself in a cave—and later displays it as proof of his fealty; he could have, after all, killed Saul when he found him in such a vulnerable circumstance.[20]

Though I have never been able to find a marionette play or folktale which treats of David's banditry, I still believe the assignment of Renaud's allegorical function is not too difficult to establish. The chivalric bandit (unlike the bandit proper) from medieval times down to our own is cut from the same cloth as the biblical bandit par excellence—David. It is not simply that he finds himself the captain of a band of roving outlaws due to some economic necessity. It is rather that his economic necessity is predicated upon the unjust treatment that he receives at the hands of an insecure ruler who is in constant fear of the adulation which the *bandito* (i.e., he who has been banned or outlawed) receives at the hands of the multitudes. Add to this the fact that Italian Catholic encyclopedias (unlike their American counterparts) invariably include David's time as a bandit as a significant feature of his early history, and it becomes less surprising that Renaud inhabits the allegorical integer that he does in the Palermitan redaction of the Carolingian Cycle.

Though probably not as explicit, or conscious, to the Palermitan audience as we will shortly find the association between Christ and the saintly Roland to be, David is the very model of the Sicilian bandit, and, thus, the Carolingian bandit par excellence, Renaud, who—like his mythical progenitor—rebels against an unjust sovereign, has to resort to theft and life in the mountains in order to survive, gathers about himself the dispossessed, and yet maintains always a sense of comic bravado and an intense loyalty to his lord who has—inevitably—been led to his tyrannical behavior by the dissembling of envious advisors. Another parallel between biblical David and Renaud may be the intensity of the male bonding that occurs in the period of banishment. Even after David has taken to the hills, his clandestine friendship with the king's son, Jonathan, continues despite the danger that it poses to David and Jonathan alike. Something of this bond adheres to Renaud in his impromptu partnership with Florindo. Yet, the story of David is especially closely related to that of Renaud in that David is a bandit second, a warrior-king first, battling his lord's enemies despite his lord's unjust treatment of him and gaining an illustrious set of arms in the process. In all these features, David presages Renaud, the bandit-knight of the Carolingian Cycle—though only one man I ever interviewed seemed to be conscious of this correspondence and, in fact, alerted me to it almost surreptitiously by pointing out the coincidence of the number of outlaws collected in both David's and Renaud's rebel bands.

Some Palermitan gentlemen of the mid-nineteenth century seem to have noticed the slippage of the ideology of bandits' lives into the epic genre and worried publicly about the effect it would have on the working classes and even went so far as to suggest that the marionette theater should be abolished. As Giuseppe Pitrè pointed out, the most loyal patrons of epic were "for the most part boys of the *popolino* [lower classes], some apprenticed, others not, in various trades. The others were youngsters and adults. ... In one place there were more urchins than youngsters; in another, more youngsters than boys. In one quarter there were more servants, waiters and scullions; in another, fishermen and fishmongers. Here there were porters [*vastasi*; *vastaseddi*], fruit mongers; there, shoeblacks, stable boys, laborers, and others of that sort."[21] Thus, their political voice would be negligble up against that of their gentlemanly detractors.

The critics saw in epic a "lurid school" in which Palermo's "plebian youth" learned the various arts of knife-fighting, thievery and rebellion: "In our theaters of the second and third order the bacchanal of some evenings reaches indecent proportions. ... The marionette theaters of our city allow too many swords and daggers to be seen by our young urchins. Is it not possible that this feast for the eyes might have certain dangerous effects on the nervous system and contribute to the high statistics for crimes of blood?" Another patriot declaimed, "Moved by love of the fatherland, we, the undersigned, protest unanimously against the secular vices of the vandalistic representations which daily take place in our marionette theaters: the lurid schools of our plebian youth. ... We do not in the least wish to ban its interesting matter but rather to reorganize its arguments, which do not bring to fruition any efforts but those which make for moral incivility among our masses. Of Renaud rebels and assassins only the Middle Ages had need. Our century seeks nothing more than honest men." Still another complained, "Hence it is not rare to see two rogues come across one another on the street and spin for themselves a genealogy of the Paladins; to wit, they gather themselves up as if they were two knights from the Middle Ages and they fly at one another: the one shouting, 'Long live Mohammed,' and the other 'Long live Jesus and Mary!' While they make a shield of the left arm, a stick in the right becomes a lance or a sword. One notes that this is one of the most common games among the boys of the lower classes who accordingly become the famous knife-pullers whom we all know so well."

Fortunately, some others among the city's erudite interceded on behalf of epic: "A few Palermitan diarists made the discovery one day that the marionette theaters were nothing more than the remains of medieval barbarism and they heatedly called for their closure. The reasoning of these blockheads was founded on the strange and rather gratuitous notion that the marionette theaters might be the schools of vice and crime in which our people learn to be highwaymen, thieves, rebels, assassins, etc. Now I ask if these fountains of knowledge who propose the closings intend to ban the chivalric poems which inspire the marionettes as well. Or why don't they cite as responsible for the rascality and crimes the poems of Boiardo and Ariosto?"[22]

Yet, epic was never all knife fights and villainy; in opposition to the bandits' lives is that other venerated genre of Sicilian popular narrative, the saints' lives. The more notable themes of that genre to find their way into epic are those involved in a progression that moves from Apparition, in which an angel brings a knight an appointment from the Lord, through Miracle, in which baptismal water miraculously appears, to

Glorification, in which a dead knight is carried away to Heaven. Central to this progression is the notion of baptismal water as the medium of purification which leads from the earthly kingdom of Charlemagne to its celestial sponsor, the heavenly kingdom of God. Whereas Renaud is the very model of the bandit-knight, Roland partakes of the nature of the martyr-saint, the qualities of which begin to appear early in the cycle but achieve full dramatic effect in the episode entitled *The Battle of Roland and Agrican*, to which we will shortly turn.

CHAPTER FIVE

On Christian Soil

The Rhetoric of Islamophobia in Sicily and Abroad

During a particularly heated interval in the Church's pedophilia scandal, I read what had to be the strangest statement in the *New York Times*. In an Op-Ed column that started off with what seemed to be a commendation of Pope John Paul II and a condemnation of Pope Benedict XVI in the face of the Church's handling of pedophiliac priests, then turned the argument on its head to suggest that Benedict had been left to clean up John Paul's messes, Ross Douthat almost off-handedly suggested that "[t]his pattern extends to other fraught issues that the last pope tended to avoid—the debasement of the Catholic liturgy, or the rise of Islam in once-Christian Europe."[1] I was startled, to say the least; it wasn't the liturgy thing, though its "debasement" didn't really seem to rise to the level of severity as, say, pedophilia. It was the suggestion that "the rise of Islam in once-Christian Europe" could be described as a "fraught" issue which Pope John Paul II, like some inattentive father, heedlessly neglected: Heavens to Betsy! Hide the burqas! Did Douthat really mean to say that?

I was instantly taken back to the earliest days of my fieldwork in Palermo when Faisal—my first friend in Sicily who, when the stock market crashed (Black Monday, October 19, 1987) and I, in a day, lost twenty dollars to every hundred that I exchanged for the, then, Italian currency: the lira—took me to the set of rooms rented out to the Tunisians and Mohammed that I previously described and thus rescued my faltering budget. I remembered fondly my first day in Sicily when the proprietress of the *pensione* I checked into suggested that, though the *pensione* was full, I might share a room with "*un bravo ragazzo*" ("a great fellow") and, after I stowed my bags, my new roommate, Faisal, took me out onto the balcony to show me the view. Our room looked out onto the famed Via Maqueda which crosses Palermo's historic center and empties, as fate would have it, just below the balcony, onto a frenzied piazza fronting the train station. Just as we stepped out onto the balcony, a horse, drawing a cart down Via Maqueda, became spooked and refused to enter the treacherous stream of traffic crushing its way through the piazza. I looked down at his terrified eyes, sheltered by blinders but fully visible from above, as Palermo erupted into a frenzy of honking horns, racing engines, and cursing motorists. I laughed aloud at this, my first image of the city before me, and Faisal affectionately pressed his cheek against my arm and shared in my reverie. We were friends from there on in.

Thus, it was natural that I bring him along one night to see a performance of the marionette theater. Unfortunately, I didn't think about it at the time I issued the invitation but—as we have seen—a mainstay of the Carolingian Cycle is the battle of the forces of Christendom—championed by the Holy Roman Emperor and his Paladins—against the infidel, Islam—championed by an array of Saracen knights: Marsilius, Falseron, Bulogant, Ferraù, and Agrican. The evening's fare was sprinkled with the usual battles, culminating in a spectacular beheading of a Saracen knight, but Faisal took everything in stride and my embarrassment was quickly quelled when he—who assimilated so easily to "once-Christian Europe" that he took the name which Sicilian friends had offered him, Fabbio, without a complaint—said, "It's just a story."

What Douthat's statement reminded me of most immediately—making me feel, once again, as I had the evening I took Faisal to the marionette theater, as if I'd been hit with a spit wad—was one that Charlemagne had spoken in the very first episode of the Carolingian Cycle, *The Death of King Pepin*. As Pepin, in a solemn council, announced his success in annihilating the Saracens who dared to attempt a conquest of France, he proclaimed:

> *I am content that peace reigns in our land, after the many wars that we have withstood against these vile Saracens who wanted to conquer France, who wanted to aggrandize the false faith of Mohammed. We have destroyed them, causing them to repent having ever set foot on Christian soil.*

How could the *New York Times*—even in an Op-Ed piece—offer up an as unabashed anti-Islamic sentiment as I would occasionally encounter in Sicilian epic where, at least, history—marked as it was by

250 years of Arabic occupation being broken only when the Norman invasion ushered in Sicily's century-long golden era—while not exactly *exonerating* such sentiments at least rendered them rhetorically comprehensible. Of course, one could claim that 9-11 was the historical antecedent to American Islamophobia—had not Islamophobia already been a cogent element of American rhetoric previous to 9-11. In America, however, as well as in Sicily, a peculiar mythological antecedent to Islamophobia comes into play: the mistaken interpretation of the Isaac/Ishmael dichotomy as the mythic precedent to Judeo-Christian/Muslim antipathy. In other words, mythologically, Isaac is viewed as the progenitor of the Judeo-Christian tradition while Ishmael is viewed as the progenitor of Islam. This mythic archetype sets the Judeo-Christian and Islamic traditions up as two eternally feuding clans: clans that have clashed in the initial expansion of Islam into Spain, Sardinia, and Sicily, the retributive Crusades, the creation of the modern state of Israel, Islamic terrorism, Christian apocalyptic fantasies, and most recently 9-11 and the resultant wars in Afghanistan and Iraq.

Yet one more image from Sicilian epic popped into my mind upon reading Douthat's statement in the *Times*: In that seminal episode of the Carolingian Cycle, *The Death of the Paladins*, as Roland, the best of the Paladins, he who had beaten back the might of Islam from the threshold of "Christian soil," readied his Oliphant, so that he might alert Charlemagne to the cataclysmic battle between the forces of Christendom and Islam, puppet devils began to glide overhead. "Look how many Saracens!" one gleefully cried. "Let's take them to hell immediately!" another rejoined. And the devils began to reap their gruesome harvest.

As I was engaged in my fieldwork, I found it to be little more than an amusing irony that during the day I would be studying a folkloric tradition in which the preeminent villain *was* a villain simply because he was Muslim—or because he colluded with Muslims—while each evening I went home to share my life with Muslims. But much later, in fact fourteen years later, with the advent of an America so often defined by the incidents of 9-11, I came to realize that back in Sicily in 1987—as in America today—I am often dealing with a rhetoric of identity: a rhetoric which defines one's group affiliation and then, in turn, represents it verbally, behaviorally, and even—and this is quite pronounced within the context of the marionette theater—materially. As we shall see, there is a definitive rhetoric of Islamophobia in the construction of Sicilian epic but it is, interestingly, subsumed within—or forms the contextual backdrop to—a more pervasive rhetorical concern: a delineation between the social constructs of obedience and rebellion along with their pre-eminent adherents, the saint and the bandit respectively. Thus, while Islamophobia pervades Palermitan epic—as will readily be seen in the episode presented in this chapter, *The Battle of Roland and Agrican*—it is not particularly virulent (in fact, I would say, less virulent than the form of Islamophobia that has taken hold in some segments of American society) and certainly not epic's main concern. But it *is* there and it's not as if one can simply—as if it were some embarrassing relative—ignore its presence. Thus, I take this moment to address Sicilian Islamophobia here. But it is not an entirely gratuitous inclusion given the topic of this study. I believe that, in many respects, it was precisely the irony of living with Muslims while studying an Islamophobic art form that led me to the recognition of the essential role of rhetoric in Palermitan epic, and it is that role—as it impinges particularly on the personage of the martyr-saint—to which I now turn.

The Battle of Roland and Agrican

Asleep in his chamber, Roland dreamt of Angelica calling out for his aid. "Angelica," he called aloud, upon awakening, "Where are you?" But, almost instantly, he realized that he had only been dreaming. "Roland," he consoled himself, "what a frightful dream I had! It was my Angelica whom I love so much! It was my Angelica who so often takes flight! It was my Angelica and she was speaking in my dream. She finds herself in danger! She was crying, 'Where are you, my Roland? I beg of you, come and liberate me!' Angelica loves me. This I know! Angelica is searching for me! Fine, Roland, what difference does it make if I stay here in Paris? And what do the affairs of my uncle, Charlemagne, matter to me if I don't have Angelica?

"Terigi," Roland called out into the darkness.

"Count Roland, command me," Terigi, Roland's loyal page, sleepily answered.

Roland: "Terigi, go immediately and prepare my horse. I wish to leave the threshold of France."

Terigi: "Fine, Count Roland, and I will prepare my horse as well because I wish to go with you."

Roland: "No!"

Terigi: "But I am your page!"

Roland: "Enough, I say! Obey me!"

And as Roland raced away from Paris, he swore not to slacken his pace until he found his Angelica. Yet it seemed to him, after three days, that he was meeting with no success. "For three days now," Roland lamented, "I have done nothing more than walk, crossing fields, woods, valleys, mountains, in search of Angelica but as often as I call for her she does not answer me. Angelica, where are you, my soul? Let it not come about that Angelica encounter Ferraù of Spain or, perhaps again, my cousin, Renaud!"

Yet, even as he spoke, he was set upon by a dragon. "What's this I see," he exclaimed. "There is a serpent approaching. Attention! My sword, Durandal, is ready to kill this poisonous dragon!" With a single lunge he vanquished his foe and, as the dragon flailed in its death throes, Roland chastised, "Ugly, venomous serpent, who knows how much anguish you have caused during your life. So long has your hide endured that not even my sword, Durandal, was able to cut it through."

Yet before he could even finish contemplating his kill, Roland heard a cry for help: "Roland, if I am not mistaken, I hear the voice of a woman crying out that someone might offer her succor! What's this I see! In the distance, there is a wicked giant leading a poor girl astray. But this girl is my Angelica! Coward and nothing more," Roland cried out as he set out in hot pursuit of his beloved's assailant. "Halt! If you don't let this girl be, sorrow will be your reward!"

But the giant, unaware that he had been spotted, continued to torment his victim: "By Magon and Trevigant, your cries are useless, inasmuch as no one will be able to hear you."[2]

Angelica pleaded, "But why have you abducted me?" And, then, upon spotting Count Roland—his visor down so that she could not know it was her own lover—careening toward her, she cried out, "I beg of you, Good Knight, come immediately and liberate me!"

Giant: "Listen, you're very pretty and I'm going to transport you to Greece, to the fair of Salonica. I will there sell you as a slave and earn my fortune in gold!"

Angelica: "Oh! Into what perfidious hands have I fallen! Help! Somebody save me!"

Giant: "Shut your mouth! Do you have a hard head? I've already told you. Nobody will hear you here."

But Roland, slipping quietly into the copse where the giant tormented Angelica, whispered, "Hey, friend, has no one ever taught you that you ought not to offend a woman, not so much as a hair on her head?"[3]

But, "Knight," the startled giant threatened, "Don't mix yourself up in affairs that don't concern you, if you don't want to lose your life."

"I understand," Roland responded calmly, "You are a man without faith and without law. Defend yourself!"

And when he had annihilated the giant, Roland, his visor still covering his face, lifted Angelica from her knees. "Oh, valorous and potent knight," Angelica exclaimed, "I thank you with all my heart for having salvaged my life from these iniquitous hands."

Roland: "I simply did my duty. Raise yourself, Angelica."

Angelica: "Oh! By my gods, Magon and Trevigant, you know my name! But who are you, knight?"

"Angelica, don't you remember my arms?" Roland asked as he raised his visor.

"Roland, embrace me!" Angelica sighed.

But when Roland began to speak of his love for her, saying, "Angelica, how beautiful you are; Angelica, oh, my soul, I have finally found you," Angelica chastised him, saying, "Roland, don't hold me so tightly. You're hurting me."

"Pardon me, Angelica," Roland stammered, "but, you must know, from the first day that I saw you at Paris, I have loved you so much. Now, tell me, why are you crying, Angelica? Why are you so sad? What is the motive for your lamentation? Also, tell me how you found yourself in the hands of this wicked giant."

Angelica: "Listen to me, Roland. You must know that I found myself on the road when I secretly left my castle, Albracca, because Agrican of Tartary waged war against me."

Roland: "For what motive?"

Angelica: "Because three times he sent me ambassadors asking for my hand in marriage. But I don't love him. I love you, Roland. And so I refused him. And he, to avenge himself, brought an army against me and laid siege to my castle, Albracca. And being alone, without father, or brothers, or friends, or family, I went out in search of valorous knights. I thought to take myself to Paris and there ask the help of His Majesty, Charlemagne. But during the journey I was abducted by this giant who had the intention of selling me as a slave."

Roland: "There is no need for you to go to Paris, Angelica, to ask my uncle Charlemagne for help. Because I, Roland, First Paladin of France, swear that I will not call myself by name, if Agrican does not lose his life under the edge of my sword, Durandal. From this moment on I swear to be your champion. Come, Angelica; we will try to embark on some craft in order to arrive all the more quickly at Albracca. Have courage! At my side no one will be able to touch a hair of your head."

Angelica: "I'm sure of it, Roland; I thank you for all you are doing for me."

Roland: "Angelica, you don't have to thank me because for your love I am able to confront an entire army. For your love, I am able to enter Hell with all my arms and to be burned alive! Angelica, for your love ..."

"Roland, don't act that way," Angelica admonished. "You're scaring me." And no sooner than Roland had complied with Angelica's admonition and stopped his wooing, she curtly said, "Now, come along, Roland." And Roland dutifully followed her.

In the meantime, at the Castle Albracca, Agrican had learned that Angelica had found a champion to fight against him: "My beloved, well-armed, gentlemen," he exhorted his troops, "We have left our land of Tartary and come here to Albracca to wage war against Angelica who had the courage and the audacity to refuse my hand in marriage. Three times, my dear companions, I sent ambassadors to Angelica, asking for her hand. And three times, she had the audacity to refuse me, to despise me, and to call me proud. But she will not receive my pardon now or ever because I have sworn by Magon and Trevigant that I will destroy Angelica's castle. And when I have her in my hands, I will have her fed to my mad dogs!" His blustering however was interrupted by the sudden mustering of his troops.

"And what are all these calls to arms?" Agrican demanded. "Mustafà! Mustafà!"

Mustafà: "Aye, aye, aye, aye, aye, my lord, command me!"

Agrican: "Mustafà, what are all these peals of trumpets, these calls to arms? Speak!"

Mustafà: "My lord, I advise you that at this moment a well-armed knight accompanies the beautiful princess, Angelica, beyond the walls of Albracca!"

Agrican: "Angelica comes in the company of a knight! But how did she ever find herself outside the walls? Mustafà, assault that knight! Then chain him and bring him into my presence!"

No sooner than Mustafà went out against Roland, he returned from his assault lamenting, "My Lord, you must know that this knight is very, very, very, very strong with sword in hand. He just goes swish, swosh, swush, and cuts off heads and arms and legs!"

Agrican: "But what are you saying! I'll go confront this knight myself! Follow me! Everybody to arms!"

And one by one, Saracen knights stepped forward to challenge Roland, only to be slaughtered, until Roland stood at the gate of Albracca facing Agrican himself.

Roland: "I suppose you must be Agrican, King of Tartary."

Agrican: "I am Agrican of Tartary. But who, by Magon and Trevigant, are you? You have killed almost half my army with the sweep of your sword. I have never seen such a potent knight."

Roland: "Listen, Agrican, know that I am Roland, First Paladin of France and nephew to Charlemagne!"

Agrican: "Ah, so you're Roland, nephew to Charlemagne! What are you doing here in this land of the unbaptized? And why are you defending a Saracen woman?"

Roland: "Listen, Agrican, I want to tell you something. You need to take down your tents and pavilions and go back to your own lands where there is certainly no lack of women to make you happy. Leave Angelica in peace. Angelica doesn't love you."

Agrican: "What are you saying, Roland! Don't speak to me in this way! Agrican of Tartary swears that I won't call myself by name if I don't skin you like the dog that you are!"

Sicilian Epic and the Marionette Theater

Roland: "Listen, Agrican, I have advised you once, and it is not my habit to repeat things a second time, leave Angelica in peace! Angelica is mine and no one is going to take her away!"

Agrican: "Vile, Roland, I'll eat your heart right out of your chest as well as that of this disgrace, Angelica!"

Roland: "Coward and nothing more! You wanted to take advantage of Angelica because she finds herself alone in the world without relatives!"

Agrican: "Roland, you will repent what you have said!"

Roland: "You wish it in vain; defend yourself!"

The battle was fierce, with neither Roland nor Agrican prevailing, but even as they fought, Roland attempted to convert Agrican to Christianity and to leave off his attacks of Albracca. Yet his words were all in vain, and the two, with night drawing in upon them, lay down exhausted in their futile efforts, falling asleep side by side on the battlefield. And on awakening, Agrican, exclaimed, "But, it's almost dawn. Do you see what a fool you are, Roland! Your god gave you the possibility of killing me in my sleep and you didn't take it!"

Roland: "Do you see what a traitor you are to your own thoughts, Agrican. I've already told you that we, the baptized, are averse to killing our enemies through treachery."

Agrican: "But this is the field of battle! Anyway, Roland, I didn't shut my eyes for a moment during the night."

Roland: "Listen, Agrican, I'm only sorry about one thing; that I didn't succeed in making you change your views. But seeing that you don't want to become a Christian, nor even to leave Angelica in peace, then prepare yourself. Because, I swear on the sacraments of God, that here, today, you will lose your life!"

Agrican: "You wish it in vain, Christian! En garde!"

And with that challenge, Roland, bristling, issued Agrican his deathblow. "Coward and nothing more," *he exclaimed.* "You are fallen! Now prepare to die!"

But, "No," *Agrican pleaded,* "Stop! Roland, I beg of you! Lower your sword. You have wounded me mortally."

Roland: "What's this I see! Agrican, from beneath your helm, I see blood issue forth onto your face!"

Agrican: "Roland, I render myself to your mercy. I am dying. But before taking myself to the other world I wish to ask of you a favor."

Roland: "Speak, Agrican! Speak to me!"

Agrican: "Roland, I beg of you, give me the water of Holy Baptism!"

Roland: "Agrican! Then I have convinced you to embrace the faith of Christ! Oh, Dear God in Heaven, what will I do without water with which to baptize you?"

Agrican: "Roland, I beg of you, I can no longer move!"

Roland: "Oh, my Good Lord, here I am at your feet! I beg of you, permit me to baptize and save the soul of this innocent."

Agrican: "Roland, I am no longer able to see with my eyes!"[4]
Roland: "Courage, Agrican, I will think how I might save you. Oh, Good Lord in Heaven, I beg of you! I have need of water in order to save Agrican!"
Agrican: "Look, Roland, I see water issuing forth from that mountain!"
Roland: "Yes, it's true, Agrican! Oh, my Good Lord, I thank you for your benevolence. And now I will take my flask and collect a little of this water so that I might baptize Agrican in his hour of need. Come, oh my faithful destrier, Vegliantin."

And in a moment, Roland went and retrieved the baptismal water, saying, even as he dismounted, "Agrican, repeat everything I say! Do you believe in the Virgin Mary?"
Agrican: "Yes, I believe in the Virgin Mary."
Roland: "Do you believe in all the Saints?"
Agrican: "Yes, I believe in all the Saints."
Roland: "And Jesus?"
Agrican: "And Jesus but, Roland, I can't last much longer!"[5]
Roland: "Joseph?"
Agrican: "Joseph."
Roland: "And Mary?"
Agrican: "And Mary."
Roland: "I commend my soul..."
Agrican: "I commend my soul..."
Roland: "In the name of the Father, the Son, and the Holy Spirit, I baptize you a Christian!"
Agrican: "Oh, Roland, I thank you."
Roland: "Oh Dear God in Heaven! What have I done? I have killed a potent knight like Agrican! Forgive me, Agrican!" Yet even as Roland mourned Agrican's death, an angel descended, saying:

> "Agrican, Agrican,
> This was your fate.
> Your pallid face,
> I return to serenity.
> And your wearied soul,
> I transport to its destiny!"[6]

A Saintly Prose

Roland, the perfect knight, is defined as such in *The Battle of Roland and Agrican* through his use of the oath ("I, Roland, First Paladin of France, swear that I will not call myself by name if Agrican does not lose his life beneath the edge of my sword!") and the boast ("I am able to enter Hell with all my arms and not be burned alive!"). But, interestingly, in this episode too are discursive elements which further set Roland apart from Renaud as the latter was depicted in *Renaud Abducts the Beautiful Clarice*. Parallelism, in *The Battle of Roland and Agrican*, is in the service of the boast, and rather than being formulated through synonymy (which, as we have seen, is used to alter emphasis), it is formulated by anaphora (the repetition of words at the beginning of successive clauses: "For your love, I am able to confront an entire army! For your love, I am able to enter Hell with all my arms and not be burned alive!"). Anaphora is always used in knightly declarations (of which the highest form is the boast) and is probably viewed as an ennobling figure by the Palermitan people because of its strong historic precedent in chivalric poetry—which any segment of the Palermitan populace would have, at some time heard, from the lips of the *cantastorie*, itinerant singers of chivalric poetry.

Another differentiation of the two cousins in these episodes involves tone. Renaud, though altering his voice figuratively, maintains a steady tone throughout his abduction of Clarice. But Roland, during his liberation of Angelica, is unable to do so. His voice wavers between the clear, resounding tone of the knight and a hoarse, at times tremulous, praise (note the repeated vocative: "Angelica!" and "Oh, my soul!") of his lady which suggests sexual excitement that is not likely to be satisfied. Dennis Tedlock has found the same use of hoarseness to denote arousal in Zuni narrative, notably in the tale entitled *The Girl and the Protector*.[7] Angelica, in response to Roland's arousal, quickly relinquishes the supplication most proper to a damsel in distress and adopts in its stead the protest ("Roland, don't hold me so tightly. You're hurting me," and, "Roland, don't act that way! You're scaring me") and finally the harsh imperative ("Come along, Roland!") to which Roland acquiesces with brute silence. Frankly, Roland here seems a compendium of all the faults a Palermitan man might lay upon someone who doesn't keep his wife or fiancée in check: he is used, controlled, hen-pecked, and apparently cuckolded.

The distinction between Roland and Renaud in this instance speaks to notions of masculinity that pertain both to epic and to Sicilian (but perhaps especially to Mafioso subcultural) social relations. And the variable voices of the two heroes are emblematic of their different fortunes in love. Renaud, the "Mafioso," is reliably successful in the pursuit of love: in fact, in a telling sequence of episodes, Angelica has drunk from the Fountain of Disdain—created by Merlin to cure Tristram of his love sickness—before glancing at Roland and she, thus, flees his embraces; then, again, her glance chances to fall upon Renaud after she has drunk from the Fountain of Love—another of Merlin's artifices—and she becomes completely enamored of him. He, unfortunately, has drunk from the Fountain of Disdain just before glancing back at her and finds Angelica's attentions abhorrent. Thus, while Roland continuously suffers the indignity of Angelica's haughty indifference, Renaud has had Angelica, at least for a time, distractedly chasing after him. Roland, the "*Occhi Storti*" (Cross-Eyes), unlike Renaud (the Mafioso), is too often bumbling in his pursuit of love. Not only has he vowed not to have conjugal relations with his wife, Alda the Beautiful, until he has conquered Spain (which in itself would seem a noble oath if everyone did not know that he would never accomplish that deed), but also his pressing displays of affection keep Angelica in flight. Roland's misfortunes in love reach a pitch when Angelica marries the common foot soldier, Medoro, and Roland goes mad. Whereas Renaud seems the master of love, Roland, seems, in a word, a cuckold, and this circumstance—perhaps more than any other—solidifies his allegorical affiliation with Christ who, at times among Sicilian men, was viewed "as a prime *cornutu* (cuckold) for letting himself be killed in the manner of a common criminal."[8]

And it is probably not inappropriate to assert, here, that the cousins' various fortunes in love presage their various fortunes in battle. To return momentarily to the allegory that begins to be drawn out between *Renaud Abducts the Beautiful Clarice* and *The Battle of Roland and Agrican*, these two episodes, like many before and after them, depict the two heroes in almost continuous battle against bloodthirsty giants and malevolent dragons. Always hedging about the depiction of the giants—and this was even true in Palermitan epic's medieval sources—is some element of Goliath: gory oaths, supernatural powers, and near invincibility. This depiction casts the cousins simultaneously in the role of Goliath's mythic adversary: David. Likewise, always hedging about the depiction of the dragons—and this too emerges in epic's medieval sources—is some notion of the serpent of the apocalypse: He emerges from the abyss of the trackless forest (a locale that Sicilian fairy tales, in particular, demarcate as outside the province of Christendom) when the knight is beyond all the confines of God's Earthly Kingdom (the Holy Roman Empire) and can be vanquished only with the heavy blow of the knightly sword.[9] Here, the depiction casts the cousins—again simultaneously—in the role of Christ's mythic alter-ego, the Angel of the Apocalypse.

Though the cousins are depicted as synonymous in these contexts, they become differentiated in others. As we have seen above, Roland is over and again associated with Christ and martyrdom. And the examples seem off-handed and so unexpected at times. I encountered the following in Danilo Dolci's discussion of an agrarian labor uprising in postwar Sicily:

> [In t]he first cavalcade [Accursio Miraglia] rode a white horse. The guy who loaned it to him was warned not to by the opposition, but so what?... All the people were with him.... All in high spirits, shouting to their friends and hissing when they ran across members of the opposition. That morning the rich stayed indoors. There were so many kids riding double with their fathers you couldn't even count them. *And [Miraglia] looked just like Roland.* It was a joy to see this mountain of a man up there on that horse. You had to admire him. Just looking at him made you love him, and he radiated that same love back. All the kids were throwing flowers. Of course, it was just the opposite when they killed him [emphasis added].[10]

We will return to the mythic correspondence of Renaud and David a bit later. But for now, let us examine the emergence of Roland's Christlike qualities in *The Battle of Roland and Agrican* a bit more closely.

Saints' Lives

Upon arriving at Albracca, Roland single-handedly slaughters half of Agrican's army. In the words of Agrican's blathering soldier, Mustafà: "My Lord, you must know that this knight is very, very, very, very strong with sword in hand. He just goes swish, swosh, swush, and cuts off heads and arms and legs!" Only after calling several retreats does Agrican confront Roland himself. The comic gibberish of the foot soldier who, whether Saracen or Christian, acts (like his ancestor in Greek and Roman drama) the fool, is replaced by the blustering oaths of the enraged giant. All Saracens are given to gory oaths in epic, but the oaths of the Saracen giants are exceptional and probably the bequest of Goliath who swore that he would throw David's flesh "to the birds of the sky and the beasts of the earth."[11] Agrican follows in like tradition, saying, "Agrican of Tartary swears that I won't call myself by name if I don't skin you like the dog that you are!" And to Roland's rejoinder, "Listen, Agrican, I have advised you once, and it is not my habit to repeat things a second time, leave Angelica in peace! Angelica is mine and no one is going to take her away," Agrican continues his blustering oaths, crying, "Vile, Roland, I'll eat your heart right out of your chest as well as that of this disgrace, Angelica!"

The two begin to fight in single combat but as neither is able to prevail and night is beginning to fall, they call a truce. As they bed down on the field of battle, the two begin to speak. Roland, impressed by Agrican's great strength, attempts to convert him to Christianity, saying that he could be of great service to Charlemagne. Agrican refuses. In the morning, they exchange words typical on the one hand of the Christian knight, on the other of the Saracen, but as the battle is decided they forego their knightly discourse in favor of a more saintly prose. Once Agrican receives his deathblow, he is more amenable to Roland's proselytization. In the face of epic's archetypal miracle, the appearance of baptismal water, both Roland and Agrican reject their knightly figures for figures more characteristic to the martyr-saint. Agrican, beyond undergoing a transformation in tone from the gruff, throaty quality of the Saracen to the clear, resounding quality of the Christian knight, switches from the familiar (actually derisive in the mouth of an enemy) form of address signaled through the use of *tu* (you) to the polite (or deferential) form of address signaled through the use of *voi*. Moreover, the figures which inform his voice include supplication ("Roland! I beg of you! Lower your sword!" and "I render myself to your mercy") and penitence ("Give me the water of Holy Baptism"). Roland's transformation is signaled through direct allusion to liturgy. Such allusion is characterized, however, by paraphrasis (the foreshortening of the liturgical act through concentration on its essential formulae) and contamination (the reformulation of the liturgical act through noble diction). Among the liturgical acts which Roland invokes are prayer ("Oh my God, here I am at your feet"), the Creed ("Do you believe in the Virgin Mary?"), and Benediction ("In the name of the Father, the Son, and the Holy Spirit").

The transformation of knight into saint is quite natural in Sicily, where a number of prominent saints are integrated into the Carolingian lineage as well as the Carolingian Cycle. In the words of the storyteller (*contastoria*), Salvatore Ferreri: "All the stories I know deal with genealogy; they begin with Constantine and they finish with Colloandro. Then I take them up again. If you want to know the entire genealogy, I will give it to you in a few words: Constantine, his son, Fiorio, then Fiorillo, then Fieravante. Fieravante bears Giberto; Giberto, Michele; Michele, Luigi; Luigi, Pepin; Pepin, Charlemagne. And at this point the genealogy ends with Roncevaux.... [But] Charlemagne bears a son as well and his name is Durando. Durando bears a son and names him Luigi. Luigi bears ... Sinilbaldo, the father of our patron, Santa Rosalia."[12] Thus two major Saints, Constantine, who Christianizes Rome, as well as Rosalia, the patron-saint of Palermo, are reckoned in Palermo as the ancestor and descendant, respectively, of Charlemagne. Thus, we might turn to their stories in order to see how saints' lives intrude upon the epic stage.

In the *Life of Constantine*, as presented by Achille Greco, heir to the nineteenth century progenitor of the Palermitan marionette theater, the emperor, afflicted twelve years with an incurable leprosy, is caught condemning Christians to death and preparing to bathe in the blood of six children to appease his affliction. The cries of the children arouse Constantine's compassion and he sets them free. Thus, Saints Peter and Paul appear to him in a dream and, commending his compassion, tell him to send for the hermit, Sylvester, who is fetched from his grotto by Constantine's captain and brought to court. Upon Sylvester's entrance, Constantine describes the twelve years' illness and the constant irritation it causes him, then recounts his vision of Saints Peter and Paul. "Can you propose any remedy?" he asks.

"Become a Christian. The water of baptism will wash away your disease."

The emperor agrees, and Sylvester fetches a cup of water with which he performs the sacrament of baptism, pouring the water over the kneeling emperor whose leprous scabs instantly fall away from his body. Constantine, in his ecstasy, embraces Sylvester and declares him bishop over all bishops—that is Pope of Rome.[13]

The life of Palermo's patron, Santa Rosalia, I have only as any Palermitan might: in bits and pieces from various sources. Not only is she

Five: On Christian Soil

Santa Rosalia's sanctuary in a grotto within Monte Pellegrino, just on the outskirts of the City. Photograph by Bengt Nyman, wikipedia.org.

said to be the daughter of Sinilbaldo, descendant of Charlemagne, but also the niece of William the Good, fourth Norman king of Palermo. She, curiously enough, seems to represent a synthesis between the two major claimants to Sicily: the papacy, which claimed Sicily as its gift, first from Constantine and then again from the Carolingian dynasty,[14] and the aristocracy, which claimed Sicily as its inheritance from the Norman kings. She fled the luxury of the court in preference to a life of quiet penitence and contemplation in a grotto on Monte Pellegrino, a limestone promontory which rises on the western fringe of Palermo. In 1624, as a plague ravaged the city, she appeared to a lone hunter on the mountain and instructed him to retrieve her bones, which had been encased in translucent stone by the water which dripped from the roof of her cave. The hunter carried her bones into the city, whereupon the plague ceased. Rosalia was declared the city's patron, and a shrine was built around her grotto on Monte Pellegrino.

The impact that saints' lives such as Constantine's and Rosalia's had on epic becomes most apparent in the progression of themes from Apparition through Miracle to Glorification not only in *The Battle of Roland and Agrican*, as we have just seen, but also in the seminal episode of the Carolingian Cycle, *The Death of the Paladins*, to which we will shortly turn. But, before moving on to that episode, I wish to return briefly to the role of rhetoric in the Carolingian Cycle at Palermo. With the introjection of saints' and bandits' lives into epic, the juxtaposition of knights and masques, detailed in previous chapters, becomes more pronounced. The saint is corollary to the knight: noble but, through his at times slavish adherence to the law of obedience, tragically flawed; the bandit is corollary to the masque: perhaps a bit coarse but ennobled by his insistence on the right of rebellion. Further, inasmuch as the detailing of the saint's voice is based on the characteristic diction of the Palermitan cleric and, likewise, the detailing of the bandit's voice is based on the characteristic diction of the Palermitan Mafioso, the conceptual framework with which epic's audiences assess saint and bandit accrues to—or is rhetorically transferred back to—the cleric and the Mafioso.

It is, in the final analysis, by means of this transference that the Palermitan audience rhetorically recasts epic in its own image and, thereby, allows epic to comment upon Palermitan social order—making the Carolingian Cycle, in the process, its own. I suspect that if we had access to the various voices that populated those societies that initially composed the Carolingian Cycle—or, for that matter, the Trojan or Arthurian—we would find similar processes at play. Though I suspect, as well, that this is an analysis for which the tools will be forever lacking. So leaving that impractical analysis behind, let me return briefly, instead, to the rhetoric of Islamophobia, which will play a significant role as the Carolingian Cycle moves inevitably toward its apocalyptic conclusion.

The Rhetoric of Islamophobia Revisited

The rhetoric of Islamophobia is apparent in a society that has historically used the term Christian as a synonym for human being and Turk as a synonym for barbarian, and, not surprisingly, it forms a mainstay of Palermitan epic: note Renaud's justification for abducting Clarice—that is, to keep her out of the hands of the Saracen Francardo—and Roland's patronizing rebuke of Agrican—that is, his declaration that Christian knights, unlike Saracens, don't kill their adversaries in their sleep. Such rhetorical strategies serve to establish a sense of social identity based on Christian affiliation and anti-Islamic antipathy. But we mustn't be so harsh with Sicily that we fail to look at ourselves or, to put it in more biblical terms, we ought not to behold the mote that is in our brother's eye but consider not the beam that is in our own.

Perhaps nothing throws into bold relief the rhetoric of Islamophobia in America more than the discussion which erupted over the proposed *name* for the Islamic community center that was to be built near Ground Zero in Manhattan: the Cordoba House. A small group of politicians of a very singular political stripe claimed, without any evidence to back them up—because, in fact, none exists—that the name evoked an Islamic conquest of a Christian land: Spain. In fact, that connotation was solely a western Christian construct—evocative of the medieval conception of "Christian soil" that occasionally intruded upon Sicilian epic or Ross Douthat's lament over the rise of Islam in "once-Christian Europe"—ascribed (again, without a shred of evidence) to Islamic culture.

In fact, in the Islamic context, the proposed name, Cordoba House, connotes something almost diametrically opposed to such signification.

Cordoba was the ancient capital of Muslim Spain, al–Andalus (Andalucia, in modern Spanish); the concept of al–Andalus throughout a good portion of the Islamic world (that is both in the Maghrib—contiguous with Islamic North Africa—and the Mashriq—contiguous with Islamic southwest Asia) exists in the folkloric realm—especially in the genre of folksong referred to in both the Maghrib and Mashriq as Andalusian—as emblematic of a Golden Era when the Islamic world entered its Enlightenment (a full 700 years before Christian Europe) and during which Muslims, Christians, and Jews lived in harmony under a benevolent Islamic caliphate.[15] Sicily, and particularly its capital of Palermo (called Balerm during the Islamic period) offered a similar multicultural environment as that present in al–Andalus throughout the Arabic occupation and well into the Norman and Hohenstaufen (western Imperial) occupations that followed: here both eastern and western Christian coexisted with Islamic and Jewish populations, creating—as we have seen—a vibrantly multicultural mosaic that was manifested in art, architecture, language, law and socio-political structure; it was in fact the Islamic model of tolerance practiced in both al–Andalus and Muslim Sicily that was adopted by Sicily's Norman and Hohenstaufen dynasties but not—notably—by the Spanish crown, which fell further and further under the sway of the intolerant Inquisition not only at home in Spain but also abroad in Sicily. Thus, the name Cordoba House rhetorically specifies coexistence: not conquest.

To return, then, momentarily to Douthat's lament over Pope John Paul II's benign neglect of the pressing issues of Christendom (the pedophilia scandal, the "debasement of the liturgy," and the rise of Islam in "once-Christian Europe"), it seems apparent that the editorialist is not simply engaging in a charming bit of medievalism—hearkening back to the concept of "Christian soil"—but he is also rhetorically linking theological liberalization, pedophilia, and cultural tolerance. In fact, he suggests—following a traditionalist line of thought—that theological liberalization (embodied in the doctrines of Vatican II) created a permissive environment (Douthat refers to this as the theological "silly season")[16] in which pedophiliac priests could somehow justify their behavior to themselves more readily and Europe could blithely discard its Christian heritage. This line of thought—that is to say, this rhetorically constructed connectivity of disparate things—seems questionable if looked at carefully. Theological liberalization, while questioning some of the harsher tenets of Christianity such as eternal damnation for recalcitrant Christians or—for that matter—non-Christians, certainly doesn't offer a justification for priestly pedophilia of all things. To suggest that it does is a misrepresentation. In the meantime, a greater Islamic presence in Europe has nothing to do with a liberal theology (or—obviously—pedophilia). It has rather to do with the consequences of European colonial history and immigration patterns in a globalizing economy—that very economy that, to a great extent, has led to the demise of Palermitan epic. To surreptitiously attach the burgeoning Islamic presence in Europe to theological liberalization is disingenuous at best—and seems likely to stoke the peculiar brand of Islamophobia that is currently taking hold in Europe—Sicily included—with its sometimes more virulent American cousin. Yet, here we may be straying too far from rhetorical strategies and too near to party politics. It might be best to simply point out, in closing, that the rhetorical linking of unlinked issues has troublesome consequences both in Sicily and America and, I suspect, I would never have noticed it had I not, without thinking too much on the ramifications, invited my friend Faisal to the marionette theater one day.

Chapter Six

The Carolingian Cycle

The Three Matters

Though, as we have seen, the Carolingian Cycle became—with time—the seminal product of the Sicilian folkloric repertoire, it wasn't, in truth, only Sicily that became enchanted by the feats of Charlemagne, Roland, and Renaud. It was rather all medieval Europe. In fact, around the year 1200, the poet Jean Bodel set forth the three matters most suitable to courtly treatment: the matters of Rome, Britain, and France. The matter of Rome centered upon the Trojan Cycle: the fall of Troy, the subsequent peopling of Europe, and the consolidation of the Roman Empire. Not only Aeneas went forth to father Rome but, as various authors have pointed out, a number of Roman territories in Italy, France and England had Trojan ancestors as well. We read in *Sir Gawain and the Green Knight*, for example, that Felix Brutus left Troy to found Britain. Even an early Sicilian people, the Elymians, were reported by Thucydides to be of Trojan origin. The matter of Britain dealt with the Arthurian Cycle in which the knights of the Round Table witnessed the passage of spiritual authority (symbolized by the Holy Grail) from the descendants of Troy (Arthur, Gawain, and Gareth) to the descendants of Jerusalem's Joseph of Arimathea (Perceval, Lancelot, and Galahad). Once again, a Sicilian connection was postulated for the matter of England. As we have mentioned above, Arthur was said to be trapped beneath Mount Etna, the belching volcano a palpable symbol of his eternally festering wounds. The matter of France centered upon the Carolingian Cycle, in which Charlemagne and his hand-picked knights, the Paladins, pursued the purified (that is to say, Holy) Roman Empire. To the matter of France, Sicilians feel their greatest connection, considering themselves the heirs of the Carolingian dynasty by means of their Norman rulers of the eleventh and twelfth centuries, one of whom, Roger

II, made the correspondence between himself and Charlemagne explicit by being crowned king of Sicily on December 25, 1130.

While Bodel makes generic distinctions between the three matters, suggesting that the matter of Rome is instructive, the matter of Britain light and entertaining, and the matter of France, simply put, noble (it deals, after all, with the king of France, God's "sergeant on Earth"),[1] it is apparent that some criterion led him to gather them together, to define them as a set. This criterion, I would suggest, was the concept of history. The matters comprised the epic history of Europe, that is a history which combines various legendry with Christian mythology in order to evoke the apocalypse: a progression of formation (the emergence of the Roman Empire), destruction (the eclipsing of Trojan Arthur by Jerusalem's Lancelot/Galahad/Perceval complex) and re-formation (the emergence of Charlemagne's Holy Roman Empire).[2] The apocalyptic overtones of this progression might have been especially attractive to Sicilian audiences, given the often rigid social strictures under which they labored and the almost continuous penchant for subverting, either through secret organizations or out-and-out rebellion, those strictures. Moreover, the matter of France, dealing as it did with the battle between Christendom and Islam, was especially trenchant for Sicilians, who saw their homeland pass from two centuries of Arab rule to become, under Frederick II, the seat of the Holy Roman Empire.

The Song of Roland

Perhaps more than any other episode of that third matter, *The Song of Roland*, as the poem was denominated by the Norman invaders of England, or *The Death of the Paladins*, as the Sicilian version came to be known, captures the imagination of its audiences, Sicilian and otherwise. The episode itself has known historical antecedents. On August 15, 778 A.D., Charlemagne's army suffered a humiliating defeat described perhaps 50 years later by Einhard the Frank, a member of Charlemagne's court:

> At a time when this war against the Saxons was being waged constantly and with hardly an intermission at all, Charlemagne left garrisons at strategic points along the frontier and went off himself with the largest force he could muster to invade Spain. He marched over a pass across the Pyrenees, received

> the surrender of every single town and castle which he attacked and then came back with his army safe and sound, except for the fact that for a brief moment on the return journey, while he was in the Pyrenean mountain range itself, he was given a taste of Basque treachery. Dense forests, which stretch in all directions, make this a spot most suitable for setting ambushes. At a moment when Charlemagne's army was stretched out in a long column of march, as the nature of the local defiles forced it to be, these Basques, who had set their ambush on the very top of one of the mountains, came rushing down on the last part of the baggage train and the troops who were marching in support of the rear guard and so protecting the army which had gone on ahead. The Basques forced them down into the valley beneath, joined battle with them and killed them to the last man. They then snatched up the baggage, and, protected as they were by the cover of darkness, which was just beginning to fall, scattered in all directions without losing a moment. In this feat the Basques were helped by the lightness of their arms and by the nature of the terrain in which the battle was fought. On the other hand, the heavy nature of their own equipment and the unevenness of the ground completely hampered the Franks in their resistance to the Basques. In this battle died Eggihard, who was in charge of the King's table, Anshelm, the Count of the Palace and Roland, Lord of the Breton Marches, along with a great number of others. What is more, this assault could not be avenged there and then, for, once it was over, the enemy dispersed in such a way that no one knew where or among which people they could be found.[3]

Evidence for an oral tradition centering on this event consists mainly of an early eleventh-century French custom of naming brothers Roland and Oliver,[4] William Malmesbury's mention of a *cantilena Rollandi*, a song of Roland, which was sung before the Battle of Hastings (A.D. 1066) in the Norman invasion of England, and the *Nota Emilianense*, a late eleventh-century addition to a Latin chronicle. The *Nota* reads:

> In the year 778 King Charles came to Saragossa; at that time he had twelve nephews ... with him, and each of them had three thousand armed horsemen with him; among them were Roland, Bertrand, Ogier of the Short Sword, Guillaume of the Hooked Nose ... Oliver, and the bishop Turpin. Each one, with his followers, served the king one month of each year. It so happened that the king stopped at Saragossa with his army. After a short time he was counseled by his men to accept a number of gifts so that the army might not perish from hunger and could return to their homeland. This was done. The king then decided that for the safety of the men of the army, the courageous warrior Roland should remain with the rear guard. But when the army traversed the Port of Cize, at Roncevaux, Roland was killed by the Saracens.[5]

Beyond this evidence, the formulaic density of the oldest extant manuscript of *The Song of Roland* (MS. Digby 23, ca. 1125–70)—35.2 percent according to Joseph J. Duggan's analysis[6]—argues that jongleurs (itinerant singers of narrative poetry in French) were primary participants in the song's composition and dissemination.

In *The Song of Roland*, Charlemagne has captured all the cities of Spain except for Saragossa, which is under the rule of the Saracen king, Marsilius. He holds a council where he accepts Ganelon's advice to permit Marsilius the option of converting from Islam to Christianity rather than suffering a siege under the walls of Saragossa. Roland, nephew to Charlemagne and stepson to Ganelon, nominates his stepfather as ambassador to Marsilius, and Ganelon accepts the nomination but vows to avenge himself upon his stepson for the nomination means almost certain death. At the court of Marsilius, Ganelon betrays Roland, suggesting that Marsilius might get the better of the Christian forces if he pays tribute to Charlemagne, then attacks the rear guard of the army as it heads back to Charlemagne's court at Aix in France. Ganelon will arrange that the twelve Peers (Charlemagne's finest knights) including Roland (the best of the Peers) will be in the rear guard. At Roncevaux, a pass in the Pyrenean mountains, the rear guard of Charlemagne's army is ambushed by Marsilius' forces. The odds are overwhelmingly against the Peers, and despite Oliver's plea that Roland blow his horn and alert Charlemagne to the treachery, Roland vows to fight to the death. Only when Roncevaux becomes littered with the corpses of Christians and Saracens alike, does Roland deign to blow his horn, knowing that Marsilius' forces have been broken.

> Roland has brought the oliphant up to his mouth,
> He grasps it firmly, he sounds it with all his
>   might.
> The mountains are high and the sound travels a
>   great distance,
> They heard it echo a full thirty leagues away.
> Charles heard it, all his men too.
> The King said: "Our men are giving battle!"
> But Ganelon contradicted him:
> "If anyone else said this, it would seem a great
>   lie!"
> Count Roland, with pain and suffering,
> With great agony sounds his oliphant.

> Bright blood comes gushing from his mouth.
> The temple of his brain has burst.
> The sound of the horn he is holding carries very
>   far,
> Charles, who is going through the pass, hears it.
> Duke Naimes heard it, the Franks listen for it.
> The King says: "I hear Roland's horn!
> He'd never sound it if he weren't fighting."[7]

Arriving at Roncevaux, Charlemagne sees the result of Ganelon's treachery; Roland and the Peers are dead. Back at Aix, Ganelon is tried. He claims that he has justly avenged himself upon his stepson but it is deemed that he has also betrayed his sovereign, Charlemagne, in the process. He is condemned to be quartered by four war-horses.

Here we find that the oral tradition has infused history with myth, transforming Charlemagne's rear guard's assailants from Basques into Saracens and adding a traitor to a list of twelve Peers. Moreover, we find the special patronage that the archangel offers Roland, who, as his mythic counterpart does at doomsday, sounds his horn in the earthly apocalypse of Roncevaux. The ambush in the Pyrenees has taken on apocalyptic overtones, conflating legend with myth (and in effect, knight with saint), overtones which will remain a defining characteristic of the Carolingian Cycle throughout its history.

The apocalyptic history embedded in the Carolingian Cycle is well grounded in European millenarianism. Millenarianism—"the hope of a complete and radical change in the world which will be reflected in the millennium, a world shorn of all its present deficiencies"[8]—reached one of its many zeniths in eleventh-century France, where the millennium was often understood as a return of Charlemagne and his Peers, a return—that is—of the Holy Roman Empire.

> A great mass of folklore had in fact been accumulating around the formidable figure of the first Carolingian. Charlemagne had come to be seen as above all the heroic champion of Christ, the tireless defender of Christendom against the armed might of Islam; and in the second half of the eleventh century it came to be almost universally believed that he had once led a crusade to Jerusalem, put the infidel there to flight and reinstated the Christians who had been expelled. More than one chronicler tells how the crusaders of 1096 travelled along the road which Charlemagne was supposed to have constructed on that occasion. Moreover it was also widely believed that Charlemagne had never died at all but was only sleeping, either in his vault

at Aachen or inside some mountain, until the hour came for him to return to the world of men. It was easy enough for popular preachers, recruiting for the Crusade, to combine these tales with Sibylline prophecies and to lead the common people to see in Charlemagne that great Emperor who was to shake off his slumber, overthrow the power of Islam and establish the age of bliss which was to precede the End.[9]

The Cycle's Migration

The history of Charlemagne, Roland and the Paladins (as the Peers came to be called) was augmented throughout the twelfth and thirteenth centuries by a number of chansons de geste (Old French epics). Bertrand de Bar-sur-Aube in *Girard de Vienne* (ca. 1200–1220) suggests that there are three gestes (deeds) which comprise the chansons (songs): that of the King of France, which centers upon Charlemagne's campaigns (most notably against the Saracens), that of Doon de Maiance, which centers upon various of Charlemagne's rebellious barons (including, beyond Doon, Renaud de Montauban), and that of Garin de Monglane, which centers on the establishment of the House of Orange (variously allied and at odds with the Carolingian kings).[10] It is notable in this context that the character of the bandit had already crept into the Carolingian Cycle under the guise of the rebellious baron (*Les Quattre Fils Aymon*, also known as *Renaud de Montauban*) and that the comic possibilities of the young knight's descent among the people had already been recognized (*Mainet*, discussing the young Charlemagne's descent among the people). Thus knight, saint, bandit, and some representative of the people (though with the *villein*, or peasant, rather than the masque, or urban laborer, providing the model) had already come into coincidence in the Carolingian Cycle by the twelfth century.

The dissemination of the Carolingian Cycle (coincident with the movement of jongleurs) is attested to in Italy by a group of manuscripts dating from the thirteenth and fourteenth centuries and written in the Franco-Venetian dialect. These texts include the tales of *Berta de li Gran Piè*, *Karleto* (overlapping *The Death of King Pepin*), *Berta, Milon e Rolandin* (overlapping *The First Adventures of Rolandin*), *Aspremont*, *Renaud de Montauban*, *L'Entree d'Espagne* and *La Prise de Pampelune* as well as *The Song of Roland*. This version of the cycle thus encompasses the early history of the young Charlemagne as well as that of the infant Roland, follows their growth into manhood (including their first battles), moves on to the revolt of Renaud and his brothers against Charlemagne and finally to the events leading to the battle of Roncevaux. It culminates with the battle itself. Yet, it is difficult to ascertain the extent to which Sicilian poets (either popular or courtly) included such matter in their repertoire because the surviving texts are nearly devoid of reference to Carolingian material. However, one poem, composed by Cielo D'Alcamo—a Sicilian poet active in the thirteenth century—tellingly has a seducer declare to his quarry that he loves her with "the heart of a Paladin," phraseology that suggests that Carolingian material had found its way into Sicily's popular tradition. Further, Sicily's Capo d'Orlando (Cape Roland) and Monte Oliviero (Mount Oliver) were associated (wrongly or rightly) with the Carolingian heroes' legendary sojourn in Sicily, at least according to Godrey of Viterbo, as early as the twelfth century.[11]

During this early dissemination of the Carolingian cycle, the barons that populate its stanzas become differentiated into two great houses: the name Maiance becomes attached to a house of traitors of whom Ganelon is the exemplary member, while the name Clermont becomes attached to a house of noble rebels whose members include the brothers Milon, Aymon, and Bueve, Milon's son Roland (who rarely rebels himself), and Aymon's son Renaud (the rebel par excellence). Moreover, the houses of Paris, Saragossa, Maiance, and Clermont become during this period more completely intertwined (primarily through numerous marriages) so that Bertrand's distinction between the *gestes* of the king on the one hand and Doon de Maiance on the other no longer applies. Thus, beyond the coincidence of knight, saint, bandit, and villein, the Carolingian Cycle is demarcated by a coincidence of Christian knight (Paris), rebel baron (Clermont), traitor (Maiance), and Saracen knight (Saragossa).

In the late fourteenth century, the center of production for chivalric narrative moved to the south, centering upon the courts at Florence and Ferrara. Such production was effected primarily by the pen (though the influence of jongleurs played a role at least in disposing the new audiences toward the genre) and continued well into the sixteenth century.[12] Among the more prominent works which came to bear on Sicilian epic were Andrea da Barberino's *I Reali di Francia* (ca. 1380–1420), Luigi Pulci's

Six: The Carolingian Cycle

Il Morgante (ca. 1460), Matteo Maria Boiardo's *Orlando Innamorato* (ca. 1490), Ludovico Ariosto's *Orlando Furioso* (ca. 1502) and Torquato Tasso's *Rinaldo* (1562).

Roughly contemporary with these works were the *cantastorie*, singers of the new chivalric romances, who appropriated the art of the jongleurs but sang in their own Italian dialects. Their activity is attested to in the Veneto, Tuscany, and Sicily as early as the sixteenth and as late as the eighteenth century.[13] With specific regard to Sicily, the poet A. Alfano mentions in 1568 that the stories of Roland and Renaud are to be found in the public squares,[14] and the Marquis of Villabianca states in the eighteenth century that

> The poor blind and blind in one eye, who (as is well known) are accustomed to the trade of singing and reciting both sacred and profane Orations on the streets and above all improvising poetry in honor of the saints which is usually narrated outside the temples and in the squares of the various quarters during the plebian festivals of the city, are the same popular poets called the *Cyclici Poetae* [the Cyclical Poets] who took their place among the ancients of Italy in the antique times of the Greeks and the Romans. One finds a good selection of the pieces and compositions of these base poets of the vulgate through me, Villabianca, in the little volume of my writings numbered 82 [no longer extant]. For the most part these are Orations of the blind and recitations of songs, ridiculous and produced in a Sicilian comic poetry, and among those which have seen the light of publication the most valuable are ... *The Contented Cuckold, The History of Meschino* [from the geste of Garin de Monglane], *The Bankrupt Merchant, The Demonic Tempter, The History of Orlando*, ... and others.[15]

By the nineteenth century, the repertoire of the Sicilian *cantastorie* was inspired mainly by police and accident reports in the local newspapers.[16] Thus, they became prime vehicles for the bandits' lives.

The Italian literary works, which represent a thorough treatment of the Carolingian Cycle, diffused through Sicily either directly, through numerous reprintings, or indirectly, through the recitation of the *contastorie* (storytellers or speakers, rather than singers, of epic). The *contastorie* practiced their declamatory art in the open air of the public squares. They often held a literary source (or perhaps a summary in manuscript) in one hand during the recitation and quite often a makeshift sword with which to punctuate their narrative in the other. Their repertoire as well as their method of recitation had much in common with that of today's puppeteers. It was substantially based on the Carolingian Cycle and performed serially. Its descriptions of battle were punctuated by a particular rhythm (consisting of a simultaneous strike to the pavement and a heavy accent on the first syllable of a line followed by a strict staccato of evenly stressed syllables descending in amplitude), which seems a possible source for the puppeteers' method of stomping the floor of the stage in a succession of rhythms during battles. And, as Antonio Pasqualino points out, the puppeteers' penchant for stopping an episode at a particularly chilling moment might be an economic stratagem learned from the *contastorie*.[17]

The first mention of a Sicilian *contastoria* occurs in 1837, when Vincenzo Linares dedicates a novella to Maestro Pasquale. Linares description of Pasquale follows:

> This is the famous Maestro Pasquale, the narrator of the most pleasurable stories that have ever been heard. Roland, Renaud, ... "the women, the knights, the arms, the loves, the courtesies, the bold adventures he sings." ... From his mouth flows forth a river of eloquence, a delight, a fragrance that enchants and moves the hearts of his less than tender listeners.... The old man is impassive as a usurer, more inspired than a poet, always agreeable and loquacious; his tales are sprinkled with easy banter, he becomes excited, he shouts, he foams at the mouth, ... and when fancy transports him, he rises from his chair, brandishes a wooden rod and acts out the duel between his characters.... And when he has excited the desire of his listeners to hear his tale to its end, the episode is finished. So he keeps his listeners agitated, in suspense, obliged to return the next day with the small donation that admits them to the spectacle.... If Maestro Pasquale sang verse instead of speaking prose, ... he would be a rhapsode, a bard of our own times.[18]

The last *contastoria* to perform in the public squares of Palermo was don Peppino Celano, whose years of activity extended from 1936 to 1953 and who was happily occasionally recorded by—among others—the famed American folklorist Alan Lomax.[19]

The *cantastorie* (singers) and *contastorie* (storytellers) must not have worked in completely different traditions because even in the late nineteenth century certain of the *contastorie* interspersed their declamatory prose with Sicilian octaves that were sometimes sung. These octaves are at times direct translations from Ariosto's *Orlando Furioso* but at others apparent inventions on the part of the *cantastorie* preserved in the repertoire of the *contastorie*.[20] Moreover, the art of *contastorie* and the puppeteer (despite the lack of a narrator in the latter) is quite similar and must have often come into coincidence. It is notable in this context that don Peppino Celano not only practiced the art of the *contastorie* but also that of the puppeteer.[21]

A Multi-Faceted Tradition

Yet another route of transmission carried the Italian renditions of the Carolingian Cycle to the last repositors of epic, the Sicilian puppeteers: the popular press of nineteenth-century Sicily. Most notable among the editorial efforts that provided material for the marionette theater was the publication of Giusto Lodico's *History of the French Paladins*, issued in installments from 1858 to 1860. Lodico's book is a monumental compilation of the Italian works mentioned previously, as well as a host of others, written in prose. It is an extensive treatment of the cycle, Lodico's professed purpose being to gather the sources of the *contastorie*'s history which had been scattered by the winds of time.[22] The book, which underwent numerous reprintings from 1862 on, opens with the events leading to the assassination of King Pepin (father of Charlemagne) and closes in the aftermath of the battle of Roncevaux. Though its publication came four decades after the institution of the Sicilian marionette theater, its popularity was sufficient to eventually transform the theater's treatment of the Carolingian Cycle.

In order to illustrate the interdependence of the various sources of the Carolingian Cycle in Palermo, I will offer a comparison of the council in which Pepin's illegitimate sons, Lanfroi and Olderigi, plot their father's assassination from (1) *The Death of King Pepin* by the last storyteller, don Peppino Celano, (2) Giusto Lodico's *The History of the French Paladins*, (3) a notebook from the puppeteer Natale Meli inscribed on the cover as "First Notebook of the Kings of France by Giusto Lodico," and (4) *The Death of King Pepin* by the puppeteers Girolamo Cuticchio and Sons.

1. The Storyteller: Don Peppino Celano

Here is the scene as presented in the storytelling tradition.

> But one day, Lanfroi and Olderigi were **thinking**, ea---**ch** of the brothers, and this is what they said: "Brother, **think** how King Pepi---n, our fa---**ther**,

had our mother, Elisetta of Maiance, killed, **burned alive!** Because he had betrayed her with **Berta** de la Gran Piè.

"**Be---rta** is dead! Because we have had her killed, **poisoned**, with the permission and the aid of our relatives of the House of Maiance. What do you say about **thi---s**, beloved brother, Lanfroi?"

Lanfroi answered, and said, "But we are alone. We are unable to confront the men of our father. There is **Berna---rdo of Chiaramonte**. There is old **Mora---ndo of Riviera**. There is the **fa---ther** of **Girardo**. There are so many old barons, and certainly they will defend our father.

"We need to send a letter to our **uncle**, Grifon. With him there is also **Gina---mo of Bagliona**. It will be necessary that **all** the members of the House of Maiance give us aid because **we**, after all, are the sons of King Pepin, that **hunchback**, that **u---glyness** who killed our mother. But at the same time, beloved brother, that we kill King Pepin, we must **assure ourselves** of the throne of Charles."[23]

2. The Popular Press: Giusto Lodico

The same scene as presented in the Sicilian popular press.

A year after the death of Berta, the two bastards of King Pepin (to wit, Lanfroi and Olderigi) were speaking together about the governance and as that one of the city of Maiance, Grifon, was always advising them, Lanfroi said, "Certainly the governance of France will not be ceded to us after the death of King Pepin but instead to Charles. And while Grifon always promises us his protection, we need to kill King Pepin and Charles. But first of all, let's send a letter to advise Count Grifon for he will gather the people who will give us succor."[24]

3. The Notebook: Natale Meli

The following text is from the notebook of Natale Meli inscribed on the cover as "First Notebook of the Kings of France by Giusto Lodico" and on the first page as "First Script of the History of the Kings of France beginning with 'Being old, King Pepino was counseled by his barons to take a wife in order to have an heir.'" Puppeteers commonly keep these notebooks in order to recall the major features of each episode. Whereas Meli cites important bits of dialogue from Lodico by page number, I have here included the cited portion directly within the text of the notebook, and set it off from Meli's text with quotation marks.

A year after the death of Berta, Lanfroi and Ulderigi [Olderigi] were speaking of the governance, and that one of the city of Maiance was advising them. Then Lanfroi says: "Certainly the governance of France will not be ceded to

Six: The Carolingian Cycle

us after the death of King Pepin but instead to Charles. And while Grifon always promises us his protection, we need to kill King Pepin and Charles. But first of all, let's send a letter to Count Grifon, for he will gather the people who will give us succor." The two come to an agreement and they go to write letters to Grifon of Maiance.[25]

4. THE PUPPETEERS: GIROLAMO CUTICCHIO AND SONS

Lanfroi and Olderigi's council in Girolamo Cuticchio's version of *The Death of King Pepin* is the closest passage to Lodico in the entire episode. Thus it presents an especially cogent example of the puppeteers' synthesis of the *contastorie*'s declamatory art with Lodico's narrative. However, it is extremely rare for the puppeteer to follow Lodico's language so closely.

> *Olderigi: My dea---r bro---ther, Lanfroi---,* **how** *do you like the fact that our fa---ther,* **King Pepin,** *loves our brother,* **Charles,** *so much more than us!* **Do** *you know what I think? I think that our fa---ther would like one day to leave his crown to* **Charles** *even though the crown of France belongs to* **us.**
>
> **Certainly** *the governance of France after the death of King Pepin will not come to* **us,** *but instead to* **Charles;** *and while Grifon always promises us his protection,* **we need to kill our father, King Pepin, and also Charles!**
>
> *But first of all we need to advise Count Grifon of Maiance, for he will gather the people who will give us succor. With his aid, we will make ourselves rulers of all France!*
>
> *Lanfroi: All right, Olderigi; I agree with you. And now we shall send a letter to Grifon of Maiance. And as soon as he promises to* **prote---ct us,** *we won't waste any time in killing our father in his bed, and also Charles.*[26]

What is it about the Carolingian Cycle that has exalted it so in the Sicilian imagination and has given its heroes the singular status of ancestral genii to the Sicilian people? What has allowed these knights—Roland and Renaud—and their ladies—Angelica, Alda the Beautiful, and Clarice—to become the template upon which the Sicilian people adjust and readjust, formulate and reformulate, vitalize and revitalize simultaneously their social order and (as we shall see) the religion which sanctifies it? Whenever a legend endures across historical epochs and cultural divides there must be something in it that captures the psyche or, more properly, causes the psyche to respond to it with familiarity, empathy, even pathos. I do not deem to know exactly what it is in the Sicilian psyche that so responded to the Carolingian Cycle in more than the briefest outline. I do know, for instance, that other European populations were similarly affected by the cycle at different times, and to some extent, I believe, the cycle's apocalyptic character was partly responsible for this; apocalyptic narrative seems to take on a life of its own in times of cultural turmoil: witness contemporary Americans viewing the attack on the World Trade Towers by (to the minds of Islamophobists at least) modern Saracens as the beginning of the fulfillment of prophecies of the end-time offered in Revelation or the clamor which the supposed "mosque at Ground Zero" elicited. Another factor, beyond the apocalyptic overtones, which seems to have captured the Sicilian imagination is the tension between obedience and rebellion that is continuously played out in the Carolingian Cycle: this tension has at times carried as much significance to contemporary Palermo as it has to the feudal Europe which spawned it.

That the Carolingian Cycle found its way to become not only one item but the dominant item of so many Palermitan folkloric traditions is finally a testament to its agility, the same agility that allowed the cycle to remain in the European oral tradition for over a millennium and that continues to allow the Palermitan people, even those who have never read Lodico, heard a *contastoria*, or seen a marionette play to be able to describe the cycle from beginning to end. I believe that one possible explanation for the Carolingian legend's ability to engage so many audiences over both successive historical epochs and significant cultural divides, as has the Trojan and Arthurian legends before it, is its malleability, its ability to be meaningfully rewritten by each successive generation and each distinctive culture. It is this malleability which creates of it, in my reading, living epic: epic still current in a society's oral tradition and meaningful to that society's social order. This malleability has allowed the Carolingian Cycle to become a kind of template upon which Palermitans—without fear of recrimination or damnation—simultaneously rescript society and Christianity to suit their particular taste.

Chapter Seven

The Song of Roland in Sicily

A Tragic Flaw

The version of this legend extant in Palermo to this day has been forged by the same processes that forged earlier versions. Literary treatments have intermingled with the recitations of Palermitan storytellers and puppeteers and, I think more importantly, the whole has been reshaped by the expectations and aesthetic demands of the Palermitan people. That the Carolingian Cycle looms so large in the Palermitan imagination is a credit to the Palermitan storytellers. I have already mentioned that Maria, the shopkeeper whose store was on my street, learned the entire cycle through her brothers' retellings. I spoke to another woman whose father was a habitué of the marionette theater and would as well read to his children nightly from Giusto Lodico's *History of the French Paladins*. I talked to people in their late forties who remembered a storyteller declaiming his histories on the Piazza Bonanno, a square not far up the Corso Vittorio Emanuele from the Norman Cathedral. Even the young students at the University of Palermo, while not generally having a full knowledge of the cycle, had some memory of the battles of Roland and Renaud, sometimes from village festivals, others from their parents' discussions. Here, then, is recounted the most important of those battles, the Palermitan retelling of *The Song of Roland*, known in the city of Palermo as *The Death of the Paladins*.

> *The Death of the Paladins*
>
> Charlemagne, his voice trembling momentously, opened his council: "Roland, my nephew," he announced, "constrained by a solemn oath, advised my beloved brother-in-law, King Marsilius of Spain, to either leave the key of Spain to Paris or to render himself subject to my crown. But rightly, Duke Naimes of

Bavaria said that I might send as ambassador my brother-in-law, Count Ganelon of Maiance, to convince the Spaniards to accept the water of Holy Baptism."[1] *And even as he finished speaking, a soldier entered the throne room to announce Ganelon's return from his embassy: "High Emperor, Charlemagne, at this moment Count Ganelon of Maiance presents himself."*

"Receive him," Charlemagne commanded, "with every honor."

And, as the soldier led him into the throne room, Ganelon prostrated himself before the emperor: "Your Majesty, here I am at your feet. I have completed my mission, oh Lord."

Charlemagne: "Raise yourself, Brother-in-law, Count Ganelon. I would like to know the outcome of your embassy."

Ganelon: "Your Majesty, I presented myself to the three Spanish brothers to whom I have given your command: That is, to either give up Spain or to convert to Christianity. War has broken out in their souls, oh my Lord. And they have decided to convert to Christianity in order to retain their kingdom."

The Ascension of Roland: Note the water rushing from the rock which Roland strikes with his sword, Durandal, as he dies. The mitered figure is Bishop Turpin, who hears Roland's dying confession, and the man at his side should be Renaud, returned from his exile just in time to participate in the Battle of Roncevaux. From the collections of the Antonio Pasqualino Museo Internazionale delle Marionette, photograph by author.

Seven: The Song of Roland in Sicily

At this auspicious announcement, the Paladins shouted their assent, whereupon Ganelon, emboldened in his design, continued with greater fervor: "For their part, oh my Lord Charlemagne, they will accept the water of Holy Baptism in the valley of Roncevaux. Moreover, oh my Lord, they insist that only the Paladins, and not the governors of Trebisond, much less an army, be present."

At this last announcement a murmur went up ominously among the Paladins, but Ganelon continued unabashed. "I have promised that the armies, both Arabian and French, will halt four leagues distance from the Valley of Roncevaux. This is the answer that the Spanish brothers, your brothers-in-law, have given me; they desire baptism but only from the hand of Bishop Turpin."

Charlemagne answered, "I am content in the knowledge that Marsilius, Bulogant, and Falseron will accept the water of Holy Baptism. But I don't understand the motive of your advice concerning the Valley of Roncevaux?"

Ganelon: "They don't want to convert to Christianity in their own land, that is, in Spain, or more precisely, at their court in Saragossa, and so bring shame and dishonor to their own people."

Astolphe: "If your majesty will permit me to speak, I would like to say a few words to Count Ganelon."

Charlemagne: "Speak, Prince Astolphe of England."

Astolphe: "Ganelon, I believe you have taken the part of the pagans and, I know well, if treachery lies beneath your words, Roland will never achieve the crown of Spain."

The Paladins murmured at this speech, but Charlemagne reprimanded the speaker, saying, "Astolphe, I insist that you hold your tongue. Do not dare to offend my brother-in-law, Ganelon, inasmuch as he, in the blessed Church of All Saints, took a solemn oath to remain faithful to my crown and to all France. Therefore I insist that each one of us ready himself without rancor so that—at the earliest possible moment—we might leave Paris, and take the road to Roncevaux."

After the council, Astolphe took Roland aside, and Roland queried him as to his intentions, saying, "I would like to know, Astolphe, why you are always so suspicious? Now you have given me a sign to wait for you; what is it that you want to tell me?"

Astolphe defended himself, saying, "Roland, as you well know, there are many caves in the Valley of Roncevaux. Therefore, Ganelon, without a doubt, has orchestrated some treachery against the Paladins. After all, why does he invite only the Paladins and not the entire army?"

"Astolphe," Roland persisted, "You haven't understood a thing. The honor of assisting in the baptism was given only to the Paladins of France. And perhaps Marsilius is afraid to allow the entire French army to come to Spain because of the reaction it might have on the Spanish people. I'm convinced that it's better to bring a people to Christianity than to conquer a crown."

And, then, turning to Oliver, Roland asked, "What do you think, my cousin?"

"Roland," Oliver answered, "I have doubts as to the sincerity of Ganelon of Maiance. I'm more in accord with Prince Astolphe on this matter."

Roland: "Look, let's summon my stepbrother, Balduin. There's no better test of Ganelon's sincerity than to know whether he, Ganelon's son by birth—unlike me who became Ganelon's son only when he married my mother, Berta—will go to Roncevaux. Certainly he would not send his own flesh and blood to his death. Balduin, come here, beloved brother."

"Dear Brother, Roland," Balduin courteously responded, "you called for me. What is it that you have to say?"

Roland: "Listen, Balduin, I want to know if you will come with us to Roncevaux."

Balduin: "But what are you asking? Am I not also a Paladin of France?"

Roland: "Certainly you are! But we would like to be certain. Would you mind, please, going to your father, Count Ganelon, and getting his confirmation?"

Balduin: "I'm ready to do so, dear brother. I'll go and return shortly."

"Now," said Roland, turning to Astolphe and Oliver, "if Balduin is coming with us, then we'll know that there is no treachery."

Balduin returned without a moment's hesitation to assure Roland that he as well would attend the baptism at Roncevaux: "I'm here at your service, Roland," he announced. "I found my father, Ganelon of Maiance, your stepfather, and he told me that I would be together with you at Roncevaux."

And as Balduin departed, Roland chastised Astolphe and Oliver for their suspiciousness.

Yet, even as the Paladins prepared for the journey to Roncevaux, one noble knight, Ricciardetto, refused to join in the festivities. "Ricciardetto," he said to himself, "everyone speaks of feasts. Everyone prepares himself for the journey to Roncevaux. But all these feasts, all these preparations, don't concern me at all. I feel in my soul the lack of my brother, Renaud. The entire world believes that Renaud is dead. But Renaud is not dead. Renaud lives. I know it! Very well! Without advising Ganelon, without advising anybody, I'll leave the threshold of Paris. I'll take the road before me and I won't return without Renaud at my side." And, that very night, Ricciardetto found himself in the trackless forest, searching out his brother. "Ricciardetto," he lamented, "I do nothing more than call for Renaud though nobody answers me. But just now I see in the distance a cave where I can rest for the night. Yes, I feel tired. The weight of my arms is crushing my spirit."

Yet, even as he fell asleep, his cousin, the necromancer Malagigi, appeared to him in a dream. "Cousin Ricciardetto," Malagigi whispered. "Banish your sadness. Renaud lives and is enveloped in grace. Certainly, you will find him in Armenia. And because the Most High has designated as martyrs all those who defend him in his land, you will bring him to Roncevaux: Not as a hermit but as a formidable warrior."

And as Ricciardetto slowly awakened, he murmured to himself, "Ricciardetto, I dreamed ... or perhaps ... No! It wasn't a dream. It was Malagigi! Renaud lives! 'Near the country of the King of Armenia, in a cave you will find your brother, Renaud, and you will bring him to Roncevaux.' Yes, this is what Malagigi said to me. Ricciardetto, I must take to the road that will lead me to the country of Armenia."

And Ricciardetto continued his journey, coming finally to another cave where he found a lone pilgrim on his knees in prayer. "Listen," Ricciardetto said to the pilgrim, "I pray of you, if you are without deceit, answer me. Who are you? What is your name, oh pilgrim?"

Pilgrim: "Knight, what do you desire? For whom do you seek in this place?"

Ricciardetto: "I seek a human being who one day made the entire universe tremble. His name is Renaud."

Pilgrim: "Renaud? But who are you? Why do you seek out Renaud?"

Ricciardetto: "I seek out Renaud because we are of the same blood, born of the same father and the same mother. Everybody says that Renaud is dead. And a few have had the audacity to say it with a smile. All right, then, I'm Ricciardetto!"

"And Brother," the pilgrim answered, "I am Renaud!"[2]

Renaud: "Ricciardetto, your presence here is a great marvel to me. However did you find me in Armenia?"

Ricciardetto: "Listen to me, Renaud, I want to recount these things to you. You must know that the Emperor Charlemagne has sent Ganelon of Maiance to the court of Spain in order to oblige the Spanish brothers to convert to Christianity. And Ganelon, returning to the court of his majesty, recounted that he had convinced the three Spanish brothers to abdicate the faith of Mohammed and to convert to Christianity. Very well, Marsilius is ready. Bulogant and Falseron, with the entire Spanish people, are ready to accept the water of Holy Baptism in the great plain of Roncevaux. Thus, I left Paris and went in search of you. During the journey, I dreamed that I saw Malagigi, our cousin, and he said to me, 'Ricciardetto, Ricciardetto, rouse yourself! Have courage that Renaud is living! You will find him in a cave in the country of Armenia. And you will bring him to Roncevaux!' Come, Renaud, leave your penitence! Return to your old trade! During the journey you will find your faithful destrier, Bayard!"

But Renaud disdainfully answered, "Brother, Ricciardetto, perhaps you have forgotten that I left my arms in Paris when I rendered myself subject to Charlemagne. Yet if you remember well, after the death of my wife, Clarice, I swore that I would no longer carry arms, that I would no longer do combat, that I would no longer kill people! And now, what is it that you ask of me, brother? I am sorry for my children, for my brothers, who are going to die for Charlemagne, or rather by means of the treachery of Ganelon of Maiance, but ..." And breaking off his complaint in mid speech, he exclaimed, "What's this I see! A celestial light! A messenger from God! Oh God, I commend myself to your keeping!"

At once, an angel appeared before the brothers, saying, "Renaud, it is the *wish of the Highest God that you leave your penitence and return to your old trade. Roncevaux will be your last adventure and, since no other will furnish you with a good set of armor, take this one! At the command of God, I took it from Raimond! For your sword, Fusbert, I have substituted the famous Balisard which I took from Guidon! On your journey you will find your Bayard who will for the last time be your mount. This is what I want of you, and this is what I command of you!"*

"My God," Renaud exclaimed as the angel disappeared, "I am moved by this celestial illumination. God wants me, God commands me, and I must dress myself in this fearsome armor in order to arrive at Roncevaux the more quickly! My children will be there, my brothers and the Paladins will be there, all for the honor of Christ!"

Yet even as Renaud readied himself for the impending battle, Roland, on the plain of Roncevaux, stood bewildered and confused. "I don't understand," he said half aloud, half to himself, "how it is that the Spanish brothers are not here to attend us. Brother-in-law Oliver, you know these mountains well. Cross over to that ridge and look into the ravine beyond to see if anyone is there."

"Brother-in-law Roland," Oliver answered, "I'll go immediately."

And even as he went to scout out the ravine, the sound of war drums and the Saracen call to arms reverberated throughout the plain: "To arms! To arms!" the Saracens cried; "Death to the Christians! Death to the Paladins of France!"

Just then, Oliver came running back: "Roland! Brother-in-law Roland!" he called. "We are dead! When I arrived at the top of that ridge, I observed, coming out of the mountains, giant knights, under arms, shouting 'Death to the Christians! Death to the Paladins of France!'"

Roland, in the face of the impending catastrophe, attempted to rally the troops: "Paladins!" he shouted, "faithful heroes of Christ! Do you prefer to die as honorable champions or live calmly in a bottomless pit of shame? This is the day which will make clear to the world that our hearts never trembled in the face of our enemies! Marsilius, Bulogant, and Falseron believe that they have snared us and that we will flee at the sight of them. They will be served by their falchions, but we have our swords to defend ourselves, to die, to vindicate ourselves until the last drop of blood!"

But Oliver pleaded with him to follow a different course of action, saying: "Roland, listen to me! We cannot succeed against the Saracens! Blow your horn! Blow your horn and alert Charlemagne to this treachery!"

Yet Roland refused, saying, "Brother-in-law Oliver, perhaps we will die, but our death will cost the enemy his blood. If we call for the help of Charlemagne, the enemy will gain spirit with the belief that there is fear in our hearts. We will save God from such infamy and we will make the pagans understand that we, dying, will have won by their shameful treason! If you do not agree with what I have said, if you do not wish to die under the sword, if you do not wish to be crowned with glory, if you prefer shame rather than victory, you may declare yourself at this very moment. If otherwise, ready yourself for battle.

Seven: The Song of Roland in Sicily

My Paladins, I well know that each of you is valorous and that Saint Michael will help us in our peril."

And with his rallying cry, the two armies collided.

In the heat of the battle, Roland encountered Buiaforte, but as Roland was about to dispatch him, Buiaforte pleaded for his life: "Stop, my Lord!" he cried, "I render myself subject to your sword! Don't kill me! I am Buiaforte, son of the King of the Veglia of the Mountains whom Renaud holds as a brother."

Roland: "What's this I hear! You stopped my sword just in time! Tell me; why are you battling against the French inasmuch as you are the son of Renaud's greatest friend?"

Buiaforte: "You must know that my father is dead and that I was carried into Spain by King Marsilius. And now, Count Ganelon of Maiance has come and arranged all this treachery. And now all of us are stationed here, waiting for your arrival, so that we might kill you."

Roland: "Then my cousin Astolphe was right! Oliver was right! Listen, Buiaforte, how is it that when the pagans see my brother, Balduin, they flee from him?"

Buiaforte: "This one carries the device of Ganelon of Maiance. Everyone, recognizing this device, knows that he must not kill him."

Roland: "I understand. Listen, Buiaforte, for the love of my cousin, Renaud, I am sparing your life. But I warn you: Do combat no longer against my brothers. Because if we meet on the battlefield once more, I swear, I will not spare your life a second time."

And as the battlefield became littered with corpses, Roland confronted Balduin with an accusation of treason but Balduin, incensed at the suggestion, threw his father's device to the ground. He was instantly set upon by a closed rank of Saracen knights, and, as he lay dying, he declared to Roland, "Now that I am dead, you may judge if I ever was a traitor."

Roland wept bitterly at his stepbrother's death, but his grieving was abruptly halted by the sight of Oliver in the throes of death. Roland, flying to his side, cried, "Oliver, it isn't possible! Even you have decided to leave me to the war that we have fought together, and never once before did you leave my side. Oliver, you asked me earlier to sound my horn and I didn't do so. Your death is my shame! But now I will do your will; I will blow my oliphant! I'll attempt to save at least your sons, Grifon the White and Aquilant the Black. Where is my destrier, Vegliantin?"

At Roland's call, Vegliantin came at a gallop and brought with him Roland's horn. "Vegliantin," Roland called softly, "You who do combat more than the others, come. The Paladins are dead. Nearly we alone remain. I am going to blow my horn."

And even as he readied his oliphant so that he might alert Charlemagne to Ganelon's treachery, devils began to glide overhead. "Look how many Saracens," one cried gleefully. "Let's take them to hell immediately," another rejoined. And the devils began to reap their gruesome harvest.

And as Roland surveyed the bloodied battlefield, he was overwhelmed by the carnage. "These parts have gone to the dead," he lamented. "There is only Bishop Turpin who defends himself with his sword in hand. Oliver! I will sound my horn for you!"

Three times, Roland blew his oliphant, but on the third mighty peal, the vein in his temple burst. "My God," he cried out, "what has happened to me! My chest is burning! My face is bathed in sweat! Vegliantin, I beg of you; take me to where I might find a little water."

It was then that Renaud and his brother, Ricciardetto, came upon the carnage at Roncevaux. "My brother Ricciardetto," Renaud said, "here we have finally arrived! From here we can observe the Valley of Roncevaux. Here is the tomb of the valorous of France! And this the day that Malagigi predicted so often. So many dead! So many Saracens! But we have nevertheless arrived in time to die at the side of our relatives, at the side of our sons!"

And with these words, Renaud jumped into the thick of the battle, encountering first Buiaforte. That knight, as he had before with Roland, begged Renaud's mercy. "Mercy, my Lord! I am Buiaforte, Son of the King of the Veglia of the Mountains whom you count as your best friend! Spare me!"

But, "He who does battle against my sons is no friend of mine," Renaud said grimly, smiting Buiaforte with his sword. And with the slaying of Buiaforte, Renaud ran to the aid of Roland and Bishop Turpin. Yet, upon Renaud's arrival, Roland was already at the threshold of death.

"Vegliantin, where are you taking me?" he asked weakly of his destrier. "Stop, for the love of heaven. I can't go any further. I have a thirst that is burning my breast." And true to his master, Vegliantin stopped, but as suddenly as he stopped, he collapsed: "Vegliantin," Roland roared in his anguish, "even you have left me. You, who wanted to commit his last service to his master, you too are dead. Faithful and valorous destrier, you who have given your last efforts to conduct me to safety, if I have ever done you an injustice during your life, forgive me. You have suffered so much pain in the perdition of the faithful Paladins, and you must abandon me now as the others have done before you. Where is Oliver? Where are Grifon the White and Aquilant the Black? Where are Duke Naimes, Ruggiero, and all the others? You, Durandal, didn't do your duty. You who were forever at my side! I will then break you on this rock, thusly!"

And in a last burst of strength, born of anger, frustration, and pain, Roland struck a solitary rock with his sword Durandal. But, "Good Lord," he exclaimed as he did so; "What's this I see! My sword doesn't break, but water issues forth from the rock! This is the water of our Lord! I wish to drink of it!" And even as he did so, Bishop Turpin, finally resting his sword, approached and, fast upon his heels, Renaud and Ricciardetto.

"I hear the voice of Bishop Turpin," Roland gasped. "Then you are alive! Where are my brothers? Where are my companions, Oh Bishop Turpin?"

But before Turpin could speak, Renaud stepped forward.

Roland: "Renaud, I can't believe my eyes! But you were dead!" And, as he spoke, Renaud threw himself upon his cousin and kissed his parched lips.[3]

"Listen Renaud," Roland continued, "have you seen? Roncevaux is covered with our relatives."

Renaud answered, "Roland, my sons, Giovane and Giunetto, are also dead in the conflict, and my brothers as well. Therefore we all have reason to cry at this, our disgrace. Now we will see if Charlemagne holds Ganelon so tightly to his breast as if he were a person of faith."

But Roland was distracted from Renaud's speech. "What's this I see," he suddenly gasped: "A celestial light! This is a sign from God!"

And an angel descended to Roland's side, saying, "Roland, Roland, poor little one."

"Where are my companions who have fought at my side?" Roland asked.

"These are among the Saints," the angel answered, "and they don't at all wish to return to you. If you want to live, God will give you more men of excellent valor."

"No," Roland sighed, "since the Lord will take care of old Charlemagne, I pray you, oh celestial messenger, take me to where my Paladins are. I want to become one of their number. Bishop Turpin? I want to confess myself."

Turpin: "Renaud, Ricciardetto, remove yourselves."

Roland: "No! I want to confess in front of everyone."

Turpin: "Very well. Speak out. What are your sins?"

Roland: "Bishop Turpin, I repent having killed don Chiaro, a Christian. I repent having challenged my uncle, Charlemagne, with a glove. And lastly I repent ... having left my wife a virgin.[4] Good Lord in heaven, I can barely see with my eyes! Where are you? Renaud? Ricciardetto? Bishop Turpin? I believe that I am dying. But at least I will die with my right hand toward Spain. Then, when my uncle Charlemagne finds me, he will know that I died as a hero and not as a coward!"

Yet even as he spoke, the angel gathered Roland in her arms and carried him heavenward, saying:

> "Roland, Roland,
> Such is your fate.
> Your pallid face,
> I return to serenity.
> And your wearied soul,
> I transport to its destiny!"[5]

Roland and Renaud

The opening council of *The Death of the Paladins*, undoubtedly the most important council of the entire Carolingian Cycle inasmuch as it opens what the angel herself later denominates as the "last adventure," is replete with the voices of the sovereign, Charlemagne, the traitor, Ganelon of Maiance, and the noble rebel, Astolphe, Prince of England, compeer to both Roland and Renaud. The voice of the sovereign is at once noble and foolish. While it participates in the stylized address characteristic of council, it is in the final analysis defined by an altered declamatory style moving away from the sovereign's normative hortatory address and toward a confused musing ("But I don't understand the motive behind your council ..."), which would be more consonant with the masque scratching his head in bewilderment than the sovereign meditatively stroking his beard. The voice of the traitor is determined by a strong nasal tone, an overuse of the vocative ("Oh Lord!"), the declaration of submission ("Here I am at your feet," which in conjunction with the traitor's act of throwing himself to the floor is rather affected, to say the least), and a strong element of insinuation ("*your* brothers-in-law") which is proved effective when Charlemagne silences Astolphe on the grounds that he is speaking against another of his brothers-in-law, Ganelon himself. The plan to baptize Marsilius, Bulogant and Falseron in the Valley of Roncevaux is accepted, and even Roland, when Astolphe repeats his accusations against Ganelon, refuses to listen, saying that he "is convinced that it is better to carry Christianity to a people than to conquer a crown." Once again, Roland, the martyr-saint, is headed for disaster.

In the meantime, Ricciardetto's clandestine meeting with his brother in a cave, the traditional hiding place of the bandit, serves to emphasize Renaud's rebellious nature:

> *But Renaud disdainfully answered, "Brother, Ricciardetto, perhaps you have forgotten that I left my arms in Paris when I rendered myself subject to Charlemagne. Yet if you remember well, after the death of my wife, Clarice, I swore that I would no longer carry arms, that I would no longer do combat, that I would no longer kill people! And now, what is it that you ask of me, brother? I am sorry for my children, for my brothers, who are going to die for Charlemagne, or rather by means of the treachery of Ganelon of Maiance, but ..." And breaking off his complaint in mid speech, he exclaimed, "What's this I see! A celestial light! A messenger from God! Oh God, I commend myself to your keeping!"*
>
> *At once, an angel appeared before the brothers, saying, "Renaud, it is the wish of the Highest God that you leave your penitence and return to your old*

Seven: The Song of Roland in Sicily

> *trade. Roncevaux will be your last adventure and, since no other will furnish you with a good set of armor, take this one! At the command of God, I took it from Raimond! For your sword, Fusbert, I have substituted the famous Balisard which I took from Guidon! On your journey you will find your Bayard who will for the last time be your mount. This is what I want of you, and this is what I command of you!"*

Previous to the miraculous appearance of the angel, which evaporates Renaud's hostility, further aspects of Renaud's bandit voice are apparent in the above passage. In his attempt to refuse Ricciardetto's entreaties, Renaud affects a facetious tone and his general use of irony gives way to pure sarcasm ("Perhaps you have forgotten …" and "If you remember well …"). Irony and sarcasm are perhaps the most effective weapons in the bandit's verbal arsenal for maintaining his reputation of toughness and gaining in the process the respect of his peers. Yet, even these are of no avail against the angel's more potent persuasion, punctuated by a heavy use of the imperative to emphasize that she is there at the Lord's command, and her almost exalted declaration of Roncevaux as the last adventure.

The two brothers set out together for Roncevaux, whereupon the scene shifts to the valley itself. Christians and Saracens close ranks and the battle begins. Roland slaughters a host of Saracens in single combat before he arrives to Buiaforte.

> *In the heat of the battle, Roland encountered Buiaforte, but as Roland was about to dispatch him, Buiaforte pleaded for his life: "Stop, my Lord!' he cried, 'I render myself subject to your sword! Don't kill me! I am Buiaforte, son of the King of the Veglia of the Mountains whom Renaud holds as a brother."*
>
> *Roland: "What's this I hear! You stopped my sword just in time! Tell me; why are you battling against the French inasmuch as you are the son of Renaud's greatest friend?"*
>
> *Buiaforte: "You must know that my father is dead and that I was carried into Spain by King Marsilius. And now, Count Ganelon of Maiance has come and arranged all this treachery. And now all of us are stationed here, waiting for your arrival so that we might kill you."*
>
> *Roland: "I understand. Listen, Buiaforte, for the love of my cousin, Renaud, I am sparing your life. But I warn you, do combat no longer against my brothers. Because if we meet on the battlefield once more, I swear, I will not spare your life again."*

However, when Renaud later encounters Buiaforte on the field of battle, the outcome is decisively different.

> *Renaud jumped into the thick of the battle, encountering first Buiaforte. That knight, as he had before with Roland, begged Renaud's mercy. "Mercy, my Lord! I am Buiaforte, Son of the King of the Veglia of the Mountains whom you count as your best friend! Spare me!" But, "He who does battle against my sons is no friend of mine," Renaud said grimly, smiting Buiaforte with his sword.*

With this final declaration of just retribution, Renaud slays Buiaforte, even as Roland, about to obtain his predestined beatification, sets out in search of water to quench his burning, blood-flecked lips.

It is Roland's pardoning and Renaud's slaying of Buiaforte, son of the King of the Veglia of the Mountains, which ultimately differentiates the two cousins. The warrior-saint is defined by his preference for obedience to the sovereign and forgiveness of his enemies, while the warrior-bandit is defined by his insistence upon rebellion and just retribution. And it is ultimately the warrior-saint's destiny to die, precisely because of his privileging of obedience and forgiveness, and the warrior-bandit's destiny to live, precisely because of his privileging of rebellion and vendetta. *The Death of the Paladins* brings together all the strands of Palermitan epic. Obedience, on the one hand, the law of the knight, and by extension, the law of the saint, is shown to be an untenable and deadly law. While it may express the aristocratic ideal of honor, its inevitable conclusion is etched in tragedy. Vengeance, on the other hand, the law of the people, and by extension, the law of the bandit, is shown to be a tenable and life-sustaining law. While it flies in the face of the aristocratic ideal of honor, it conforms to the ideal of honor extant among the people, the famed Sicilian *omertà*, and more importantly, it is, again, for the people, a necessity to the maintenance of life. Here, in all its finality, is the reason why the people sometimes disdain Roland and call him *Occhi Storti*, Cross Eyes. His stubborn adherence to the law of obedience makes of him one who is not of their party but represents another class altogether: the clergy. And here as well is why Renaud is almost universally adored. His preference for vendetta over obedience, a preference that is underscored by his nickname, the Mafioso, makes of him one who, though pertaining to a different class of society than that of the people, pertains, at least, to that class which—because of some of the graver difficulties of Sicily's tumultuous history—is more contiguous with the people: the Mafia.

Chapter Eight

Social Order and the Fairy Tale

Kinship

Two elements of Palermitan social organization are essential to understanding the Palermitanization of the Carolingian Cycle: kinship and class. Kinship, in Palermo, functions almost as a commodity, a means of making it in a sometimes harsh environment. The nuclear family is, under certain circumstances, paramount and it doesn't take long to realize that Palermitans, like other southern Italians, feel their greatest responsibility to its members. But this seminal social unit is very quickly expanded to include grandparents—at times residing in the household with the family proper—and grandchildren. These latter can easily reside in the household as well, especially if their parents are young, without regular employment (not an uncommon circumstance at Palermo during my stay), and therefore unable to afford their own apartment. As one can easily surmise, this situation may place a son-in-law or daughter-in-law in the household.

Yet, the Palermitan's sense of duty to the nuclear family and its most immediate expansions doesn't lead to the infamous amoral familism—an ideology of supporting the immediate family to the detriment of extra-familial cooperation—postulated by Edward Banfield in his now mostly discredited study of peasant society in Basilicata.[1] Banfield's observations sound very much like what the conservative elements of the southern Italian middle class say when speaking of the working classes—both rural and urban—and I suspect he was listening too intently to that class's prejudices. I once had a Neapolitan businessman, when I suggested that Banfield's thesis might not be based on observation of the peasants themselves, exclaim, "But it is! That's just how these people live!" Rather, the emphasis on the nuclear family allows the Palermitan social fabric a certain degree of fluidity so that Palermitans can easily expand their social network along non-kin, or what anthropologists often call fictive kin, lines.

The most notable element of this fictive kin expansion is the tradition of *comparatico* or co-parenthood. When a man or woman stands up as godfather (*cumpari* or *patrino*) or godmother (*cummari* or *madrina*) to a child at baptism, he or she becomes co-father (Italian, *compare*; Sicilian *cumpari*) or co-mother (Italian, *comare*; Sicilian, *cummari*) to that child's parents. In actuality, this long string of *cumpari* and *cummari* extends well beyond the limited set of individuals who stand up as godfather or godmother to a child to include any individual of the adult population upon whom one can depend. As a Sicilian-American woman from Brooklyn put it: "Oh, everybody in the neighborhood was *cummari*!" The terms *cumpari* and *cummari* can draw just about anyone—

A sign on a street corner in Palermo: A Marionette Theater Is Here. Photograph by author.

Eight: Social Order and the Fairy Tale

brothers, sisters, aunts, uncles, cousins, good friends (and some of these perhaps even *padroni* or bosses who can better one's station in life)—into the system of fictive kinship, and a system of mutual obligations, a kind of impromptu mutual aid society, emerges as a result. Shepherds will watch out for one another's sheep. Farmers, whether sharecroppers or small landholders, will cooperate in the harvest or threshing or milling. The *cumpari* who is also the *padrone*, or boss, can be expected to select you for day labor in either the urban or rural context. In the world of urban workers, your *cumpari*—if he is well placed—may help you obtain that ever elusive commodity: a job. While the explicit Sicilian kinship system functions like our own, or what anthropologists call the Inuit kinship system, privileging the nuclear family through having separate terms for mother, father, sister, and brother, but lumping aunts (whether mother's sister or father's sister), uncles (whether mother's brother or father's brother), and cousins each under its own term, *comparatico* functions more like the classic Hawaiian kinship system, in which everyone in the parental generation is called by the same terms used to refer to mother and father and indeed take on many of the parental functions to all children in the group. This circumstance seems the very opposite of amoral familism and allows a certain social agility that could be adaptive to the forbidding and unforgiving political-economic environment that Sicily's history of foreign occupation often enjoined upon the local populace. It essentially says that you have kin everywhere and anywhere upon whom you can count in times of extremity.

Beyond the structures of kinship and *comparatico*, which so characterize Palermitan social order, is the concept of class. As in all stratified societies, an almost infinite number of occupations are subsumed in Palermo under a limited set of classes, not unlike India's subsuming of its innumerable *jatis* (occupations) under its four *varnas* (castes). But whereas in most preindustrial European societies (that is, before a clearly delineated middle class emerged), that set of classes included three, the aristocracy (today, better read as the ruling class), the clerical class, and the people (often understood as the working people, and especially, the working poor), at Palermo, a fourth class had to be added to the list: the Mafia. None of these classes was completely discrete and self-contained—that is to say there was always a fluidity of class functions at Palermo so that a function normally pertinent to say, the clergy, might at times have been pertinent as well to the aristocracy; thus, any essentializing definition of Palermitan class structure is fraught with problematics. Further, there was always some limited mobility between classes, and in many ways the apparent chasm that separated them was somewhat greater in the imagination than in practice. Interestingly, fairy tales in Sicily almost take this proximity of classes as their starting point. Thus, the peasant or urban laborer who marries a prince or a princess in Sicilian fairy tales has a greater resonance than he or she might in, say, England.[2]

In fact, though I have thus far neglected fairy tales in this study, I suspect that they functioned historically much as did epic in Sicilian society—as a critique of class structures. The reason that I was unable to include them to any great extent in this study, thus far, is the unfortunate circumstance that those fairy tales which formed an integral part of the narrative repertoire in the Palermitan region seem to me to remain only in a vestigial form—almost devoid of the dialogic aspects that permit the rhetorical analysis which anchors my analysis of the marionette theater. There are happily, however, exceptions.

The Beautiful Annichia

There is, in one instance, a curious tale that arises in the context of Sicilian American society and, though not offered as a fairy tale per se, it contains most of the apparatus of the Sicilian fairy tale—including the magical captivity (marginally naturalized rather than ostentatiously supernatural) of three recreants and the obligatory moral signification that goodness exists not as a result of but rather in spite of class affiliation. The story is reported in Jerre Mangione's memoir of his Sicilian American community in Rochester, New York, *Mount Allegro*. And though offered in English, one can readily see the social critique that is its mainstay. Told by Mangione's favorite family raconteur, Uncle Nino, the tale of a modest peasant girl and the debauched *galantuomini* (gentlemen) of the village is reported as if it were a historical instance back home in Caltanissetta, Sicily. It opens when the beautiful and resourceful—though impoverished—Annichia marries, despite her peasant origins, the illustrious Baron Albertini.

Eight: Social Order and the Fairy Tale

Baron Albertini was rich and handsome and was besieged by women of his own class but, except for purposes of casual love-making, he showed no interest in any of them. One day while riding through the fields on a hunt, he saw a girl about fifteen years old spinning in the sunlight. Her raven-black hair fell over her shoulders like a dark cascade and, when she turned her face toward him, he fell in love with her and resolved right then and there to make her his wife.

The girl's mother was a peasant widow who made her living by weaving, and it was difficult at first for her to believe that a man of his education and wealth could have honorable intentions toward her daughter. "I think I have a good idea of what a person of your class means by "marriage," she told him bluntly. The Baron begged her to believe that he wanted, more than anything else in the world, to make her daughter Annichia his legal wife.

"Very well," the widow said. "I'll give you my daughter in marriage, but first you must prove your good intentions. You must first provide her with the means of an education. Although she is fifteen years old, she has never been to school. The only things she can do are cook and weave and, as your wife, such knowledge would be useless. No matter how much you loved Annichia, you would soon become bored with so uneducated a wife."

The Baron complimented the widow on her great wisdom and agreed to follow her suggestion. And so it was that Annichia, the poor weaver's daughter, was sent to the best schools in Italy. She did remarkably well, and within five years she had lost all traces of her peasant upbringing and could read and write as well as anyone who had been born of a rich family. Although she now combed her hair on top of her head, she was still as appetizing as ever to the Baron and he promptly married her.[3]

Yet, the baron's closest friends mistrusted the morality of a peasant girl who found herself married to an aristocrat, and three of them, upon learning that the Baron was indisposed on a business trip to Palermo, decided to try their luck with the beautiful Annichia. Each, in his turn, found the means to earn an invitation to the Baron's villa, feeling assured that he would be able to seduce the naive—if elegantly educated—peasant girl. And each, in his turn, was spirited by Annichia into a darkened room where he found himself captive. From a loose floorboard in the room above, Annichia had her maid ask if her captives were hungry. "Yes, of course," came the reply. Then followed the most elegant retribution. "My mistress instructed me," the maid declared, "to tell you that if you wish to eat you must earn your food. Here is the spindle her mother used in her poorer days," she said, lowering it on a piece of string. She also threw him a package of fiber. "And there is your material," she added brightly. "You will be paid according to the work you turn out. Now remember, [Gentlemen], if you want to eat, you must spin." And, in the course of the days that followed, three gentlemen, very unused to manual labor, learned to spin tolerably well. If a lowly peasant girl could learn to be a lady, certainly even a gentleman, it seemed, could be prevailed upon to work for a living!

Though offered as history, the tale of Annichia has all the earmarks of the classic Sicilian fairy tale, from the first appearance of a raven-haired beauty (spinning no less) to a member of a higher class (in this case, a titled gentleman rather than a prince) while out on the hunt, through the trebling of the central motif (the three nearly magical punishments exacted upon Annichia's detractors), to the triumph of she who is naturally modest and good (i.e., displaying the most honored attributes of maidens in Sicilian fairy tales). In each of these features, the story brilliantly crystallizes all the elements that Sicilian culture values: family, community, class consciousness and affiliation, the sense of right and wrong, and—following naturally upon the heels of what is right and wrong—the meting out of the appropriate reward or punishment.

In fact, Sicilian fairy tales might seem a funny kind of animal to those more accustomed to their German and French cousins. They're certainly magical, but the magical apparatus doesn't seem to be nearly as elaborate as that which we find in, say, the Brothers Grimm. Rather, Sicilian fairy tales continuously accentuate the social: whereas one witnesses the brutal misadventures of the throw-away boy or the ash-girl as in other fairy tale traditions, the affiliation of these protagonists is more clearly delineated in the Sicilian variety. They are representatives of the lower classes rather than simply abused and orphaned individuals. Further, the same saints and bandits that populate epic find their way with some regularity into Sicilian fairy tales. In this, Sicilian fairy tales act much like a sister genre to Sicilian epic. But whereas Sicilian epic was entirely a masculine pursuit (so much so that, as I have previously noted, one of my female informants was offended at my inadvertent suggestion that she had ever visited the marionette theater), Sicilian fairy tales, while not being exclusively the province of women, seem most often to be a notable part of a feminine narrative repertoire—and the protagonists tend to more often, at least in my experience, be women

Eight: Social Order and the Fairy Tale

and girls. It is interesting in this context that while all the various genres we have explored thus far actually formed a part of the puppeteers' repertoires, fairy tales did not, though certainly a certain fairy tale ethos found its way into epic just as a certain epic ethos found its way into Sicilian fairy tales. One more point: whereas Christian allegory permeates the world of Sicilian epic, it seems utterly lacking from Sicilian fairy tales or—at least—the selection that I have encountered.

A quick note before moving on to one more tale: the following translation is not literal! Inasmuch as this tale, in particular, depends upon a number of statements and rejoinders—some of them rhymed and others playing on puns and/or word games—there is no way to literally translate this tale and properly catch up its significance. I have tried to stay as true to the wordplay—if not to the literal terminology—that characterizes the original story as well as possible but have had to offer myself a bit more liberality than I would normally take in translating Sicilian folktales for an English-speaking audience. In large part, the translating dilemma is here self-made. I particularly chose this tale for its dialogic aspect, thus complicating the process of presentation but better illustrating the multivocality that probably characterized Sicilian fairy tales in their original environment.

The Talking Belly[4]

Gentlemen! It is said that, once upon a time, there was a king and a queen. And this king and this queen had an only son who, having achieved the age of eighteen, was pressed by his father to take a wife. Yet the crown prince demurred, saying, "Your Majesty, it's too soon for me to think of marriage!" Still, the king persisted in his demands and the crown prince kept repeating, "Your majesty, it's too soon!" Then, one day, to stave off his father's constant badgering, he added, "Listen, if you want me to marry, I'll marry! But only if you find me a girl with a talking belly!"

So the king rang for his royal councilors and here they all come! "My Lords, what advice can you give me? This obstinate son of mine says he will marry but only if I find him a girl with a talking belly! I don't want to give my beautiful kingdom away to just anybody! What say you?"

And a noble councilor—old and very wise—arose, saying, "Your Majesty, this is what I advise. Summon twelve of your most noble lords along with twelve of your best court artists and send them out to all the corners of the earth—one to Portugal and one to Brazil, one to Spain and one to France—and that lord who finds a girl with a talking belly must commission his artist to paint her portrait and deliver it into your own hands. If, then, her appear-

Sicilian Epic and the Marionette Theater

ance is pleasing to your son, all is well! If, on the other hand, her appearance is disagreeable to him, you'll never hear a word of a girl with a talking belly again!"

So this is what the king commanded: Twelve noble lords, each with his own court artist, departed for this place and that. And among these—you must know—was the illustrious Prince of Butera, who took with him a masterful painter. And these two, along with the Prince's faithful servant, travelled far and wide, until they were caught, one night, in a dreadful downpour that came on with a fog so thick that they couldn't even see the road before them. They hurriedly took refuge in the dense forest which loomed up on the road's either side and soon lost their way. Only when the storm subsided did they find their way out of the dark forest whereupon they espied an old man plowing the earth. And the Prince called out, "I greet you, Man of the Share!"

To which the old man replied, "And I greet you, Man of the Sword!"[5]

"And to what abode do your two legs carry you?" the Prince continued.

"To the same abode that one day soon my three legs will," the old man rejoined.[6]

"Can you see it from this far off?" the Prince asked.

"Better than I will one day soon see it before my very nose!"

"And is there snow on yon mountain peak?"

"With time! With time!" the old man laughed.

Then, the good old man rose up from his work and invited the travelers back to his home, where a single daughter sat busy at her loom. And the Prince of Butera politely asked, "What manner of cloth do you weave for your lord?"[7]

But the girl curtly replied, "Nothing that has aught to do with the sword!"

Whereupon her father, turning to where his daughter sat at her work, asked, "Good daughter, where has your mother gone?"

"To view the world through the eyes of one who has never seen it before!"[8]

"And your grandmother?"

"To view the world through the eyes of one who will see it no more."[9]

And, even as she spoke, her mother and grandmother returned, whereupon the small party sat itself down to eat. But, as they did so, the Prince whispered to the artist, "If this girl has a talking belly, she'll undoubtedly become the wife of the crown prince. She doesn't have so much as a single defect!"

That very night, as the Prince, having dropped his candle and put out its wick, went searching about the darkened house for a match, he happened upon the old man's daughter where she lay asleep in her bed. Feeling about blindly in the dark, he inadvertently brushed the girl's belly with his hand, whereupon it cried, "Touch me not! I am promised to the Crown Prince!"

Well, you can imagine what happened next! The Prince of Butera returned to his own room and said to the artist, "Listen to what I have discovered! There, within that very room, lies a girl with a talking belly!"

"Very well," the artist replied, "tomorrow, when the family awakens, I'll begin my portrait. And, then, we'll take it to the king!" And, in the morning,

Eight: Social Order and the Fairy Tale

after the artist had painted the girl's portrait in miniature, the Prince of Butera hung it about his neck with a bit of cord and asked leave of his host to depart, saying, "Within a few days, we will see one another once again."

One by one, the various nobles—along with the court artists—returned with their portraits to the kingdom and, when they were all reunited, they held a council during which the crown prince found some fault with each and every portrait. But, then, the Prince of Butera arose and pronounced, "Your Majesty, if you find something to dislike in this portrait, you'll never take a wife!" And, then, he handed the Crown Prince the miniature that hung about his neck.

"This one I like very much," the Crown Prince said, "but does she have a talking belly?"

"Yes, your Majesty!"

"Then this one I'll marry!"

Thereupon, a lovely gown was prepared for the girl as well as four carriages to transport a dozen ladies-in-waiting to dress her in her new finery and bring her to meet her future husband. And when he saw the four carriages—carrying the Prince of Butera, the ladies-in-waiting, and all manner of servants, what could the good old man believe other than that the entourage was coming for his daughter! Of course, the Prince of Butera confirmed as much, telling the old man that the Crown Prince intended to take his daughter as his wife. The ladies-in-waiting readied the girl, bathing her and dressing her in a sumptuous gown, whereupon the girl—weeping somewhat in anguish at leaving her family, somewhat contentedly at the future which awaited her—took her leave of her father and mother and stepped into a carriage.

Arriving at the royal palace, the King, the Queen, and the Crown Prince were waiting expectantly for her. And when she stepped down from the carriage, the Crown Prince took her by the arm and led her into a grand ball held in her honor.

That evening, before each went to his or her own bed (after all, they were not yet married), the Crown Prince took his mother, the Queen, aside and said, "Your Majesty, this evening, as the damsel lies asleep in her bed, enter her chamber and touch her belly to see if it truly talks." And the Queen, of course, did her son's bidding. Well, you can imagine what happened next! No sooner than the Queen had touched the girl's belly, it cried out, "Touch me not! I am promised to the Crown Prince!" The Queen hurriedly withdrew her hand and went directly to her son. "Don't worry, my son," she said. "You've found that for which you were searching!"

The next day, they all went to the Royal Chapel and the two were married.

Now, let's leave them to their revelry and turn our attention elsewhere! There were, once upon a time, two cumpari,[10] the best of friends, and merchants both! Now, these two cumpari loved one another as if they were brothers born of the same sire and dam. They were, in a word, inseparable, and one of these had a very fine mare. So, one day the one went to the other, and said, "Cumpari,

I have to travel—as we like to say—up to Monreale. Would you kindly loan me your mare?"

"Yessir, Cumpari,"[11] *the other happily replied.*

So the one merchant took the other's mare and rode her up to Monreale. But listen to what happens next! While there, in the stable where he had berthed her, the mare had a foal, and the one who had borrowed her, allowing her to rest sufficiently to recuperate from her parturition, traveled back down to Palermo and though he returned the mare to his cumpari, he kept the foal for himself! Now the servant to him who owned the mare saw what had happened and reported it all to his master. "But how could my cumpari treat me so abominably," the owner of the mare said to himself. And he forthwith went to his friend.

"Cumpari," he asked, "how—in the name of San Giovanni—could you treat me in this way?"[12]

"But what are you saying, Cumpari? Since she was in my hands when she gave birth, the foal is mine."

Well, naturally, to make a long story short, the merchant who was cheated of his foal went to the one time Crown Prince, now the King, precisely he who married the girl with the talking belly! And upon entering the throne room of the Royal Palace, he told his entire sad story but the king found in favor of his one-time friend. The poor, cheated merchant left the throne room crying like a little boy but, as he did so, who should he encounter but the girl with the talking belly. She was now the Queen!

"But why are you crying?" she asked.

"Your Majesty," he said, "let me tell you what has happened to me just now at the hands of your lord!"

"Don't be dismayed," the girl with the talking belly told him. "Dry your tears and leave the palace by this secret staircase.[13] *That way, no one will know that I've advised you. Now, let me tell you how to proceed. Tonight, at the stroke of midnight, place yourself at the bottom of this staircase and begin to cry for help. The king will send his guard to investigate and, when you are brought before him in the throne room, you must—in answer to his query as to what ails you—say, 'Your Majesty, the fish are rising out of the sea and climbing the mountains,' to which he will ask, 'But how is that possible?' At that moment, you'll know what to say!"*

The poor cumpari did exactly as the girl with the talking belly advised and, upon being brought before the king and asked what ailed him, he said, "Your Majesty, the fish are rising out of the sea and climbing the mountains," whereupon the King asked, "But how is that possible?"

"And how is it possible," the poor man blurted out before he even knew what he was saying, "that you gave my foal to my one-time friend?"

With that, the King awarded the foal to the cheated cumpari, and so everything ended well at the court (while we still are drifting in a boat without port)!

Eight: Social Order and the Fairy Tale

Fairy Tales and Epic

Notice how clearly differing perceptions of class affiliation play themselves out in this fairy tale. Here, as in the almost innumerable variations on the theme of a poor peasant girl married to a king that populate Sicilian fairy tales, the king manifests an obvious inability to carry out his duties in a just manner, whereas his lowly born wife simultaneously manifests the sense of justice that should animate the nobility and the good common sense that is a necessity of the commoner in a perennially unjust society. No allegory; no cryptic threats. Just good, native, intelligence.

In this context, there is one last episode of *The Talking Belly*, which I didn't include inasmuch as it is offered almost in outline in the original. The king, upset at his wife's interference in his kingly prerogative, banishes her from the royal palace, telling her to take whatever she likes. Not to be dismayed, the girl with the talking belly takes all the materials and servants she needs in order to construct a magnificent palace directly across the square from the king's (a motif, of course, not only reminiscent of the *Tale of Aladdin* but also innumerable Sicilian fairy tales), and, one night, having tricked the king through the use of a sleeping potion to spend the night in her palace, she declares, upon his awakening, "You told me to take whatever I like. Very well! I like you and you I took!" So impressed was this nobly born king that he turned over the reins of the kingdom to his wife and her superior—or might we say native—intelligence.

Here, as in the various Carolingian stories we considered, a notable rhetoric of identity is at play. First, the girl with the talking belly's father and next the girl herself are demarcated by the use of what we might call gnomic utterances, mysterious statements that might not seem sensible until we think about them a moment and, thus, find the meaning behind the mysterious words. Note that the use of such phraseology might be particularly historically laden at Palermo, where the populace—as any besieged populace—had to be able to speak its mind (for its own sanity) but speak it carefully (for its own safety). This is the very essence of native intelligence. The clearly noble characters, in contrast to the lowly born, speak with a refined politeness which could, within the context of relations between the aristocracy and the people, seem simultaneously intrusive and patronizing. For instance, when the Prince of Butera questions the girl as to the nature of her activity at the loom, her response suggests that his queries are both intrusive and perhaps even unseemly. Interestingly, the characters whose voices are actualized through gnomic utterance are precisely those who carry the burden of intelligence in the story. Those whose voices are actualized through an encumbered gentility are often—in a word—stupid. This message is driven home when the king—who had foolishly proclaimed that the colt belonged to the man who had borrowed rather than owned the mare—offers the reign of the kingdom to his lowly born queen. Interestingly, and I'm not entirely sure what to make of this, in *The Girl with the Talking Belly*, the voices of the representatives of the people—in contradistinction to those of the aristocracy—are reminiscent of those mysterious utterances that characterize the realm of Faerie in a number of Arthurian tales. Perhaps, then, the characters who populate Sicilian fairy tales share an ideological, if not actual, kinship with the likes of Morgan le Fey, Merlin, and the mysterious consort of Sir Launfal in Marie de France's famous tale.

As a momentary aside, the apparent lack of allegory in the Sicilian fairy tale—as opposed to what appears to be its sister genre, epic—seems to me significant. Perhaps the investment of the sacred world of mythos (i.e., the myth) in the magical world of the fairy tale (i.e., the folktale) is what creates the hybrid epic (i.e., the legend). In other words, it may be that legend—and this may be particularly marked in that variety of legend that we refer to as epic—is the result of a kind of dialectic between myth and folktale. Perhaps, then, all legend is at least partially characterized by allegory and, in one way or another, the gods are always lurking behind legend's human—though certainly heroic—characters. If so, it would seem likely that whereas both myth and folktale should be found in most foraging and horticultural societies, legend would tend to more often inhabit the narrative repertoires of complex agricultural and mercantile societies. Indeed, both Iroquoian and Indian legend—at least—seem to confirm this notion. In the Iroquoian legend which authorizes the league among the Seneca, Cayuga, Onondaga, Oneida, and Mohawk nations, the heroes Peacemaker, Hiawatha, and Adodarhoh carry unmistakable shades of the Iroquoian gods Grandmother, Elder Brother (Good Mind), and Younger Brother (Evil Mind) whereas Iroquoian folktales seem to lack this mythic leveraging. And in the *Mahabharata*, each of the preeminent heroes, the five Pandava brothers, as well as their unrecognized brother, Karna, certainly carry shadings of the gods who are in fact their fathers. Bhima, for instance, seems in many respects the incarnation of his father Vayu—the Wind—and shares many of that god's martial characteristics with another of Vayu's sons: Hanuman. We can go even further in this analysis: The vying of the Homeric heroes in the *Iliad* does seem to mirror the vying of the gods on Olympus, and it does seem, as well, that the accommodation Achilles, Agamemnon, and the others make to some degree of shared authority is precisely what prevails among the deities (even if Zeus, like Agamemnon, attempts to lord it over the others). And I would be remiss if I didn't point out that the quest for the Holy Grail is most fully achieved by he who is most Christlike of all the Arthurian heroes. It would be interesting to see if other legendary traditions share with the Carolingian Cycle, the *Legend of Peacemaker*, the *Mahabharata*, perhaps even the *Iliad* and the Arthurian Cycle this same indebtedness to myth. If so, it would seem in the nature of legend to take the social analysis characteristic of folktales and, through melding it with the sacred essence of myth, raise it to the level of political analysis. In fact, the analysis—and we might even say critique—embedded in the Carolingian Cycle (like that in *Peacemaker*, the *Mahabharata*, and the *Iliad*) is preeminently political in nature.[14]

Class

While in both epic and fairy tale one sees how deeply classes interpenetrate one another in Sicilian society, Sicilians have always had a general feel for the independence, singularity, or—perhaps better—unitary existence of each of their social classes. As a result, there has always existed, for each of Palermo's prevailing classes, a very specific set of defining criteria, which I will here try to delineate, starting with the aristocracy. The concept of an aristocracy is somewhat vitiated by the historic context of modern Sicily. However, throughout most of her history, and certainly during the period in which epic was a prominent feature of Palermitan folklore, the aristocracy was a firmly entrenched class of Palermitan society, slowly transforming itself from a military caste in the Norman period to the bureaucratic ruling class it had become by the Spanish occupation.[15] Yet, it was never a class defined simply by "noble birth." Finley attempts to delineate it during the period of the Spanish viceroys.

> At the end of the eighteenth century the titled aristocracy consisted of 142 princes, 788 marquises, and about 1500 other dukes and barons, quite apart from the boasters of pretended titles that were sufficiently common to be legislated against. About twenty families among this nondescript proliferation possessed overwhelming economic power. Although for convenience one may speak of "the aristocracy," this was naturally not a homogeneous group. The owners of new creations, for example, were still divided by a special degree of snobbery from older titles, and viceroys disregarded this difference at their peril. Some nobles were very rich indeed; most were poor. A very few were cultivated *grands seigneurs*; many more were entirely illiterate. There was a down-at-the-heel provincial nobility who failed to afford life at Palermo, as well as a new and more mercantile aristocracy in the growing town of Catania. Most prominent of all, however, were those who lived grandly in the capital and were the petty sovereigns of some feudal estate which they perhaps never visited. ... [For these, k]eeping up appearances was a costly and time-consuming activity. A carriage, or preferably two, was obligatory, and by the 1740s this fact was causing serious traffic problems in Palermo. [The agronomist] Balsamo vainly wished that the nobles would occasionally ride through their own farms on horseback instead of taking their daily journey along the marine front with their liveried equipages; but appearances were everything and the afternoon drive was mandatory.[16]

The Sicilian aristocracy didn't disappear along with the Italian monarchy's dissolution after World War II, but its effect, already long weakened by that time, certainly became less noteworthy to the Sicilian people. Today, as a social category, the aristocracy or nobility may be better read, following Crane Briton's denomination, as the ruling class: "the politicians, the important civil servants, the bankers, the men of affairs, the great landowning nobles, the officers of the armed forces, the priesthood, perhaps even some of the intellectuals. Formal nobility of the blood has in the Western world usually been a much too narrow test of membership in a ruling class."[17]

The clerical class can be conveniently defined: it consists of all functionaries of the church. Yet, in Sicily, the history of the clerical class particularizes that class' meaning to both society at large and epic. Sicily,

Eight: Social Order and the Fairy Tale

as has already been mentioned, was considered by the Papacy and Sicilians alike to be the gift of "first Constantine and later the Carolingian kings" to the Papacy. Thus, one could rule Sicily only at the invitation of the Pope. And, indeed, such was the case with the Normans: "In 1059, Pope Nicholas II authorized these warlike if not very obviously Christian freebooters to govern as much of Southern Italy as they could conquer; and [they] in return agreed not to recognize the religious authority of Constantinople," this despite the fact that those Christians who survived the Arabic occupation were Greek Orthodox. As a result of this investiture, "the Church remained part of the royal prerogative, and the King enjoyed the title of 'Apostolic Legate,'" allowing him to create dioceses and appoint bishops. William II, the fourth Norman king of Sicily, perhaps to contest the authority of Walter of the Mill, the archbishop of Palermo and a champion of papal authority, even created a second archbishopric in Monreale, just five miles from the capital[18] and adorned it with a cathedral to rival that at Palermo, perhaps because Walter, in an attempt to exercise papal authority, ordered that the body of William's grandfather, Roger II, the second Norman king of Sicily, be buried in Palermo's cathedral. Monreale became the burial place of William and his father as if to say that even in death these sovereigns remained aloof to papal authority. A recognition of the intensity of the power struggle between William and Walter remains even today in a number of folktales that attempt to explain the relative ornateness of the interior of Monreale vis-à-vis the relative austerity of the interior of Palermo's cathedral and the relative ornateness of the exterior of Palermo's cathedral vis-à-vis the relatively austere exterior of Monreale, a tale which was proudly told me by (among others) a young priest as we explored the sarcophagus of Emperor Frederick II within the dim recesses of Palermo's cathedral together.

Likewise, as we have seen, the papacy, in fear that the Hohenstaufen dynasty, heir to the Norman kings, might overshadow it, invested Charles of Anjou with the kingdom of Sicily, only to see its machinations crumble with the Sicilian Vespers. Again, in the early years of the eighteenth century, "[c]ontroversy [was] touched off by a minor incident ... when the Bishop of Lipari excommunicated certain local officials who had taxed a consignment of beans without realizing they were Episcopal property and so exempt. When the Pope supported the Bishop, the Spanish Viceroy retaliated by pointing out that the Pope's authority in Sicily was limited by ancient custom and would always require validation by the crown."[19] The precise admixture of church and royal authority in the context of Sicilian affairs was, thus, never a settled matter. Sicilian kings and viceroys stocked the cathedrals and monasteries with their relatives, and, along with the barons, the king or viceroy, and the communes, the church was a major landholder, controlling at times 10 percent of the land worked by Sicily's peasantry.[20] Thus, as a class, the clergy was so deeply intertwined with the aristocracy, at times vying with it and at others colluding with it, that it came to be seen by the Palermitan people as an arm of the aristocracy.

The terms *popolo* or *popolino* refer to the working people of Palermitan society and cover the great bulk of the city's population. Though this class has throughout Palermitan history displayed innumerable variation (that is to say, there is much stratification within the category and at times great disparity of wealth), the term overwhelmingly implies the working poor. It seems to contain within itself the comprehension that life at Palermo has often been fraught with difficultly: not enough food to eat, dramatically limited access to manufactured items, and a labor history wildly fluctuating between grueling work and no work at all. Even in the modern period, for example when I was doing my fieldwork, unemployment at Palermo could hover at 50 percent. All this is to say that historically, at least, the life of the people has been difficult at Palermo and to a certain extent continues to be so today.

The delineation of Mafia—probably as a result of the ever present difficulty of the existence of the working poor—as a distinct class of Palermitan society is not uncommon either in the academic or the popular imagination. It is not a large class—but, then, neither is the aristocracy or, for that matter, the clergy—yet it is a class that has had a distinctive effect on Palermo's history and, moreover, it consists of a set of people who clearly do not pertain to any of the standard classes of Palermitan society. That is to say, Mafiosi are clearly not members of the aristocracy or the clergy, and it cannot be maintained with any surety that they actually work for a living—though they are, as we have seen, associated with the people in the popular imagination even as the clergy is with the aristocracy.

It should be noted here that the term Mafia means something quite different in Sicily than it does in the United States; it would probably be best rendered by a term suggesting urban (as opposed to rural) band of thieves. Thus, I tend to use the term Mafioso for an urban outlaw and bandit for a rural outlaw. As a model for the bandit I take the young shepherd who was gunned down in the city of Palermo during my stay. He was unattached to any group, but simply came to the city of Palermo, obtained a gun, and began robbing stores. He was killed by two undercover police officers who happened to be in a store he was robbing. His image in the newspaper, lying dead in the street, a large pool of blood centered on his chest, a smaller pool, perhaps the result of the flow of blood from his chest, centered on his groin, is still fresh in my memory. The Mafioso, rather, seems to be more at home in the city and more gregarious in his vocation. He also seems less destined to die than the bandit. Charles Tilly makes a similar distinction: "To the extent that they operate on their own, without protection, those who kill and plunder are bandits. There are bandits in Sicily now; at times the island has been infested with bandits. They differ from *mafiosi* in two important regards: (1) they do most of their work through the direct use of force; the *mafiosi* only employ force when someone steps out of line; (2) they do not belong to long, reliable, and protective patron-client chains. To the extent that they are successful, in fact, bandits tend to be drawn into *mafia*. When they begin to build up their own power domains, bandits threaten *mafia*; the operators of *mafia* then co-opt ... or destroy them."[21]

While the comprehension of the Mafia as a distinct class of Palermitan society is common, as we have seen, to scholars and Palermitans alike, its genesis remains quite elusive. Anton Blok sees it emerging from the rural *gabelloti*, men culled from the peasantry to keep order on the great estates of absentee landlords. These *gabelloti*, who used strong-arm tactics primarily to dominate their fellow peasants but secondarily to maintain their own necessity to the landlords, seemed to emerge during the long reign of the Spanish viceroys when it became more the custom to maintain a palace at Palermo (near the court and under the watchful eye of the viceroy) than to manage one's estate.[22] It would then be a simple step to transfer some of these *gabelloti* and their strong-arm tactics to the city. Certainly, they could serve their masters' interests there as well as in the country. And it would come as no surprise that some elements of this class would split off from their masters to become entrepreneurs of a sort. In fact, we know that barons living in the city used criminal gangs at times when they rebelled against the viceroy (or so the Spanish government claimed). Whether these gangs were synonymous with the *gabelloti* or not is difficult to say.

Perhaps so direct a lineage from rural *gabelloti* to urban Mafiosi is too exacting, inasmuch as Palermo has had a long history of secret societies. The legend of the Beati Paoli, to which we will shortly turn, discusses one such society in the period of the viceroys and the Inquisition. Palermitans I spoke to see the Mafia as another, albeit newer, secret society—one that like the Beati Paoli before it, yes, redressed wrongs but one that also got out of hand. Then again, an obvious theory for the emergence of the Mafia is to take epic's merging of bandit and Mafioso as truth. Thus, the Mafia would simply be—to some extent, at least—the transformation of the rural bandit to the urban environment where greater organization and concerted action would be necessary than in the country. Still, all the Mediterranean world has had its bandits, and none (or very few others out of Southern Italy) has developed anything like the Mafia. It seems to me most likely that the Mafia emerged out of all three agencies—*gabelloti*, secret societies, and bandits—coming together simultaneously in the face of what was essentially severe colonial policy—that is to say occupation—and becoming in time its own peculiar class of Palermitan society. Once entrenched in Palermo's social order, the Mafia became a sort of alternate aristocracy, one born of the people and thus often, by default, their champion.

Perhaps the greatest obstacle to understanding Mafia as a discrete class of Palermitan society is the notion of Mafia as a pervasive, hierarchical organization. Yet, over and again, close analysis suggests that, historically at least, Mafia has not functioned in such a way—until perhaps, and this is truly hypothetical, very recently. Anton Blok's painstaking ethnographic analysis—based on intensive interviews of members of a Sicilian village in an attempt to reconstruct social networks (sets of dyadic relationships within the social order)—offers the best explanation of the emergence of the view of Mafia as a syndicate.

> It is worth noting that the term "*associazione a delinquere*" was invented by the judicial authorities to facilitate the mass arrests of *mafiosi* during 1926 and 1927 carried out by Mori, Prefect of Palermo at the time. Regarding its meaning, Mori writes in his memoirs: "...[I]t sometimes happened that after

long, careful and close inquiry we had succeeded in collecting strong evidence against numerous individuals who had been guilty of crimes committed some time before. However, the state of flagrancy having elapsed, it was not legally possible for the instruments of the judicial police to act on their own initiative. Under the ordinary criminal procedure the collected evidence should have been transmitted to the judicial authorities, who would then take action as they were competent to do after having followed the prescribed procedure (interrogations, confrontations, etc.), which meant that they could only act after having raised the alarm sufficiently to render all the criminals in that particular district immediately undiscoverable, and in consequence to induce all those who had given denunciations, indications, testimony, etc., to retract all they had given. In order to avoid this it was necessary to create a state of flagrancy which would allow the instruments of judicial police to act directly. This was obtained by formulating the offence of "association for criminal purposes," particularly on the ground that the same individuals committed the same crime. This was a permanent state of crime and, therefore, flagrant; and on this basis we proceeded to make a sudden and simultaneous round-up with all the necessary subsidiary action and denunciation to the judicial authorities [citation omitted]." Thus, to be a member of such a "group," a legal fiction, created from above, was defined as a criminal offence. No specific indigenous term exists to denote an assemblage of *mafiosi* in areas larger than the local commune. Each village or town had its own *cosca* [group]. Its members exploited a distinct and limited territory. This territory generally coincided with the commune itself.[23]

Blok believes, in fact, that the phrase which Sicilian villagers used to describe Mafiosi, *amici degli amici*, that is friends of friends, is especially apt in characterizing the loose Mafiosi networks that he charted in the rural hinterland of Palermo.[24]

CHAPTER NINE

City Legend and Secret Societies

Of Priests and Brigands

The central integers of the social order enumerated above consist, then, of the aristocracy and the people, juxtaposed by the fact that the former rules and (at least historically) fights while the latter is ruled and (when that scarce commodity is available) works. The secondary integers, the clergy and the Mafia, are juxtaposed sociologically by their affiliation with the primary integers, the clergy with the aristocracy and the Mafia with the people, and ideologically by the two laws that govern their existence: obedience for the clergy and vendetta for the Mafia.

But the ideological juxtaposition of the clergy and the Mafia must have been rendered more subtle in the minds of the people, with whom our analysis is most concerned, by certain correspondences between these two latter classes; for instance, as Jerre Mangione and Ben Morreale observe for the peasantry of the *Mezzogiorno*, or southern Italy (and this observation is as valid for the region's urban poor as well): "Until the fever of emigration virtually evacuated entire villages, the peasantry had only two routes of escape from the rigid, self-confined atmosphere prevalent in the rural districts of the *Mezzogiorno*. One was the priesthood, which offered a free education, social prestige, and the possibility of moving beyond the village. A second, more popular route was brigandage."[1] Further points of correspondence between the clergy and the Mafia consist in the fact that both participate in positions of authority vis-à-vis the people in the Palermitan social hierarchy, albeit the former is a legitimate authority and the latter illegitimate, and both are specified by particular gender relations. The clerics, of course, are not subject to relations with women, while the bandits are relegated to all-male societies.

Nine: City Legend and Secret Societies

Interestingly, in their narrative contexts, the knight-as-saint is variously depicted as unlucky in love and henpecked (Roland's crossed eyes seem to be an aspect of the love madness—or, fascination—he suffers over Angelica), while the knight-as-bandit is variously depicted as being in control of and mildly indifferent in his relations with women (Renaud, after all, has Angelica running after him in his coldest moments).

To comprehend the ramifications of social order delineated above, we must look at two final stories: the first, a city legend (to which we will immediately turn); the second, a bandit's life (which we will consider in the following chapter). The legend, that of the *Beati Paoli*, I have taken from a nineteenth century literary retelling, that of Vincenzo Linares, which quickly found its way back into the Palermitan oral tradition. Such is the way of Palermitan folklore. The literary tradition feeds off the oral tradition, which reincorporates the literary retellings back into itself. The *Beati Paoli* tells of a mysterious group which Palermitans see as a precursor to the Mafia. It thus shares generic affiliation with the bandits' lives to which we will shortly turn.

The Beati Paoli

The night of December seventh, here in Palermo as elsewhere, ushers in the Feast of the Immaculate Conception. One hundred and more years ago, it was our custom during that nocturnal vigil, as it still is, to light the sky with fireworks, to shoot off our muskets, to sound our fifes and bagpipes, and, in the company of the Sacred Image of the Immaculate Virgin, to betake ourselves in a throng from the Church of Saint Francis to the Cathedral, then back again. On this particular night, so many years ago, there was, among the participants of the procession, a man enveloped head to toe in his mantle and wearing his beret pulled down so low as to almost cover his eyes. He kept close to a young damsel whose beauty was not lost to the growing darkness.

"Oh," the damsel exclaimed to her companions, as if she had encountered some malignant spirit, "Let's get closer to the Sacred Virgin," and she flitted away like a sprite flying among the clouds. But the man in the mantle and beret kept her in view, keeping first to her right side, then to her left, aligning his direction anew whenever she attempted to evade him. When she almost became lost in the multitude that surrounded the Virgin, the man laid hands upon her. The boldness of this gesture, and the addition of some indiscreet words which he directed toward her, caused her to cry out, and her cry instantly brought to her side a young gentleman: "Corrado," said the damsel, offering her arm to the young man who had come so quickly to her defense. "Leave him be, I beg of you. It is only that lost soul, Prospero."

Prospero was an ill-bred vagrant without means, without honor, a drunkard, a sink of vice, a swaggering villain. One day, he happened to find himself near Costanza, which name had the lovely damsel, and he felt himself aroused by an unquenchable flame. He began to follow her, to importune her incessantly, and now, he took advantage of the press of the crowd to assault her. Corrado, wishing to avenge such an outrage against Costanza's innocence, unsheathed his sword, but Prospero drew his knife. The companions of each of the combatants jumped into the fray, and blows began to fall. Prospero was slightly wounded on the left cheek, and what began as a light scuffle quickly escalated into a full-blown contest. Women began to weep. The people, in a throng, began to flee, then to stampede. Men, women, and children, shouting, scattered in all directions. Within minutes the panic had spread throughout the city, and the darkness of night nurtured and teased it into a terror. The threats of thieves, the cries of the wounded, and the stealthy tread of assassins mingled in the night and no one could do anything about it, for, in these times, the Royal Court was feeble: Two authorities—the nobility and the Inquisition—dominated, the one by force, the other by prestige. The government of the Spanish viceroy was too weak to restrain the disorder. It wielded a heavy hand against the poor people but could exert no control over the barons or the ministers of the Inquisition. Prospero, who along with all the other vagrants of the city had adapted to the times, profited by the chaos of the stampede and slunk off into the night like a famished wolf hounded to distraction by the shepherds' guard, gnashing his teeth and vowing revenge.

Corrado loved Costanza, and he who saw the girl would have understood why. Here, in Sicily, beauty still retains its Greek origins varied slightly over the generations by a gentle and smiling climate, a warm and fertile land. Here, all is vegetation; all is life. So beauty is vivid and precocious as the eastern sun. And while a lovely English damsel needs twenty years or more to feel the joys of love, here the virgin of twelve pales and blushes in its face. Costanza was in the flower of her youth: Innocent with an open and loving heart. She was an orphan, having lost her father, and the vulnerability of her station in life inflamed all the more the gentle feelings which Corrado held for her.

Corrado was the son of a prince, a potent and feared lord. But he was without the haughtiness, pride, and arrogance that so marked the nobility—including his own father—of that dark era. He was tall and handsome, with a masculine and agreeable appearance, olive in complexion, so that he seemed the god Ares incarnate. Yes, he was noble, but not destined for richness. The inheritance of his father was not to be his. It all pertained to his elder brother. Primogeniture was the custom of the time; the first son was the sole heir of the father. Corrado, the second son, was destined to choose between the surplice and the sword. Because of his strength and courage, he inclined toward the life of a soldier, but in the service of Spain? To serve Spain would be to give up every noble sentiment. In Sicily, the Norman eagle no longer took flight. Nor did the splendid court of the Hohenstaufen remain. No longer did Frederick II beckon the learned and benevolent men from all corners of the Earth. The princes of

Nine: City Legend and Secret Societies

Aragon and Castile, rather than nurturing the splendor of this precious piece of their dominion, kept our destiny in check from the continent. For now, Corrado found all his happiness in the arms of Costanza, whose aged mother blessed their nuptials under the cloak of night. Such were the convenient nuptials of an unlucky love, celebrated at home without friends and without ceremony.

One evening, a few days after the events previously narrated, Corrado betook himself in disguise to the house of Costanza. To avoid the scrutiny of his parents, he was enveloped in the mantle and beret of one of the servants of his father's palace. It was late. As he approached Costanza's door, he encountered a figure wrapped likewise in a mantle, and before he could even ask, "Who are you?" he saw a knife flash before his eyes. Yet, in the ensuing struggle, Corrado overpowered his assailant who—in an instant—evaded Corrado's grip and fled. And in his fury, Corrado failed to hear Costanza, who looking out her window for Corrado, cried out when she caught sight of the combat. Through the deserted streets of the city, Corrado pursued his assailant until he finally took him.

"Vile traitor," he shouted, "who battles only with a man's back," and he unsheathed his sword as his assailant lunged at him with his knife. Corrado, a master at arms, evaded the knife and, feeling his sword pierce tendons and nerves, wounded his assailant in his treacherous wrist. The bitter strike caused the assassin to drop his knife and flee into the night. Corrado gave chase again, determined to finish off his assailant, but the darkness and the tortuous windings of the streets thwarted his design.

He found himself alone on a deserted plain over which presided a great walnut tree. It was near the Church of Saint Cosimo. He looked about himself but could not see a living soul. He listened but heard only the wind rustling the dry leaves of the walnut. The clock in the city's bell tower struck midnight, and Corrado saw a man, mantled like himself and with a beret on his head, walk to the bottom of the plain and fire a gun. Soon another, dressed in the same mantle and beret, appeared. Then a third. And finally perhaps a dozen or more men, all in mantle and beret, fell in and ordered themselves in a single straight rank.

A thousand thoughts racked Corrado's mind: "What are these men doing in a place so lonely and deserted? Is my vile assailant hidden among them?" And still more men joined the group, a few taking note of Corrado, almost hidden in the shadow of the walnut. "Look at this fool," one joked, "lurking under the walnut!" "Is he one of us?" another asked. "Of course," the first answered, "look at the mantle and the beret. How could he not be one of us?" They approached him, saying, "Didn't you hear the clock strike midnight, Brother? It's time. Let's go!" And he went with them.

They crawled through a small portal scarcely three palms high, and no sooner than the door had shut behind him did Corrado shudder, feeling as if he had been enclosed in a tomb. They descended by five or more steps, cut from stone, *and entered an obscure and humid chamber. In front of them rose an altar with a crucifix, lighted by a sole lamp. From there, they walked along a corridor, the walls of which were lined with daggers, crossbows, pistols, and all manner of arms, until they entered a large grotto carved from the living rock.*

Now in a state whose existence is dependent on the division of its citizens into classes, on the atrocities of the Inquisition's "articles of faith," on an engorged and debilitated government, it is no wonder that a tenebrous congregation of men might gather itself, intent on redressing, to a certain extent, justice: Efforts inept, illegal, violent, but in consequence of the oppression and ignorance of the times. Men convened in the shadow of mystery and founded another authority to defend themselves against the open violence of the barons and the secret violence of the Inquisition. They gathered to exercise their despotic and secret prerogatives under the name of the Beati Paoli. Men of the people—artisans, sailors, townspeople, marketers—formed this terrible body which appropriated to itself the right to adjudicate the actions of men, to reexamine judicial decisions, to rectify the miscarried justice of the authorities.

And so it came about that Palermo contained within her fold two authorities: The one legal, the other illegal, but both unreasonable, both enveloped in terrible mysteries, with the significant difference that while the one bedecked its barbarous justice in public ceremony, the other hid its judicial proceedings under the veil of darkness; while the one intended to bring mankind back into Christ's fold through torture and burning its victims at the stake, the other attempted to rectify such callous injustices. The first was the tribunal of the Inquisition. The second was the Beati Paoli.

Thus, Corrado found himself in the chamber of the secret tribunal, dressed like the others in black mantle and beret, and regarding the scene before him with a mixture of horror and fascination. And as he did so, an aged man—whose face, though parched by years of hard labor in the sun, could still not hide a profound sorrow—appeared at the chamber's door. He wore the garments of a peasant and in his debilitated body and withered limbs, one saw the signs of age and misery: "Tomasso, is it you?" asked the Chief of the Beati Paoli. A profound sigh escaped from the breast of the old peasant as he took the beret off his hoary head. "Sir," he pleaded, "I have need of your assistance." "We remember well the service you have rendered us," the Chief exclaimed. "Even if age has prohibited you from participating in our convocations, you will find no lack of succor here. What disgrace has fallen on the house of worthy Tomasso?"

"My only remaining son," Tomasso wailed, "Antonio, a creature of only sixteen years, my joy, my delight, the only hope of my poor wife and me, was hunting and passed into the preserve of the lord of our village, not realizing that it was prohibited to enter there. He was set upon by the lord's mastiffs, and constrained, for self preservation, to fire upon them, he killed one. The others ran yelping back to the palace, and the lord's wardens, like lions, fell upon my poor son. He was taken and arrested and thrown into a cell in my lord's dungeon, where he is put to daily torture."

Nine: City Legend and Secret Societies

"Good old man," said the Chief, "you will find justice. Our work is secret, but our hand is ready and powerful. This case is already decided in your favor and against the perverse lord who has dared to disturb the peace of an honest family." "Yes, he will lose his life," assented the Beati Paoli in a single voice, and the rattle of arms, ratifying the decision, reverberated throughout the chamber. And hopeful tears ran down the old man's cheeks as he was escorted from the chamber.

Next, one of the Beati Paoli reported on the successful execution of a vendetta: "The hypocritical minister of the Inquisition who wanted to dishonor that good family," he began, "has had such a good lesson that he will not return to its torment. I caught him as he was descending a staircase, dressed as a damsel. With a large and knotted club, I applied a good medicine to his shoulders. He collapsed, rolling down the staircase and at every jolt he let out a shriek like a mouse caught in the mouth of a cat so that he attracted all his neighbors who—seeing that brute in damsel's dress—chased him with shouts and whistles, kicks and pushes, and so accompanied him all the way home."

Yet even before the laughter that such an image evoked, subsided, Prospero stepped forward, saying, "I suffered a violence at the hands of Corrado, who has seduced and taken from me my beloved Costanza. Look. I still bleed. It was but a few minutes ago that I escaped his sword. Must we always be victimized by the powerful? Must we watch helplessly as they first ravish our women, then insult and threaten us? I ask for vengeance." "You have it, without argument," came the answer. "Corrado will die."

But, "Companions," reprimanded the Chief, "don't let yourselves be moved by anger. We must reflect carefully. Justice is needed. We must see if the conduct of Corrado ..." Yet, before he could finish speaking, the cry went up: "He's a rogue!" "He's a noble!" "He's arrogant!" "He has offended our companion! Yes, he must die!" the Beati Paoli shouted in unison. Corrado, paralyzed with fear, was delivered only by the close of the convocation.

And in the meantime, Costanza? No sooner than she became aware of the voice of Corrado, she hurled herself to her window. And how deep was her fright upon hearing the tumult and the blows? She shrieked in horror and, gasping for breath, ran for the stairs, but suddenly her strength fled her body and she slumped to the floor unconscious. Two days passed, and Costanza was beside herself in worry. Her house occupied a solitary station on a lonely beach, and every commotion that convulsed the city—and there suddenly seemed so many—filled her with trepidation. The oddest of all began with a sudden clamor, then traded whispers here and there, and finally a confused prattling. Bit by bit, however, the noise became more distinct and finally it broke out in a great explosion of shrieks and shouts. Flying to her balcony, Costanza saw an agitated mob running through the streets. At its head was an old man wearing a robe and vestments after the style of Joseph, the father of Jesus. He had a long beard and wore his hair long as well. And he claimed he had been sent by God to redeem the people, to take away their misery and to restore to them *their former abundance. He seemed inspired, spouting forth frenetic words both vigorous and seditious that urged the crowd to avenge their injuries. A great crowd of women came running after him, weeping and wailing. But the Saint suddenly flew into a rage and, coming directly under Costanza's window, flashed a threatening glance in her direction.*

At that moment, a troop of Spanish soldiers, their crossbows at the ready, descended on the mob. Suddenly, the street erupted in a tumult of voices, threats, curses, hideous laments, whistling arrows, and flashing daggers. The people let loose with a volley of stones, and from the roofs and windows of the surrounding houses, the Palermitans, both men and women, pelted the soldiers with roofing tiles, firewood, pieces of broken furniture, anything that would come to hand and serve as a weapon. Suddenly, a troop of Spanish cavalry, their sabers drawn, charged upon the crowd, dispersing it in a bloody rout. The mob, armed with clubs and temporarily emboldened by their numbers, staged a momentary reversal, surging in upon the Spaniards, but they soon succumbed to the greater arms and were routed once again.

The Saint continued to urge on the crowd, wandering here and there amid the tumult, until he suddenly tumbled to the ground, muddying his robe and losing his beard and hair. With his face fully exposed, someone in the crowd recognized him, shouting, "Hallo! Do you see this? It's Prospero! Look! The imposter! The drunk! He wanted us to believe he was a saint. He wanted ... Lord knows what he wanted. To rob us? To murder us?" Yet even as the crowd pondered the meaning of Prospero's deception, the Spaniards charged in upon them once again, and the women, men, and youths, discouraged at yet another shattered hope and, beat down by the continuous onslaught of the soldiers, withdrew, advanced, withdrew once again, and then like a swarm of bees knocked from its hive, mustered once again elsewhere.

As night fell, a profound darkness enveloped the city's high domes and campanili, then covered the sumptuous palaces, and finally descended on the immense expanse of the sea. The chill that precedes a snow made the air gelid, and not a single star could pierce that frightful gloom. Suddenly, a small boat shot out of the darkness, hugging the shore. Four strong arms governed its movement, uncertain and halting, in the onslaught of wind and wave. A man wrapped in a heavy mantle stood at the prow, insensible to the wind that battered his face, but glancing behind him from time to time, as if he were in fear of pursuit. The boat came to rest on the bank just before Costanza's house, and the man, tugging his mantle about his shoulders, stepped under Costanza's balcony and called to the damsel in a low voice. Costanza's spirit danced in her breast. "Corrado," she exclaimed, her voice tremulous with the wave of joy that washed over her as she hurtled herself down the stairs. And as she fell into his arms, she burst into convulsive tears.

Corrado told her of the dangers that threatened them. He spoke of Prospero's attack, which he had miraculously survived. He spoke of his parents' discovery of their love, how they flew into a rage, how they imprisoned him in a castle with threats that he would never be released unless it was to take ship to Spain. It had been arranged in the meantime that Costanza would be abducted from her mother's house and obligated to take in marriage one of Corrado's father's vile servants. An honorable servant of the house, however, had advised Corrado of his father's plans and provided Corrado the means of escaping the castle. A boat manned by his armed retainers awaited them, ready to save them from the persecution of Corrado's father for at least this one night.

Corrado threw his mantle over Costanza's shoulder and fitted his beret on her head in order to hide her long hair. Thus, disguised as Corrado's servant, Costanza prepared to leave her mother's home. Yet, as she and Corrado stepped out the door, two men, hidden in the shadows of the street, let loose the arrows from their crossbows. In a moment, the earth was stained with blood and a corpse lay across Costanza's threshold.

The traitors, pursued by Corrado's retainers, fled toward the plain of Saint Cosimo, where they disappeared. The city's bell tower struck midnight, and once again the mysterious men, enveloped in their mantles and wearing their berets low over their eyes, entered the secret grotto, fell into formation, and were called to order. As the terrible congress opened, one man reported, "Corrado has been killed and justice vindicated." "Not yet," cried one of Corrado's band, which flooded the grotto with Corrado at its head. "Not yet, you despicable traitor. But it will be vindicated—and that soon—with your death!" Corrado was alive. The arrow meant for him had killed instead his poor Costanza, who fell to the earth drenched in blood and breathed her last breath in Corrado's arms.

Prospero grew pale at the sight of Corrado, and the Beati Paoli took up their arms but the grotto was surrounded by guards, and the Beati Paoli, taken by surprise and outnumbered, were routed. Thus the terrible congress was dispersed, the secret entrance to the grotto walled in, and Prospero hanged for the murder of Costanza, as the Inquisition redoubled its efforts and the barons jealously defended their privileges.[2]

The Beati Paoli and the Mafia

While I have never seen the Beati Paoli performed (or even heard a recording of a performance), Antonino Uccello has happily provided a notebook version of the play script (*copione*), which he obtained from the Canino family, the same family of puppeteers which provided Uccello the notebook script of the bandit's life, *The Life and Death of Antonio Di Blasi, alias Testalonga*, presented in chapter four. All the episodes of Linares' version of the Beati Paoli presented above are noted in the play script with the exception of the infamous injustice committed by the minister of the Inquisition (and the punishment that was exacted upon him). Perhaps it was included in the play since notebook versions are no more than mere outlines. What is, of course, notably missing from the notebook is any suggestion of the dialogue with which the action of the play was filled out. Certainly, it would not have looked terrifically like the ongoing commentary that Linares offered in his short story. There is, interestingly, however, a line in the notebook that gives some indication of how the play's dialogue might have been constructed. When Costanza is murdered by Prospero, the play script reads: "Corrado swears vengeance and departs."[3] Of course, Corrado's voice—as configured by the puppeteer—is forever lost to us but, I suspect, it would not sound terribly different from that of Roland when he swears vengeance—very knightly in tenor. It would then seem not too great an analytic leap to suggest that the voice of the vagrant Prospero would be configured very much along the lines of the marionette theater's characteristic bandit.

It is difficult to imagine the circumstances that could have given rise to such an organization as the Beati Paoli. Perhaps, as Linares suggests, the double authority of the state and the Inquisition was too much for the people to bear without some form of redress. Palermitan historians continuously chronicle the excesses of foreign nobilities, but the cruel effect of the Inquisition on Palermitan society is almost unimaginable.

> The Holy Office became extremely rich through benefactions, but especially because it confiscated the possessions of any victim. Such confiscations were, of course, a strong incentive to zealous prosecution, and people complained that not even tradesmen who were owed money by a heretic could collect once the Inquisition had marked him for their own. Informers, on the other hand, might obtain one-tenth of the proceeds of any successful prosecution, and since anonymity of informers was kept, many people must have found this an effective and profitable means of paying off private scores.... The Viceroy sometimes reached the point of complaining that Inquisitors used their position for personal financial profit and spent too little time on matters of faith. Certainly their wealth was considerable, a fact which facilitated the recruitment of laymen as assistants or familiars. Ferdinand in 1510 had said that there should not be more than twenty of these lay officials in each large city, but in 1577 the Viceroy put their number at over twenty thousand and it was still growing.[4]

Nine: City Legend and Secret Societies

Little wonder, then, that the people had to develop extraordinary means to combat such excesses; yet there is a continuous undercurrent in the discussions of secret organizations suggesting that while they rectify injustices they as well create their own. Thus, the ambivalence that Linares' literary retelling of this city legend displays is characteristic of the Palermitan view of the Beati Paoli and, incidentally, the Mafia. Linares' own statement that "when the exercise of power fears no law, no accountability, no publicity, then abuses are inevitable"[5] suggests that it is Prospero rather than the Beati Paoli who is faulted with a miscarriage of justice. Nonetheless, the Beati Paoli are still predominantly looked upon with favor by the Palermitan people. A woman, in response to a foreigner's complaint about the high crime rate in Palermo, said to me, in exasperation, "Up north there are terrorists. Here we have the Mafia. The terrorists will kill anybody. The Mafia will only kill you if you do something wrong. Which is the more honorable? Excuse me. I think the Mafia.

"I'm talking about the true Mafia," she quickly added, "the Mafia when it was more like the Beati Paoli."

While the element of romance and the moral ascendancy of an (albeit penniless) prince in this story occludes the issue, the legend deals once again with the relations between the people (as Linares says: "artisans, sailors, townspeople, marketers") and the nobility (both foreign and native, secular and clerical). Additionally, in the *Beati Paoli*, the clerical class (depicted as the rapacious Inquisition) is seen as an arm of the aristocracy, while the Mafia (depicted in this instance as its symbolic precursor, the Beati Paoli) acts as the ally to (not to say, the strong arm of) the people. Thus, as the aristocracy and the people become more clearly juxtaposed and defined in narration, so too do their respective allies, the clerics and the Mafiosi.

Further, in the *Beati Paoli*, the people are more clearly detailed through their alliance with the Mafia. Their proper sphere of action is, like his, vendetta. The apparent collusion between the people and the Mafiosi that occurs at Palermo is natural. Urban Mafiosi (like their rural brethren, bandits) are, after all, the sons of the people and can expect sanctuary among them. Further, sons are expected to turn over at least some of their earnings to their fathers and—maybe especially—their mothers. And sons who happen to be Mafiosi are subject to this custom as well. Moreover, both urban and rural society in Sicily, as elsewhere in Europe, was characterized—Banfield's assertions aside—by extensive kinship networks (both actual and fictive) among which reciprocity—hedging one as it does against catastrophe—was the economic ideal: that is to say, the amoral familism that Banfield isolated in Basilicata probably never—as I suggested earlier—existed. Rather, Banfield was apparently unable to penetrate or gain access to the places where societal cooperation actually—and absolutely necessarily—occurred. Thus, some of the Mafioso's earnings would be spread beyond his immediate family: here, again, *comparatico*, or fictive kinship should have accrued benefit for the community at large (not to mention offered refuge for the Mafioso, who was, in a very real sense, every mother's son). In Sicily, then, the natural alliance between the people and the Mafia—or, in the rural arena, between peasants and bandits—is somewhat accentuated by the characteristic structure of social relations. Finley describes the perplexity that was experienced by the Austrian authorities in their short-lived occupation of Sicily in the early eighteenth century as a result of this seemingly unnatural alliance as it impinged upon Sicily's rural populations: "There was little to stop large bands of outlaws roaming the countryside; for though bandits sometimes levied a contribution on the peasants, they were protected by an environment that considered law breaking a respectable activity. One indication of this may have been the popular religious cult of the *Decollati*, in which prayers were offered up to executed criminals, and shrines were erected for their dismembered relics. A more practical consequence of this extra-legal mentality was noncooperation with the police. The Austrian authorities had been baffled to discover that 'to be a witness in any kind of criminal action brought unspeakable disgrace even on the most abject member of society.' Clearly *omertà* [the Sicilian code of honor which demands silence in the face of police interrogations] was not founded on fear alone."[6]

Conclusion: The Last Adventure

A Curious Interlocutor

On my first visit to a Palermitan marionette theater, a young boy, his face brightening with surprise, said to me, "But you speak like a soldier!" He then turned to his friends and reiterated, "But he speaks like a soldier!" I did not understand it at the time, but he was telling me that my Italian was like that of an outsider, like that of someone *not* from Palermo. When that understanding finally came, several weeks later, there came fast upon its heels another: when the soldier is the very model of the foreigner, the city is in a state of occupation.

In fact, my time in Palermo coincided with that of the Maxitrial (*Maxiprocesso*), a group trial of nearly 500 Mafiosi (more than 300 of whom were eventually convicted) in a judicial chamber built especially for the event in Palermo's infamous Ucciardone Prison, a prison chilling enough to have been immortalized in one of the many prison songs that forms an integral part of Sicily's folk music:

> The prison at Ucciardone was well built
> And those who built it knew their business;
> It is surrounded on all sides by a great rampart
> Broken only by windows out of which one can merely look.
> The hot summer sun sears its inmates' souls.
> And the cruel winter is even harder to bear.
> I am imprisoned in this great dormitory where,
> Even if my mother comes, I am not even allowed to hear her voice.[1]

The Maxitrial was probably precipitated by—more than any other event—the infamous 1982 assassination of the Prefect of Palermo, General Alberto Dalla Chiesa. The place where he was gunned down had

Conclusion

become a notable shrine by the time of my arrival in Palermo in 1987. During the trial, the city was patrolled by soldiers from throughout Italy, and though I have never been able to ascertain the figure, one soldier, who manned the turret of a tank positioned outside one of Ucciardone's fortified gates, told me that there were two soldiers from each region of Italy, giving a total of some 180 Italian soldiers altogether, but, I believe, he was talking about soldiers proper. Other counts I have been offered, which may have included soldiers of different units as well as police have numbered well over 1,000. In no case—whether the more reserved 180 or the wildly emphatic 1,000 plus—could I ever authenticate a number but I can say that, simply on the basis of my own observations, the military presence was notable. When walking past the gates of Ucciardone, the observation that guns were trained upon you was unavoidable and I, like a number of my friends, unconsciously avoided suspicious movements—such as taking our hands out of or inserting them into our pockets until we were out of view of the tanks. Ironically, the soldier I had the opportunity to speak to—at such length that we overstayed our time in the *Giardino Inglese*,[2] talking over the events that had entangled the city, and had to climb over the perilously sharp spikes of the locked gate—had, earlier on the same day, had his gun trained on me. He would have never taken note of me, perhaps, had I not been—unusually, for me—wearing a notoriously American piece of clothing, a baseball cap. It was he who confirmed to me that the nearly instinctive avoidance of suspicious movements while passing the Ucciardone Prison was not ill-advised, for he claimed that while manning the turret, he—as well as his fellow soldiers—was always on the lookout for unusual, particularly sudden, movements. And, as if to authenticate the nefarious connotations of such movements, Sicilian prison songs enshrine "a ritual expression of Mafia jargon 'Sleight of Hand' [literally, *tira mano*] which refers to the offering of a challenge through placing one's hand in his pocket or beneath the breast of his shirt, mimicking the gesture of pulling a knife."[3]

The effect that the Maxitrial had on Palermo reverberated long beyond its duration. The two prosecutors upon whom the success of the Maxitrial rested, Giovanni Falcone and Paolo Borsellino, were assassinated—by spectacular bombings which seemed to be rigged as much for effect as revenge—within two months of one another in 1992. Then,

Conclusion: The Last Adventure

in 1993, their assassin, Salvatore ("The Beast") Riina, the Cosa Nostra's *capo di tutti i capi*, or boss of all bosses, from Corleone, he who had masterminded the assassinations, was captured near his Palermo villa after two decades on the run. Finally, in 1995, Palermo's airport was renamed the Falcone-Borsellino Airport, a fitting tribute to the brutal slaying of these two men and the changes exacted on Palermitan society at least partially as a result.[4]

An American report of the Maxitrial, interestingly, managed to capture not only the significance of the trial to the life of the city but also—and no doubt incidentally—the rhetorical sweep of the Mafioso's voice, something that comes through even when translated into English:

> The most dramatic moment of the opening week [of the Maxitrial] came when Luciano Liggio, reputedly "the boss of bosses" of the Sicilian Mob, sent a tremor through the courtroom when he stepped to a microphone at the bars of Cage 23 and boomed out, "I'm releasing my lawyers from this case!" Liggio's Mafia "family," based in the Sicilian town of Corleone (which gained notoriety in Mario Puzo's *The Godfather*), was the first to jump massively into the drug business. Liggio is charged with four murders and drug trafficking. His voice heavy with sarcasm, he told the court he had read that some of the accused did not deserve to be defended. Said Liggio: "I want to support that view by renouncing my defenders." Judge Giordano shot back, "The law requires you to be defended."[5]

I don't wish to overstate the situation in which Palermo found itself during my stay there; it was not as if Palermitans were seething with resentment over the Italian military presence and cowering beneath the soldiers' carbines as the Maxitrial proceeded. The presence was just something that—given the way it so poignantly cited Palermitan history—one noted. In fact, Sicilians generally see themselves as Italians and perhaps even, today, Europeans, as well as Sicilians and have a vested interest in an orderly, law-abiding society. But at the same time, it is as true to say that Palermitans are keenly and quietly aware of the significance of an Italian (or, for that matter, any non-Sicilian) presence on their island and its historical implications. It is not a situation entirely dissimilar to that evoked by President Obama when he cautiously but reasonably suggested, after the outcome of the Zimmerman trial had been announced, that Black Americans are not unaware of dilemmas within the African-American community but rather hopeful that sometimes their white detractors might take a moment to consider the historical genesis of such dilemmas as well as the difficulty in finding a tenable solution to them. Curiously enough, that young boy whom I encountered on my first visit to a marionette theater, one of the first of my Palermitan interlocutors, had particularly emplaced me so that I might understand the function of epic to Palermitan society: it is the negotiation of Palermo's complexly interrelated and heavily nuanced social relations. A case in point may be illustrated by looking to one of those negotiations in greater detail: that between the people and the bandit.

The alliance forged between the people and the bandit gained particular focus for me when I visited Montelepre, the hometown of the famed Sicilian bandit Salvatore Giuliano. It was a lovely day as I hiked with some friends and a small hound that had joined us somewhere beyond the village limits, in the hills surrounding Montelepre. Wild irises dotted the green slopes, and outcroppings of sharp, white stone here and there concealed shallow caves. It was easy to see how Giuliano's band of outlaws could have evaded the *Carabinieri*, the National Police, for over three years in such terrain, and as I hiked with my friends our conversation quite naturally turned to the tale—which each of us knew (as most of us knew the story of Santa Rosalia) in bits and pieces—of Salvatore Giuliano's storied career.

To reconstruct it here, I have taken what I have almost invariably heard of the story of Salvatore Giuliano to sketch out the sequence of the major episodes and, then, heavily filled in the details using the Web site of Giuliano's brother—a Web site that attempts to set the story of Salvatore Giuliano's life and death straight. I have further used a playbill from a marionette theater production of *The Life and Death of Salvatore Giuliano, Bandit* (something I have never seen or heard). The idea of using a Web site as a sort of folk artifact is by now well enough established that I don't need to spend an inordinate amount of time justifying it. It is probably sufficient to state that the generation and transmission of Web sites (particularly those that participate in the arena of popular culture) share a number of features with the generation and dissemination of folktales. Indeed, I have cited an article above that depends entirely on such analysis: Robert Glenn Howard's analysis of *The Sinner's Prayer*.

Conclusion: The Last Adventure

The Life and Death of Salvatore Giuliano, Bandit

Salvatore Giuliano, a son of the village of Montelepre, in the province of Palermo, was—by all accounts—a diligent, hardworking, and studious boy whose father, as a result of numerous excursions to the United States, had managed to buy a small parcel of land back home with which he could support his family. Yet, with World War II savaging Sicily, the very staples of life were—even for a farmer with his own land—becoming more difficult to come by: "The government, in order to cope with the crisis [of war], instituted the infamous wheat appropriation. The farmers were constrained to deprive themselves of their own harvest and to turn to the hated ration card in order to survive. It was a crime to hide wheat, but even if it were not illegal, it would not have been worthwhile, because the flour mill was under government surveillance. Thus, the greater part of Montelepre was pressed to the very edge of survival; yet a few farmers in the village's hinterland succeeded in hiding a portion of their harvest and Salvatore Giuliano, senior, built a small mill. But even then the flour he so obtained for his family was insufficient because he gave so much to the needy."

Up until this time, much of the support upon which the Giuliano family depended came from Salvatore's older brother, but when he was recalled to military duty, the entire weight of the family's needs fell upon the shoulders of young Salvatore, "just then twenty years old." Untutored in the ways of a corrupt world, Salvatore did the best that he could but, then, on one infamous day in September 1943, he "encountered a patrol consisting of two country wardens and two carabinieri [national police]. Prayers and explanations alike were useless. He was accused of smuggling two sacks of wheat, about 40 kilograms each. The authorities confiscated both his mule and his wheat." Worse yet, "they intended to arrest him and transport him to the American garrison. He ... begged to be denounced rather than arrested," and, it seemed at first, that his pleading had succeeded. But, then, an unaccountable tragedy occurred. The authorities, distracted by "true smugglers," went to investigate, leaving Salvatore momentarily unguarded. Salvatore took advantage of the moment to escape but he was shot by the carabinieri as he attempted to flee. Two bullets struck him in the hip wounding him gravely.

"One of the carabinieri, Giuseppe Mancino, was ordered to finish him off if he were still alive, but Salvatore, hearing the order, struck first, critically wounding Mancino with a pistol that he had hidden in his boot. Mancino died the following day in Palermo while Salvatore, wavering between life and death for a month, healed completely and took refuge in the hills around Montelepre." It was then that the Italian government set a force of 800 carabinieri to exact their retribution against Salvatore Giuliano. Failing in their attempt, they set about exacting their vengeance instead upon the helpless citizens of Montelepre, arresting 125 of them in retribution.

"Giuliano's father, who was among the arrested, was beaten bloody by one *of the carabinieri. Salvatore, junior, witnessed the entire scene from a hiding place and his wrath became uncontainable. He attacked the carabinieri's convoy waiting in the town square. One of the officers died and another was seriously injured. From then on, the carabinieri hunted him without rest and without mercy, but he always managed to escape. In February 1943, he made so bold as to liberate eight Monteleprenese from the Monreale jail and with them he formed his first band of guerilla warriors."[6] It was not long before his exploits drew the attention of members of the burgeoning Sicilian independence movement that emerged out of the tumult following World War II.*

"The Voluntary Army for the Independence of Sicily was the brainchild of the latifundista, *the great landowners, ingenious idealists, shrewd Mafiosi, and astute Italian-Americans hoping to create a 49th star for the U.S.A. in the center of the Mediterranean. Giuliano was made commander-in-chief of this meager army. Yet on the 15th of May, 1946, the Italian government conceded autonomous administration to Sicily. The various Mafia groups, which had given it their full support, withdrew from the separatist movement. Giuliano was left alone. But the barons and the Mafia convinced the bandit—holding out the promise of a government pardon—to fight against the left-wing parties who were vying for control of Sicily. On May 1, 1947, Giuliano's band opened fire on the peasants who had gathered at the Juniper Gate to celebrate May Day," killing eleven people and injuring many more.[7] Salvatore Giuliano had, unfortunately, fallen victim to the police and the Mafia; it was the latter, in fact, that had infiltrated his band and opened fire on the peaceful demonstrators but it was Giuliano who—only wishing to disrupt the protest—took the blame—losing the adoration and protection of the people who had always been his bulwark and support.*

"The exploitation and elimination of Giuliano should be considered one of the Mafia's masterpieces. First, the Mafia used Giuliano to create the myth of an army that never really existed, then to save the landed gentry from an invasion of the sharecroppers. Finally, when he was of no more use to the Mafia, it killed him; or rather, it had him killed, on July 5, 1950, by his most devoted friend and lieutenant, Gaspare Pisciotta. Immediately after his death in the house of the lawyer, Di Maria, Giuliano's body was dragged into the courtyard where a fictional struggle and a false killing were set up so that it looked as if the carabinieri *were responsible. Four years later, the Mafia also eliminated Gaspare Pisciotta by poisoning him with a cup of coffee while he was in the Ucciardone Prison in Palermo."[8]*

Bandits and Mafiosi

As a friend and I discussed the massacre at the Juniper Gate, in which Giuliano's band opened fire on a communist march, whether by

Conclusion: The Last Adventure

Giuliano's orders or some treacherous act within the band no one can ascertain, my friend exclaimed, "Giuliano was a fool. He was a bandit, right? Then his natural allies were the people. He should have gone to the communists; instead he went to the fascists. You see what was the result." My friend was suggesting that the massacre at the Juniper Gate was the result of treachery: the inevitable result of dealing with the ruling class (i.e., the "fascists," in my friend's terminology) rather than the people.

And it is, in fact, this eternal struggle between the ruling class and the people, explicit in Palermitan city legend and Sicilian bandits' lives, that surreptitiously invaded the Sicilian marionette theater by means of the knight-become-bandit, Renaud, to form its implicit content: the creation of an alternate and indigenous aristocracy, such as the Beati Paoli, a band of brigands, or the Mafia, one that, like the official and foreign aristocracy, taxes (and, at times, taxes sorely) the people but one that at the same time acts as the strong arm of the people when the official and foreign aristocracy oversteps the limits of its authority. I here think back to earlier conversations about the Palermitan people's preference for Renaud over Roland and the man who told me that Roland was too one-dimensional, always doing what he was supposed to do, while Renaud, he who had the audacity to rebel, was multifaceted, with more sides to his nature. And Maria who told me, "Pay attention to Renaud of Montauban. He's the good one. He always acts honorably."

But it is not as if Palermitans are a criminal lot, the perennial kith and kin of brigands and thieves. Here is why Roland, the perfect knight, is so reviled: That knight-become-saint lives by the law of obedience, a law that works well if your lord is honest, but if he becomes dishonest due to some dissembling traitor—a Judas, a Ganelon—it is your duty to rebel. Roland, in his intense loyalty to his uncle Charlemagne, could never do so, and you see where his loyalty got him. And here is why Renaud, the knight-become-bandit, is so universally adored. If your lord becomes dishonest to the point of your imminent demise another law replaces that of obedience. Your duty is no longer to your lord but to your family—and perhaps even to society at large—who demands satisfaction. In Palermo, if the injury has been particularly grievous only one manner of satisfaction is available: vendetta. In this ideological complex, in this intricate web of signification, we witness the construction of an alternate and indigenous aristocracy, an aristocracy not defined by rarified blood, an aristocracy rather of the people. Yet even this aristocracy, whether represented by the Beati Paoli, a band of brigands, or the Mafia, becomes taxing, and an ambivalence or, perhaps better, a tired resignation on the part of the people is manifested toward it.

I had few interactions with Mafiosi for obvious reasons, but one, which I previously mentioned briefly, stands out. As a friend and I were returning to her apartment one evening, the storeroom on the first floor of her apartment building was being robbed. My friend, like me, a foreigner to the city, wanted to ask the young men carting furniture and various appliances out of the storeroom what they were doing, but despite the obvious evidence to the contrary (a cut chain on the floor; legitimate workers, I assumed, use keys rather than metal clippers to get into a storeroom), I convinced my friend that the men must be workers rather than thieves; after all, everyone else was coming and going up and down the stairs as if nothing out of the ordinary were occurring. With that explanation I got her up the stairs and into her apartment, but as I attempted to convince her not to intervene, one of the men stopped his activity and did not take his eyes from mine. He smiled steadily and noncommittally, but his message was very clear: "Get her out of here."

The Mafioso, or the urban bandit, survives on a perception of calm toughness and the effective use of the threat. If toughness and the threat are the mainstays of his existence, his existence is tenuous at best. It is interesting in this context that the bandit, like the saint, is bound to die. His death is simply deferred: Witness the death of Salvatore Giuliano on the streets of Montelepre, ostensibly gunned down by the *carabinieri* but as likely delivered to that force through treachery within his own band, perhaps even on the part of his own cousin and lieutenant, Gaspare Pisciotta, and, in epic, Renaud survives the battle of Roncevaux only to die in a monastery manned by—Oh, treachery of treacheries!—monks from the hated house of Maiance.

An Expansive Allegory

In infusing epic with a native sensibility, the Sicilian marionette theater seems to have incorporated Palermitan society in its entirety:

Conclusion: The Last Adventure

engorging itself—as did the serpent at the Genius' breast—on history, economy, social order, and religion in order to anatomize and distill Palermo's essence. Its primary tool in this process is allegory, but allegory that moves in two directions simultaneously: citing at once Palermitan social organization and Christian myth. In this, we could say that epic is the intersection where myth is rendered sociologically meaningful and society is offered its mythic rationalization.

But the mythic dimension of epic that emerges in the marionette theater seems as old as the Carolingian Cycle itself. Even in the eleventh century *Nota Emilianense*, which retold the events of the ambush in the Pyrenean Mountains, we see a mythologization of a historical event. The enemy is no longer another European people (i.e., the Basques) but rather the enemy of Christendom (i.e., the Saracens). Charlemagne now has twelve nephews, analogous to Christ's twelve apostles, which in itself seems to be a reconfiguration of God's twelve tribes of Israel. By the time we arrive at the twelfth century *Song of Roland*, the allegory is complete. Charlemagne stands in the position of God the Father, Roland in the position of both Christ (martyring himself for the Father) and the angel of the apocalypse (sounding his trumpet as the earth scorches under God's numerous plagues), and Ganelon stands in the role of Judas. Even Renaud's association with the bandit-king David is established in the Old French and Franco-Venetian poems that begin to fill out Roland's story in the twelfth and thirteenth centuries.

This ancient allegory is still in effect in the Palermitan version of the Carolingian Cycle, but perhaps particular to the Palermitan version is that these knights, Charlemagne, Roland, Renaud, Ganelon, taken in their entirety, or as a corporate body, stand juxtaposed to the masques (epic's representation of humanity) as the body of the gods. This might seem peculiar at first glance, Palermo being dominated by a monotheistic religion, but Christianity—and this is notable in Palermo—is monotheistic in the same way that Hindu religion is in India. There are a number of entities residing under the general principle of godhead. In Palermo, these entities are expanded to include not only God the Father, God the Son, and God the Holy Spirit but also many of the prominent heroes of both Hebraic and Christian legend.[9] And the various attributes of these heroes might not be so much a function of what they do in the Bible but rather what they do in Palermitan folktales

Conclusion

derived from Biblical myth. That is to say, in Palermo, one finds—as did Zora Neale Hurston in African-American culture—tales dealing with Adam, Noah, God, Satan, Saul, David, Christ, Mary, Judas, Michael, Gabriel—that are often better known than their biblical precedents.

And the situation is further complicated in Palermo where, despite arguments to the contrary, one doesn't have to search too hard to find that beneath this current pantheon of Judeo-Christian heroes lurk the old Greco-Roman deities of the island. For example, as Mary Taylor Simeti points out, the month of May, sacred to the virgin Artemis, is reiterated through the Church's "dedicating the month of May to the Virgin Mary and preaching the observation of chastity in her honor."[10] The Carolingian heroes, inasmuch as they are rerepresentations of Judeo-Christian heroes, provide a kind of template with which the inalterable priestly form of Christianity can be adjusted to the exigencies of Palermitan society without committing sacrilege. Yet, in their adjusting of the template, Palermitans ultimately rewrite Christianity in their own image.[11] It may, in fact, be characteristic of societies with moderately monotheistic religions to fulfill the social function of mythology's gods with legend's heroes. In other words, we can't simply give up our gods for the sake of monotheism. If we did, we would lose the social function of the gods in the process and, thus, the social function of mythology. We must therefore augment our gods with ancient heroes, be they biblical or Carolingian or other, in order to undergo the *imitatio dei*—the reenactment of the life of the gods in the world of humanity—that is the staple function of mythology on a universal basis.

Then, in an odd sort of transference, the mythic entity that informs each of epic's characters—Roland's Christ, for instance, or Renaud's David—translates his meaning to the class of Palermitan society that the epical character represents. That is, Christ translates his meaning through Roland to the clerical class. And David translates his meaning through Renaud to the Mafia. Further, the class of Palermitan society represented by the epical character transfers its meaning back through him to the mythic entity. In other words, just as the youthful David transfers his meaning to the Mafioso through the representation of Renaud in the Carolingian Cycle, the Mafioso transfers his meaning back to the youthful David through Renaud's epic machinations. Then again, just as Christ transfers his meaning to Palermo's clerics through

Conclusion: The Last Adventure

the Carolingian Cycle's depiction of Roland, the Palermitan cleric transfers his meaning back to Christ—again by means of Roland's epic machinations. Just as myth rewrites society, so too does society rewrite myth. Allegory, in this context, sets up a kind of eternal feedback loop continuously redefining mythology's gods, epic's heroes, and society's classes and knits these gods, heroes, and men into a unified system. In the final analysis, it is this eternal feedback loop that is the lynchpin of the rhetoric of identity that emerges from Palermo's marionette theater and serves to critique the social matrix that defines Palermitan culture.

The social dimension of epic's characters emerges—as we have seen—from the careful interweaving of the themes from various genres of Sicilian folk narrative and the artful use of the tropes, speech acts, and tones which control and contain the voices of epic's various characters (i.e., dialogism). With such narrative strategies, epic's major protagonist, the knight, becomes a masque, becomes thereby of the people, becomes a saint, becomes thereby like a priest, becomes a bandit, becomes thereby a Mafioso. He ranges about his narrative space, incorporating the various personages who populate it and citing them in their own distinctive voices. It is, in actuality, his taking on of different social personae that creates the story. If the knight works, he is a masque, and the narrative involves the knight's descent among the people. If the masque fights, he is a knight, and the narrative—very much after the manner of a Sicilian fairy tale—involves the recognition of the masque's royal origins. If the knight dies, he is a saint, and the narrative involves holy war, but if he rebels, he is a bandit, and the narrative involves just retribution. I think narrative is distinguished precisely by these shifts, these metamorphoses, these reversals; they provide the recognition, the sudden flash of insight, the epiphany, which ultimately defines (and perhaps even informs) the major social relations of Palermo, those very relations that determine the interactional basis of the aristocracy, the people, the clerical class, and the Mafia. I am suggesting here that narrative itself—on the basis of its various rhetorical strategies—formulates social relations, that it creates logical connections where none have as yet existed, that it makes sense of the hodge-podge that society sometimes is, that it actually instructs people on how to behave toward one another. If it were otherwise, multi-genericity (the convocation of characters from disparate genres of narrative) and dialogism (the citation of real voices by these disparate characters) would achieve no dramatic force.

But what exactly are the connections that narrative draws? In the final analysis, one would have to say that the aristocracy is no more universally hated in Palermo than the Mafia is universally adored. And for that matter, the people no more heap uncritical acclaim upon themselves than they do anticlerical abuse upon the priest. Rather, in epic, one encounters a comprehension, a sympathy for, an appreciation of, and at times a tired resignation to Palermitan social order *as it is*. What epic does is play out the intricacies of that social order: the complex interdependencies, the nuances, the expectations. In the final analysis, I suppose that it should come as no surprise that it does not simply reflect but it also teaches social order. It is—but, perhaps today, we must say inasmuch as a vibrantly participatory world is quickly being replaced by a kind of colorless consumer monoculture[12] where there is little room for the Palermitan brand of narrativity—*was* one of the elegant means of enculturation at the disposal of the Palermitan people.

Genre and Power

One last point: If stories are a means of enculturation, if they *teach* social relations, then they are integrally related to the energy which charges social relations, that causes such relations to adhere to one another like negatively and positively charged ions: power. This devolution of power from a society's social order into its stories, I believe, is what we call genre. That is to say, genre is a comprehension of the type of social relationship under analysis in a story. If a story deals purely with the nature of aristocracy, we are involved in epic, which in its purest form does seem to idealize the dominant class of Palermitan society; if it deals, on the other hand, with the nature of the people, we are involved in farce, which, in essence, pokes fun at the perennial condition of the Palermitan working classes: tired, hungry, and overworked but perhaps unlike the aristocracy full of life. If it deals with the nature of the saint alone, we witness the salutary—even miraculous—effects of a life of quiet penitence, but if it deals exclusively with the nature of the bandit, we see the tenuous nature—and precarious hold on life—of that cham-

Conclusion: The Last Adventure

pion of the people. Yet, the peculiarity of narrative and its rhetorical impact is that we can't seem to content ourselves with just one genre at a time. Farce keeps slipping surreptitiously into epic because what we really want to see is the relationship between the aristocracy and the people. Likewise, the saints' and bandits' lives keep becoming entwined one with the other because what we're really after is a read on the penetration of authority—either the cleric's sanctioned authority or the Mafia's alternate authority—on the power of the aristocracy to subjugate and the will of the people to resist.

In fact, there seems to be an integral relationship between genre and power in epic. I here understand the major arena of genre to be narrative and the major arena of power to be social organization: genre is that coercive energy that renders the account of a potentially real event artificial; power is that political-economic energy that forges social relations. I further understand the relationship between genre and power to be of the nature of a dialectic in which each informs, legitimizes, and in fact inscribes itself within the other. Narrative then is the arena in which social relations are effectively formed. Likewise, society is the arena in which the peculiar laws of narrative voice (i.e., genre) are constituted.[13] In other words, genre is not solely a narratological but also a sociological phenomenon; likewise, power is not solely a sociological but also a narratological phenomenon. Genre, particularly in the realm of episodic accretion and voice construction is *essentially* sociological; power, particularly in the realm of configuring nuanced social relations is *essentially* narratological. In a very real sense, therefore, those individuals (whether nineteenth century Sicilian gentlemen or twenty-first century American moralists) who argue that stories can effect behavior are—at least to some extent—correct. But I—alongside that sensible if a bit heated Palermitan diarist who upbraided his fellow *galantuomini* as blockheads for seeking the closure of Palermo's marionette theaters by asking if they wished to ban Boiardo and Ariosto as well—suggest that we allow the peculiar laws of genre and power (as well as those laws which govern the intersection of the two) to run along, as they ought naturally to do, unimpeded. It really doesn't do to attempt to control the uncontrollable anyway.

For just as the coercive energy of genre is rendered impossible by a principle of contamination[14] that insists that no single genre can exist in isolation, that it must necessarily be informed beforehand by an apposite genre, such as is epic by farce, such as is the saint's life by the bandit's, so too is the coercive energy of power broken by a principle of contamination that insists that one social category presupposes another, such as the aristocracy does the people, such as the clerical class does the Mafia, that no social category exists outside the context of a relationship, and that the major directional flow of power, which constitutes the relationship, may at anytime be inverted: to the Palermitan this inversion is explicitly understood as vendetta. This is the lesson that, at the very least, the mysterious depiction of the Genius of Palermo attempts to cryptically promulgate across the many generations of Palermitan society.

In essence, what is mythologically postulated in Sicily's marionette theater is a kind of double Christ: one based on Christ proper, the other based on his Hebraic equivalent, David. At times, the obedience of Christ is warranted: Roland expresses it in his unwavering duty to Charlemagne, his pardoning of Buiaforte, and his self-sacrifice at the Battle of Roncevaux. And the Palermitan people have resignedly expressed it again and again in the face of numerous military occupations. But at times the rebelliousness of that alternate Christ, David, is warranted: Renaud expresses it when he takes to the hills and resorts to banditry, when he kills Buiaforte, that same Buiaforte whom Roland spared, for fighting with the Saracens and against the Paladins at Roncevaux, and the Palermitans express it in such "tenebrous," to borrow Vincenzo Linares' term, associations as the Beati Paoli and the Mafia.

When I finally realized what it meant to "talk like a soldier," I began to understand the function of Palermitan epic. Yet, by then New Year's Eve was upon me and my fieldwork was winding down to an unnatural conclusion; I would be leaving Palermo (broke) in about a week, and I simply had to close my notebooks and quit my studies with the decided sensation that I was not yet finished with them. As midnight, that moment of symbolic closures and openings, approached, I found myself once again on a Palermitan rooftop, a pistol in my hand, and my hostess urging me to shoot. So along with hundreds of other Palermitans, and to the accompaniment of firecrackers and bottle rockets, I shot a bullet straight into the sky. A gaggle of children, two dogs, and a duck scattered, screaming, barking, and quacking gleefully about the roof and were

Conclusion: The Last Adventure

Remnant of a bygone era directing patrons to a marionette theater. Underneath is posted an announcement for a novena and feast for the Immaculate Virgin; beyond, the slightest glimpse of a street. Photograph by author.

Conclusion

herded back to a protective overhang by my hostess, only to press once again to the edge of the roof. As each man shot the pistol in turn, I wondered if this act were simply an augment to the noise of the firecrackers and bottle rockets, an assertion of Palermitan independence, or some admixture of both. I took the pistol again as it went the round, shot once more, and ran with the children, dogs, and duck to the edge of the roof to watch Palermo grow crimson beneath a fire-streaked sky.

Appendix: The Death of the Paladins[1]

The Death of the Paladins is undoubtedly the most important of the episodes of the Carolingian Cycle to the people of Palermo. The particular version which I use in this study represents a special production undertaken by several puppet companies in concert. It represents an attempt to revive interest in the art form while there were still masters able to command the marionettes and give them voice. The puppeteers involved are Giuseppe Argento, Vincenzo Argento, Giacomo Cuticchio, Nino Cuticchio, Sir Antonino Mancuso, and Pino Mancuso. The performance occurred in 1980. Here, I offer the first scene in the original Italian as well as the raw, bare-boned translation to allow readers a sense of what the texts included in this book look like in the original.

Scene I

Carlo Magno: Gano di **Mago---nza**
  è stato sce---lto
  come **ambaciato---re**
  per andare a parlare con il mio amato cognato
  Re Marsilio di **Spa---gna!**
  Orla---ndo,
  mio **nipote,**
  legato ad un giurame---nto,
  consigliava i **spa---gnoli**
  che devono lasciare le chiavi di Spagna a **Pari---gi**
  e che si dovevano **arre----ndare**
  alla mia **coro---na!**
  Ma **giu---stamente**
  il Duca Namo di Bavie---ra
  di---sse
  che potessi mandare come ambasciatore

Appendix

   mio cognate, Conte Gano di **Magonza**
   per potere **convi---ncere** gli **spa---gnoli**
   ad accetare **l'a---cqua**
   del **Sa---nto Batte---simo!**
Soldato: C'è permesso, Maestà?

Scene I

Charlemagne: Ganelon of **Maiance**
   was chosen
   as **amba---ssador**
   to go and speak with my beloved brother-in-law,
   King Marsilius of Spai---n.
   Ro---land,
   my **nephew,**
   constrained by a solemn oa---th,
   advised the **Spa---niards**
   that they should leave the key of Spain to **Pari---s**
   and that they should **re----nder** themselves subject
   to my **cro---wn.**
   But **ri---ghtly**
   Duke Naimes of Bave---ria
   sai---d
   that I might send as ambassador
   my brother-in-law, Count Ganelon of **Maia---nce**
   to **convi----nce** the **Spa---niards**
   to accept the **wa---ter**
   of **Ho---ly Ba----ptism.**
Soldier: **Permission?**
Carlo Magno: Avanti, Soldato!
Soldato: **A---lto** Imperatore, Carlo Magno,
   in questo mome---nto.
   si presenta il conte Gano di Mago---nza.
Carlo Magno: **Riceve---telo**
   con gra---nde onore.
Soldato: Va---do,
   Maestà!
Gano (enters and throws himself prostrate at Charlemagne's feet): **Maestà,**
   E---ccomi ai vostri piedi!
   Ho **compiu---to** la mia **missio----ne,**
   O mio signore.
Carlo Magno: Alza---tevi,
   O **cogna---to** mio,
   Co---nte Gano di Mago---nza!
   Vorrei **sape---re**

Appendix: The Death of the Paladins

l'e---**sito** dell'ambasciata,
   cognate Gano.
Gano: **Maestà,**
   mi sono **prese---nto** ai fratelli **spa---gnoli**
   ai quali ho dato la vostra ambasciata;
   cioè
Charlemagne: Come forward, soldier.
Soldier: **High** Emperor, Charlemagne,
   at this moment
   Count Ganelon of Maiance
   presents himself.
Charles: Receive him
   with every honor.
Soldier: Yes, your Majesty.
Ganelon (enters and throws himself prostrate at Charlemagne's feet): Your Majesty,
   here I am at your feet.
   I have **completed** my **mission,**
   oh Lord.
Charlemagne: Raise yourself,
   oh Brother-in-law,
   Count Ganelon of Maiance.
   I would **li---ke** to know
   the **outcome** of the embassy.
Ganelon: Your Majesty,
   I presented myself to the three Spanish brothers
   to whom I have given your embassy:
   that is
   o consegnare **la spa---gna**
   o farsi **Cristiani.**
   Si è scatenata la guerra
   Nei loro **a---nimi,**
   O mio signore.
   E **per l'u---ltimo** hanno deciso
   di farsi Cristiani
   per non perdere il **reame!**
Paladini: **Bra---vo!**
   Bra---vo!
Gano: Da queste parti,
   O mio signore, Carlo **Ma---gno,**
   a---cettano l'a---qua del **Sa---nto Ba---ttesimo**
   nelle **strette gole** di **Roncisvalle.**
   Inoltre,
   O mio signore Carlo **Ma---gno,**

Appendix

  e---**sigono** soltanto **i Paladini**
  e **non** la signoria di **Trebiso**---**nda**
  tanto meno **l'ese**---**rcito.**
    • [A murmur goes up among the Paladins.]
  to **either** give up **Spain**
  or to convert to Christianity.
  War has broken out in their souls,
  oh Lord.
  And they have finally decided
  to convert to Christianity
  in order not to lose their **kingdom.**
Paladins: **Bravo! Bravo!**
Ganelon: For their part,
  oh my Lord, **Charlemagne,**
  they will **acce**---**pt the wa**---**ter of Ho**---**ly Baptism**
  in the **narrow** valley of **Roncevaux.**
  Moreover,
  oh my Lord, **Charlemagne,**
  they **insi**---**st** that only the **Paladins**
  and **not** the governors of **Trebiso**---**nd**
  much less an **a**---**rmy**
  be present.
    • [A murmur goes up among the Paladins.]
  Io ho promesso che l'armata sia Araba che quella Francese
  si fermerà
  a quattro leghe
  fuo---**ri** delle gole di Roncisvalle.
  Que---**sta** è la risposta
  che mi hanno dato
  i fratelli spagnoli,
  vostri cognate,
  che desiderano **soltanto** il **Battesimo**
  per mano del Vescovo **Turpino.**
Carlo Magno: **So**---**no conte**---**nto**
  nel **senti**---**re**
  che **Marsi**---**lio,**
  Bulogante, e Falserone
  acce---**ttano** l'acqua
  del **Santo Battesimo!**
  Ebbene!
  I have promised that the armies,
  both Arabian and French,
  will halt
  at four leagues

Appendix: The Death of the Paladins

    di---stance from the valley of Roncevaux.
    Thi---s is the answer
    that the Spanish brothers,
    your **brothers-in-law**,
    have given me;
    they desire **baptism**
    but **only** from the hand of Bishop **Turpin.**
Charlemagne: **I am conte---nt**
    in the **knowle---dge**
    that **Marsi---lius,**
    Bulogante and Falseron
    will accept the water
    of **Holy Baptism.**
    This is well done!
    [Bewilderedly] Ma non capi---sco
    il moti---vo del tuo consiglio
    essendo appunto così:
    come si trova a Roncisva---lle?
Gano: Non **vo---gliono** affatto farsi Cristiani
    nella loro terra:
    cioè
    in **Spa---gna,**
    ovve---ro
    a **Sarago---ssa**
    e **così**
    creare **vergogna** e **disonore**
    a proprio popolo.
Astolfo: Se sua Maestà mi permette la parola,
    Vorrei dire due parole al Conte **Ga---no**
Carlo Magno: **Pa---rla,**
    Principe Astolfo d'Inghilterra!
Astolfo [menacingly]: **Ga---no,**
    tu hai fatto la parte dei paga---ni
    perchè se sotto il tuo dire
    si nasconde il tradimento,
    Orlando non avrà **mai**
    [Bewilderedly] But I do---n't understand
    the mo---tive of your advise
    concerning the valley of Roncevau---x?
Ganelon: They **do----n't** want to convert to Christianity
    in their own land,
    that is,
    in **Spai---n,**
    or more precisely,

Appendix

    at **Sarago---ssa,**
    and **so** bring **shame** and **dishonor**
    to their own people.
Astolphe: If your majesty will permit me to speak,
    I would like to say a few words to Count **Ganelon.**
Charlemagne: **Speak,**
    Prince Astolphe of England.
Astolphe [menacingly]: **Ganelon,**
    you have taken the part of the **pagans**
    because if treachery lies beneath your words,
    Roland will **never** receive
    la corona di **Spa---gna!**
        • [Another murmur runs throughout the throne room.]
Carlo Magno: **Asto---fo,**
    io **e---sigo**
    che **stai zitto!**
    Non **osa---re** di offendere
    mio cognate, **Ga---no,**
    in quanto **costui**
    nella Madre Chiesa dei **Santi Uni---ti**
    ho fatto un giuramento
    di essere fedele alla mia corona
    e a tutta la **Fra---ncia!**
    Quindi **e---sigo**
    che ognu---no di noi
    si prepara lieto
    che al piu presto
    lasciare---mo Pari---gi
    e prendere il **cammi---no**
    per Roncisvalle!
    the crown of Spain.
        • [Another murmur runs throughout the throne room.]
Charlemagne: **Astolphe,**
    I insi---st
    that you **hold** your tongue.
    Do not **dare** to offend
    my brother-in-law, **Ganelon,**
    inasmuch as **he**
    in the Blessed Church of All Saints
    took a solemn oath
    to remain faithful to my crown
    and to all **Fra---nce.**
    Therefore I **insist**
    that each one of us

Appendix: The Death of the Paladins

will ready himself with gladness
so that at the earliest possible moment
we might leave Pa---ris
and take the **road**
to Roncevaux.

Chapter Notes

Preface

1. Mary Taylor Simeti, *On Persephone's Island: A Sicilian Journal* (San Francisco: North Point Press, 1986), pp. 37–38.
2. Giuseppe Pitrè, "Le Tradizioni Cavalleresche Popolari in Sicilia," *Romania* 13 (1884), p. 359.
3. In actuality, there is no Monte Oliviero today but rather a Castello di Oliveri which sits upon a promontory hard by the village of Oliveri in Messina. The topographic feature was called Mons Olivierius by Godfrey of Viterbo in the 12th century and probably did not (as Godfrey suggests) relate to the Paladin but rather to the olive groves which were a mainstay of the local economy.

Introduction

1. Leonardo Sciascia and Rosario La Duca, *Palermo Felicissima* (Palermo: Edizioni il Punto, 1974), pp. 24–30.
2. Sicilian *pupi* (marionettes), despite the fact that the term *pupi* is cognate with the English puppet, are not truly puppets but neither are they completely like modern marionettes. The main distinction between *pupi* and marionettes is that *pupi*, as we shall see, are maneuvered with two rods as well as four strings. It seems likely that at least one rod was characteristic of earlier marionettes which, in most traditions, gave up the rod for more realistic movements. Sicilian pupi, because they came to be dominated by armed knights, needed to keep the rod for the rigors of combat and, in fact, added a second for the same reason. Though I refer to *pupi* as marionettes, I refer to their masters as puppeteers and the art form as puppetry (inasmuch as marionetteers and marionettry just sound weird).
3. I have borrowed this notion of consumer monoculture, to which I will return, from Sabina Magliocco's *The Two Madonnas: The Politics of Festival in a Sardinian Community* (New York: Peter Lang, 1993).
4. Giuseppe Argento, Vincenzo Argento, Giacomo Cuticchio, Nino Cuticchio, Sir Antonino Mancuso, and Pino Mancuso, *Morte dei Paladini* (Palermo: Antonio Pasqualino Museo Internazionale delle Marionette, 1980), Audiotape.
5. Felice Cammarata, "Gli Eroi Carolingi in Terra di Sicilia," in *Storia dei Paladini di Francia*, by Giusto Lodico (Palermo: Mazzone, 1970), p. 6.
6. Antonio Pasqualino, "Transformations of Chivalrous Literature in the Subject Matter of the Sicilian Marionette Theater," in *Varia Folklorica*, ed. Alan Dundes (The Hague, Paris: Mouton, 1978), p. 191.
7. My discussion of themes relies heavily on the work of Antonio Pasqualino, especially "Transformations of Chivalrous Literature in the Subject Matter of the Sicilian Marionette Theater," cited above, and *L'Opera dei Pupi* (Palermo: Sellerio, 1977).
8. Mary Taylor Simeti, *On Persephone's Island* (San Francisco: Northpoint Press, 1986), p. 253.
9. I've liberally, some will no doubt have noticed, borrowed my diction from John Barth's *Lost in the Funhouse* here.
10. Carmelo Cuticchio and Giacomo Cuticchio, *Prime Imprese di Orlandino* (Palermo: Antonio Pasqualino Museo In-

ternazionale delle Marionette, 1987), Audiotape.

11. Sabina Magliocco, *The Two Madonnas: The Politics of Festival in a Sardinian Community* (New York: Peter Lang, 1993), p. 1.

12. Vincenzo Linares, *I racconti popolari* (Palermo: Luigi Pedone Lauriel, 1886), pp. 2–33; I am here offering a synopsis of the story which will be presented nearly in full later in this study.

13. Giuseppe Pitrè, *Fiabe e Leggende Popolari Siciliane* (Palermo: Luigi Pendone Lauriel, 1888), p. 348.

14. Interestingly, in Sicily, the dog is considered not man's *best* friend but rather man's *last* friend. To die alone with a dog is a horrible fate. Notice that Michael Corleone—in his Sicilian retirement—does so in *The Godfather* trilogy. And when Salvatore, in Giuseppe Tornatore's *Il Nuovo Cinema Paradiso*, returns from his military duty the only soul to meet him is a cringing dog in an empty piazza.

Chapter One

1. M. I. Finley, Denis Mack Smith, and Christopher Duggan, *A History of Sicily* (New York: Viking, 1986), p. 31.

2. Ibid., pp. 31–36.

3. Ibid., p. 50.

4. Ibid., pp. 3–5; Steven Runciman, *The Sicilian Vespers* (Baltimore: Penguin, 1960), p. 18.

5. M. I. Finley, Denis Mack Smith, and Christopher Duggan, *A History of Sicily* (New York: Viking, 1986), pp. 31–36.

6. Ibid., p. 56.

7. Giuseppe Quatriglio, *A Thousand Years in Sicily: From the Arabs to the Bourbons*, 2nd ed., trans. Justin Vitiello (Brooklyn, New York: Legas, 1997), p. 10.

8. Donald Matthew, *The Norman Kingdom of Sicily* (Cambridge: Cambridge University Press, 1992), p. 10.

9. M. I. Finley, Denis Mack Smith, and Christopher Duggan, *A History of Sicily* (New York: Viking, 1986), p. 53.

10. Donald Matthew, *The Norman Kingdom of Sicily* (Cambridge: Cambridge University Press, 1992), pp. 17–18.

11. Steven Runciman, *The Sicilian Vespers* (Baltimore: Penguin, 1960), p. 22.

12. M. I. Finley, Denis Mack Smith, and Christopher Duggan, *A History of Sicily* (New York: Viking, 1986), p. 61.

13. Steven Runciman, *The Sicilian Vespers* (Baltimore: Penguin, 1960), p. 24.

14. M. I. Finley, Denis Mack Smith, and Christopher Duggan, *A History of Sicily* (New York: Viking, 1986), p. 56.

15. Ibid., p. 57.

16. Ibid., p. 54.

17. Steven Runciman, *The Sicilian Vespers* (Baltimore: Penguin, 1960), p. 29.

18. Ibid., p. 28.

19. Ibid., passim.

20. Giuseppe Pitrè, *Il Vespro Siciliano: Delle Tradizioni Popolari della Sicilia* (Palermo: Edizioni "Il Vespro," 1979), pp. 11–12.

21. Diacritic marks added.

22. Steven Runciman, *The Sicilian Vespers* (Baltimore: Penguin, 1960), pp. 237–238.

23. Ibid., pp. 313–318.

24. M. I. Finley, Denis Mack Smith, and Christopher Duggan, *A History of Sicily* (New York: Viking, 1986), p. 79.

25. Mary Taylor Simeti, *On Persephone's Island* (San Francisco: Northpoint Press, 1986), p. 176.

26. The Jewish, like the Muslim and—to a lesser extent, Byzantine—population might have been substantial but it is difficult to ascertain any certain figures; especially inasmuch as the population suffered expulsion and forced conversion, particularly with the advent of the Inquisition, which cast its net so widely as to torment *neofiti* (forced converts) and non-converts alike.

27. This perception may largely be a matter of the historic imagination of the populace rather than the facts on the ground. In actuality, all these courts were comprised of external conquerors though, certainly, some courts—the Kalbid, Norman, and Hohenstaufen, for instance—could be said to have been founded on more enlightened principles of rule than others—

Notes—Chapter Two

the Angevin, undoubtedly, and probably the Aragonese and Spanish as well.

28. Antonio Gramsci, *Selections from the Prison Notebooks*, trans. Quintin Hoare and Geoffrey Nowell Smith (New York: International Publishers, 1972), p. 283.

29. M. I. Finley, Denis Mack Smith, and Christopher Duggan, *A History of Sicily* (New York: Viking, 1986), p. 74.

30. Ibid., p. 97.

31. Ibid., pp. 106–109.

32. Giuseppe Quatriglio, *A Thousand Years in Sicily: From the Arabs to the Bourbons*, 2nd ed., trans. Justin Vitiello (Brooklyn, New York: Legas, 1997), p. 10.

33. Ibid., p. 121.

34. Ibid., pp. 168–169.

35. Ibid., p. 172.

36. Ibid., p. 180.

37. Ibid., p. 181.

38. Giuseppe di Lampedusa, *The Leopard*, trans. Archibald Colquhoun (London: Pantheon Books, 1960), p. 111.

39. Ibid., p. 219.

40. Giuseppe Pitrè. *Usi e Costumi, Credenze e Pregiudizi del Popolo Siciliano*, in *Biblioteca delle Tradizioni Popolari Siciliane*, Vol. 16 (Bologna: Forni, 1969), p. 56.

41. David Basile, "Agricultural Sicily," *Economic Geography* 17, no. 2 (April 1941), p. 109.

42. For a discussion of the effects on consumer culture in Italy, particularly in the sphere of ritual, see Sabina Magliocco, *The Two Madonnas: The Politics of Festival in a Sardinian Community* (New York: Peter Lang, 1993).

43. Danilo Dolci, *Sicilian Lives*, trans. Justin Vitiello (New York: Pantheon Books, 1981), pp. 90–93.

44. This synopsis is heavily geared toward the five episodes that I present in this study. A thorough synopsis would look more like Bullfinch's *The Age of Chivalry*, in which the Carolingian Cycle, mainly of the Italian literary tradition, is summarized.

45. M. I. Finley, Denis Mack Smith, and Christopher Duggan, *A History of Sicily* (New York: Viking, 1986), p. 55.

46. Mario Puzo, *The Sicilian* (New York: Random House, 1984), p. 7.

Chapter Two

1. Antonio Pasqualino, *L'Opera dei Pupi* (Palermo: Sellerio, 1977), p. 21.

2. The family of Maiance is the Carolingian Cycle's villanous lineage, which includes besides Charlemagne's stepbrothers, Lanfroi and Olderigi, Roland's stepfather, Ganelon.

3. Both storytellers and puppeteers use a rhythmic diction punctuated with resounding strikes to render assassination as well as battle.

4. There is often an annoyance on the part of the individual receiving liturgical phrases, as if to say, "You're wasting precious time!"

5. Girolamo Cuticchio and Sons. *Morte di Re Pepino* (Palermo: Antonio Pasqualino Museo Internazionale delle Marionette, 1985), Audiotape.

6. John McCormick, Alfonso Cipolla and Alessandro Napoli, *The Italian Puppet Theater: A History* (Jefferson, North Carolina: McFarland and Company, 2010), p. 5.

7. Mimmo Cuticchio, *Storia e Testimonianze di una Famiglia di Pupari* (Palermo: Stass, 1978), p. 26.

8. Ibid., 38.

9. Ibid., 26.

10. Antonio Pasqualino, "Marionettes and Glove Puppets: Two Theatrical Systems in Southern Italy," *Semiotica* 47, no. 1–4 (1983), p. 241.

11. Ibid., 242.

12. John McCormick, Alfonso Cipolla and Alessandro Napoli, *The Italian Puppet Theater: A History* (Jefferson, North Carolina: McFarland and Company, 2010), p. 89.

13. Ibid., 87.

14. Antonio Pasqualino, "Transformations of Chivalrous Literature in the Subject Matter of the Sicilian Marionette Theater," in *Varia Folklorica*, ed. Alan Dundes (The Hague, Paris: Mouton, 1978), p. 185.

15. Giuseppe Pitrè, *Il Vespro Siciliano: Delle Tradizioni Popolari della Sicilia* (Palermo: Edizioni "Il Vespro," 1979), p. 133.

16. Antonio Pasqualino, "Transforma-

tions of Chivalrous Literature in the Subject Matter of the Sicilian Marionette Theater," in *Varia Folklorica*, ed. Alan Dundes (The Hague, Paris: Mouton, 1978), p. 184.

17. Antonio Pasqualino, *Del Testo alla Rappresentazione: Le Prime Imprese di Carlo Magno* (Palermo: Laboratorio Antropologico Universitario, 1986), pp. 444–445.

Chapter Three

1. The author of the chivalric poem *Orlando Furioso*.
2. It's not unusual to hear this sort of praise of boys on the part of women in and out of narrative.
3. Godfather, the literal translation of this term, is probably not accurate. It is used more like Brother (or Brer) in African-American folklore. It is sometimes translated as Friend.
4. Offered in the declamatory style of a town crier.
5. Notice that respect is conditioned on fear, and this from the mouth of Charlemagne's sister who, along with her son, has joined (albeit temporarily) the ranks of the people.
6. Carmelo Cuticchio and Giacomo Cuticchio, *Prime Imprese di Orlandino* (Palermo: Antonio Pasqualino Museo Internazionale delle Marionette, 1987), Audiotape.
7. Steven Runciman, *The Sicilan Vespers* (Baltimore: Penguin, 1960), p. 308.
8. Mikhail Bakhtin, *Problems of Dostoevsky's Poetics*, vol. 8 of *Theory and History of Literature*, trans. Caryl Emerson (Minneapolis: University of Minnesota Press, 1984), p. 8.
9. Jerre Mangione, *Mount Allegro: A Memoir of Italian American Life* (Syracuse, New York: Syracuse University Press, 1981), p. 51.

Chapter Four

1. Marcel Danesi, *A Basic Course in Anthropological Linguistics* (Toronto: Canadian Scholars Press, 2004), p. 147.

2. Nicolas Abraham and Maria Torok, *The Wolfman's Magic Word: A Cryptonomy*, trans. Nicolas Rand (Minneapolis: University of Minnesota Press, 1986), p. 132.

3. Ronald Loewe, "Euphemism, Parody, Insult, and Innuendo: Rhetoric and Ethnic Identity at the Mexican Periphery," *Journal of American Folklore* 120, no. 477 (Summer 2007): pp. 284–307.

4. Deborah Tannen, "Interactional Sociolinguistics as a Resource for Intercultural Pragmatics," *Journal of Intercultural Pragmatics* 2, no. 2 (July 2005), pp. 205–208.

5. Roger Abrahams, "Introductory Remarks to a Rhetorical Theory of Folklore," *Journal of American Folklore* 81, no. 320 (April-June 1968), pp. 143–58.

6. Kent Ono and John Sloop, "The Critique of Vernacular Discourse," *Communication Monographs* 62, no. 1 (March 1995), p. 22.

7. Robert Glen Howard, "A Theory of Vernacular Rhetoric: The Case of the 'Sinner's Prayer' Online," *Folklore* 116, no. 2 (August 2005), p. 175.

8. Elliott Oring, "Legendry and the Rhetoric of Truth," *Journal of American Folklore* 121, no. 480 (Spring 2008), pp. 130–131.

9. Robert Brooke and Charlotte Hogg, "Open to Change: Ethos, Identification, and Critical Ethnography in Composition Studies," in *Ethnography Unbound: From Theory Shock to Critical Praxis*, eds. Stephen Gilbert Brown and Sidney I. Dobrin (Albany, New York: State University of New York Press, 2004), p. 118.

10. Dexter Gordon, *Identity, Rhetoric, Ideology, and Nineteenth-Century Black Nationalism* (Carbondale, Illinois: Southern Illinois University Press, 2003), pp. xi-xii.

11. Deborah Tannen, "I Can't Even Open my Mouth," *Annual Editions: Anthropology 4/5*, ed. Elvio Angeloni (Guilford, Connecticut: McGraw-Hill/Dushkin, 2003), pp. 38–46.

12. Robert Glen Howard, "A Theory of Vernacular Rhetoric: The Case of the 'Sinner's Prayer' Online," *Folklore* 116, no. 2 (August 2005), pp. 175–191.

13. Girolamo Cuticchio and Sons, *Ri-*

naldo Rubba la Bella Clarice (Palermo: Antonio Pasqualino Museo Internazionale delle Marionette, 1987), Audiotape.

14. Giusto Lodico, *Storia dei Paladini di Francia*, Vol. XIII, ed. Felice Cammarata (Trapani, Sicily: Celebes Editore, 1971), p. 299.

15. The incident is described by the puppeteer Don Giovanni Filippo da Alcamo in an unpublished interview conducted by Vita Adamo and preserved at the Antonio Pasqualino Museo Internazionale delle Marionette.

16. Antonino Uccello, *Carcere e Mafia nei Canti Popolari Siciliani* (Palermo: Edizioni Libri Siciliani, 1965), pp. 12–13.

17. Antonino Uccello, "Copioni di Briganti nel Repertorio dell'Opra," *Bollettino: Centro di Studi Filologici e Linguistici Siciliani* 10 (1965), p. 356.

18. Denis Mack Smith, *A History of Sicily: Medieval Sicily 800–1713* (London: Chatto and Windus, 1968), p. 296.

19. Antonino Uccello, "Copioni di Briganti nel Repertorio dell'Opra," *Bollettino: Centro di Studi Filologici e Linguistici Siciliani* 10 (1965), pp. 359–362.

20. 1 Samuel 21–24.

21. Giuseppe Pitrè, *Il Vespro Siciliano: Delle Tradizioni Popolari della Sicilia* (Palermo: Edizioni "Il Vespro," 1979), p. 124.

22. Carmelo Alberti, *Il Teatro dei Pupi e lo Spettacolo Popolare Siciliano* (Milan: Mursia, 1977), pp. 166–169.

Chapter Five

1. Ross Douthat, "The Better Pope," Op-Ed, *New York Times* (April 12, 2010), p. A25.

2. In Sicilian epic, as in its medieval forbears, Islam is considered polytheistic with a triumvirate of main gods: Mohammed, Magon, and Trevigant.

3. Roland's voice until the final portions of this episode is marked by a certain toughness, edged with threat, that almost makes one think of the bandit (this while he is defending Angelica), but it will give way to the saintly voice of conversion.

4. The existence of the common formula, "I am no longer able to see with my eyes," is here denoted by the fact that Agrican sees the water; one thinks of laughing-eyed Aphrodite in tears.

5. Once again, impatience in the face of liturgy is expressed.

6. Nino Cuticchio and Rosa Cuticchio, *Battaglia di Orlando e Agricane* (Palermo: Antonio Pasqualino Museo Internazionale delle Marionette, 1987), Audiotape.

7. Dennis Tedlock, *The Spoken Word and the Work of Interpretation* (Philadelphia: University of Pennsylvania Press, 1983), p. 106.

8. Jerre Mangione and Ben Morreale, *La Storia: Five Centuries of the Italian American Experience* (New York: Harper Perennial, 1992), p. 234.

9. This rule was notably contraverted in *The Early Adventures of Rolandin* but for very particular purposes.

10. Danilo Dolci, *Sicilian Lives*, trans. Justin Vitiello (New York, Pantheon Books, 1981), pp. 243–244.

11. 1 Samuel 17: 44.

12. Giuseppe Pitrè, "Le Tradizioni Cavalleresche Popolari in Sicilia," *Romania* 13 (1884), p. 359.

13. Henry Festing Jones, *Diversions in Sicily* (London: Alston Rivers, Limited, 1909), pp. 266–276.

14. Denis Mack Smith, *A History of Sicily: Medieval Sicily 800–1713* (London: Chatto and Windus, 1968), p.13.

15. Jonathan Shannon, "Performing al-Andalus, Remembering al-Andalus: Mediterranean Soundings from Mashriq to Maghrib," *Journal of American Folklore* 120, no. 477 (Summer 2007), pp. 308–334.

16. Ross Douthat, "A Time for Contrition," Op-Ed, *New York Times* (March 28, 2010), p. A21.

Chapter Six

1. Jean Bodel, *La Chanson des Saisnes*, ed. Francisque Michel (Paris: J. Techner, 1839), p. 3.

2. I am here following Victor Turner's tripartite organization of expressive culture

into the states of separation (the Trojan Cycle), Limin (the Arthurian Cycle), and reincorporation (the Carolingian Cycle).

3. Einhard the Frank, *Life of Charlemagne*, trans. Lewis Thorpe (Harmonsworth, Middlesex, England: Penguin, 1969), pp. 64–65.

4. Gerard J. Brault, "Introduction," *The Song of Roland* (University Park: Pennsylvania State University Press, 1978), p. 4.

5. Pierre Le Gentil, *The Chanson de Roland* (Cambridge, Massachusetts: Harvard University Press, 1969), pp. 35–36.

6. Joseph J. Duggan, *The Song of Roland: Formuliac Style and Poetic Craft* (Berkeley: California University Press, 1973), p. 83.

7. Gerard J. Brault, "Introduction," *The Song of Roland* (University Park: Pennsylvania State University Press, 1978), p. 109.

8. Eric Hobsbawm, *Primitive Rebels: Studies in Archaic Forms of Social Movement in the 19th and 20th Centuries* (Manchester, UK: Manchester University Press, 1971), p. 57.

9. Norman Cohn, *The Pursuit of the Millenium: Revolutionary Millenarians and Mystic Anarchists of the Middle Ages* (New York, Oxford: Oxford University Press, 1961), pp. 71–72.

10. Urban Tigner Holmes, *A History of Old French Literature: The Origins to 1300* (New York: F.S. Crofts, 1937), pp. 72–122.

11. Marcella Croce, *Pupi, Caretti, Contastorie: L'epica Cavalleresca nelle Tradizioni Popolari Siciliane* (Palermo: Diario Flacovia, 1999), p. 20.

12. Pio Rajna, *Le Fonti dell'Orlando Furioso* (Florence: G. C. Sansoni, 1900), p. 18.

13. Antonio Pasqualino, *L'Opera dei Pupi* (Palermo: Sellerio, 1977), pp. 20–21.

14. Giuseppe Pitrè, "Le Tradizioni Cavalleresche Popolari," *Romania* 13 (1884), p. 346.

15. Ibid., 349.

16. Antonio Pasqualino, *L'Opera dei Pupi* (Palermo: Sellerio, 1977), p. 21.

17. Ibid., p. 20.

18. Vincenzo Linares, *I racconti popolari* (Palermo: Luigi Pedone Lauriel, 1886), pp. 76–78.

19. Antonio Pasqualino, *L'Opera dei Pupi* (Palermo: Sellerio, 1977), p. 20.

20. Giuseppe Pitrè, "Le Tradizioni Cavalleresche Popolari," *Romania* 13 (1884): pp. 366–374.

21. Antonio Pasqualino, *L'Opera dei Pupi* (Palermo: Sellerio, 1977), p. 225.

22. Antonio Pasqualino, "Transformations of Chivalrous Literature in the Subject Matter of the Sicilian Marionette Theater," in *Varia Folklorica*, ed. Alan Dundes (The Hague, Paris: Mouton, 1978), p. 190.

23. Don Peppino Celano, *Morte di Re Pepino* (Palermo: Antonio Pasqualino Museo Internazionale delle Marionette, Undated), Audiotape.

24. Giusto Lodico, *Storia dei Paladini di Francia*, Vol. 1, ed. Felice Cammarata (Trapani, Sicily: Celebes Editore, 1971), p. 44.

25. Natale Meli, *Primo Quaderno die Reali di Francia di Giusto Lodico* (Palermo: Antonio Pasqualino Museo Internazionale delle Marionette, Undated), Unpaginated notebook.

26. Girolamo Cuticchio and Sons, *Morte di Re Pepino* (Palermo: Antonio Pasqualino Museo Internazionale delle Marionette, 1985), Audiotape.

Chapter Seven

1. Charlemagne's queen, Galerana, is the sister of King Marsilius of Saragossa; Count Ganelon of Maiance is married to Charlemagne's sister and Roland's mother, Berta.

2. At this point in the recitation, the audience broke into wild applause, and one boy shouted emphatically, "Bravissimo!"

3. Once again, emphatic applause from the audience.

4. Hushed laughter spreads slowly around the room.

5. Giuseppe Argento, Vincenzo Argento, Giacomo Cuticchio, Nino Cuticchio, Sir Antonino Mancuso, and Pino Mancuso, *Morte dei Paladini*. (Palermo: Antonio Pasqualino Museo Internazionale delle Marionette, 1980), Audiotape.

Chapter Eight

1. Edward C. Banfield, *The Moral Basis of a Backward Society* (Glencoe, Illinois: Free Press, 1958). This book is almost silly and, today, predominately discredited. It actually opens with a discussion of the lack of community organizations in an impoverished peasant commune in the southern Italian region of Basilicata—a region so impoverished that its inhabitants couldn't even afford to emigrate to northern Italy, Europe, America, or elsewhere in any significant numbers—in comparison to, of all places, Logan, Utah! What was he thinking?

2. I believe a similar social critique to that which occurs in epic occurs in Sicilian fairy tales though, inasmuch as fairy tales are so reliant on plotting rather than dialogue, their rhetorical function is more difficult to ascertain. Nonetheless, Sicilian fairy tales that have been collected by Giuseppe Pitrè regularly employ, beyond their stock characters—princes and princesses—peasants, seafarers, urban and rural laborers, merchants, and—most notably—priests and thieves. Had their dialogue been retained in its entirety—something which I am unsure has happened on the basis of the Pitrè transcriptions—I suspect they might have presented a trove of rhetorical devices. Still, Sicilian fairy tales offer their own brand of insight into Palermitan social relations and, happily, an excellent English translation of Pitrè's collection now exists: *The Collected Sicilian Folk and Fairy Tales of Giuseppe Pitrè*, edited and translated by Jack Zipes and Joseph Russo (New York and London: Routledge, 2009).

3. Jerre Mangione, *Mount Allegro: A Memoir of Italian American Life* (Syracuse, New York: Syracuse University Press, 1981), pp. 141–151.

4. Giuseppe Pitrè, *Novelle e Racconti Popolari Siciliani*, Vol. 1, in *Biblioteca delle Tradizioni Popolari Siciliane*, Vol. 4 (Palermo: Luigi Pedone Lauriel, 1875), pp. 68–77.

5. Share, or Ploughshare; the original plays on a rhyme: *terra* (earth) and *guerra* (war).

6. That is, my two legs plus a cane.

7. Your father.

8. To assist—perhaps as a midwife—at the birth of an infant.

9. To a funeral.

10. Again, as we saw previously, Godfather, the literal translation of this term, is probably not accurate. It is used more like Brother (or Brer) in African-American folklore. It is sometimes translated as Friend.

11. The original reads, "Gnursi, *Cumpari*." Gnursi is a contraction of *signore* (sir) and *si* (yes). Most Italians who I have asked say it is not an uncommon word and will relate it to an American soldier saying, "Yessir," but a quick Google search leads to few hits. One terrifically interesting one that I found was comprised of the transcriptions of three Sicilian farces that were staged for the Sicilian immigrant community in New York at the beginning of the previous century. The central character is none other than our own Nofrio—but here he is a live actor rather than a marionette. Giovanni De Rosalia wrote the plays and performed the title role, and, fascinatingly, the farces were popular enough with their Sicilian American audiences to be recorded on 78-r.p.m. records released by, among other studios, Columbia. The transcriptions (along with English translations) were prepared by Joe Accardi and Art Dieli and may be found at the following web address: http://accardiweb.com/nofrio/.

12. San Giovanni (Saint John) is said by Pitrè to be the patron of *comparatico* (coparenthood): the system of fictive kinship which makes of good friends *cumpari* (cofather or godfather) and *cummari* (comother or godmother).

13. Palaces tenanted by a poor girl who has become a queen or a princess seem to always have a secret staircase in Sicilian fairy tales. This one doesn't figure any further in the story so it seems to simply be a stock characteristic. I've taken the liberty of tying it a bit more closely to the tale through borrowing a feature that I encountered in other Sicilian fairy tales where the secret staircase serves to allow the poor girl or abused princess to carry out her inevitably benevolent scheme.

14. Without, hopefully, relying overly on the ideologies of the old linear evolutionists, I suspect that this circumstance might help explain why in many hunting-gathering societies there is not a real distinction between myth and folktale. All Australian aboriginal tales, for instance, seem to participate in the realm of myth—centering on the various spiritual agents that populated Australia in the ancient time of the Dreaming. Many simple agricultural societies, on the other hand, seem to maintain a distinction between those tales that are sacred (myth) and treat therefore the exploits of gods and those that are secular and rather treat the exploits of marginally fictional protagonists. Finally, those societies—complex agricultural and mercantile—that have a clearly delineated political class—here the Iroquois come to mind—seem to add the legend, the kind of tale that invests cultural founders or heroes with the attributes of deity, to their narrative repertoire.

15. Helmut Koenigsberger, *The Government of Sicily under Phillip II of Spain: A Study in the Practice of Empire* (London: Staples Press, 1951), p. 88.

16. M. I. Finley, Denis Mack Smith, and Christopher Duggan, *A History of Sicily* (New York: Viking, 1986), pp. 128–129.

17. Crane Brinton, *The Anatomy of Revolution* (New York: Vintage Books, 1965), p. 51.

18. M. I. Finley, Denis Mack Smith, and Christopher Duggan, *A History of Sicily* (New York: Viking, 1986), pp. 55–64.

19. M. I. Finley, Denis Mack Smith, and Christopher Duggan, *A History of Sicily* (New York: Viking, 1986), p. 115.

20. Anton Blok, *The Mafia of a Sicilian Village, 1860–1960: A Study of Violent Peasant Entrepreneurs* (Prospect Heights, Illinois: Waveland Press, 1974), p. 40.

21. Charles Tilly, "Foreword." *The Mafia of a Sicilian Village, 1860–1960*, by Anton Blok (Prospect Heights, Illinois: Waveland Press, 1974), p. xx, xiii–xxiv.

22. M. I. Finley, Denis Mack Smith, and Christopher Duggan, *A History of Sicily* (New York: Viking, 1986), p. 87.

23. Anton Blok, *The Mafia of a Sicilian Village, 1860–1960: A Study of Violent Peasant Entrepreneurs* (Prospect Heights, Illinois: Waveland Press, 1974), pp. 144–145.

24. Ibid., p. 146.

Chapter Nine

1. Jerre Mangione and Ben Morreale, *La Storia: Five Centuries of the Italian American Experience* (New York: Harper Collins: 1992), p. 53.

2. Vincenzo Linares, *I racconti popolari*. (Palermo: Luigi Pedone Lauriel, 1886), pp. 2–33.

3. Antonino Uccello, *Carcere e Mafia nei Canti Popolari Siciliani* (Palermo: Edizioni Libri Siciliani, 1965), p. 180.

4. M. I. Finley, Denis Mack Smith, and Christopher Duggan, *A History of Sicily* (New York: Viking, 1986), pp. 91–92.

5. Vincenzo Linares, *I racconti popolari*. (Palermo: Luigi Pedone Lauriel, 1886), p. 36.

6. M. I. Finley, Denis Mack Smith, and Christopher Duggan, *A History of Sicily* (New York: Viking, 1986), pp. 91–92.

Conclusion

1. Antonino Uccello, *Carcere e Mafia nei Canti Popolari Siciliani* (Palermo: Edizioni Libri Siciliani, 1965), pp. 48–49.

2. The "English Garden," a small park just off the Via della Libertà.

3. Antonino Uccello, *Carcere e Mafia nei Canti Popolari Siciliani* (Palermo: Edizioni Libri Siciliani, 1965), p. 59.

4. Joshua Hammer, "In Sicily, Defying the Mafia," *Smithsonian* (October 2010), Online.

5. Michael Serrill, Erik Amfitheatrof, and Judith Harris, "Italy Slicing up the Beast," *Time* 27, no. 8 (February 24, 1986), pp. 147–152.

6. The Web site I used to fill in the details of Giuliano's story is Giuseppe Sciortino Giuliano's, *La Vera Storia di Salvatore Giuliano*. I have noted those sections that I nearly translated verbatim through the

use of quotation marks. Sciortino's Web address is as follows: http://www.sicilian.net/salvatoregiuliano/italiano.php.

7. Cooperativa Teatrale Nuove Proposte. *Salvatore Giuliano.* Enna, Sicily: Playbill, 1986.

8. Ibid.

9. This same use of Abraham, Moses, Gabriel, David, and Christ is made even in the Sunday school classes of America.

10. Mary Taylor Simeti, *On Persephone's Island* (San Francisco: Northpoint Press, 1986), p. 196.

11. They are not the only people to do so. Americans—using a less transparent medium than folklore, the sermon, rewrite Chrisitianity in their own image as well.

12. Sabina Magliocco, *The Two Madonnas: The Politics of Festival in a Sardinian Community* (New York: Peter Lang, 1993), passim.

13. Michael Buonanno, "The Palermitan Epic: Dialogism and the Inscription of Social Relations," *Journal of American Folklore* 103, no. 409 (July-September 1990), pp. 324–333.

14. This conception of contamination is predicated on Jacques Derrida's discussion of "The Law of Genre" in *Critical Inquiry*'s special issue *On Narrative*: Jaques Derrida, "The Law of Genre," trans. Avital Ronell, *Critical Inquiry* 7, no. 1 (Autumn 1980), pp. 55–81.

Appendix

1. Giuseppe Argento, Vincenzo Argento, Giacomo Cuticchio, Nino Cuticchio, Sir Antonino Mancuso, and Pino Mancuso, *Morte dei Paladini* (Palermo: Antonio Pasqualino Museo Internazionale delle Marionette, 1980), Audiotape.

Bibliography

Abraham, Nicolas, and Maria Torok. *The Wolfman's Magic Word: A Cryptonomy.* Translated by Nicolas Rand. Minneapolis: University of Minnesota Press, 1986.

Abrahams, Roger. "Introductory Remarks to a Rhetorical Theory of Folklore." *Journal of American Folklore* 81, no. 320 (April-June 1968): pp. 143-58.

Accardi, Joseph. "Images of Giovanni de Rosalia: Playwright, Poet, and Nofrio." Joseph Accardi's Web site (May 2010): http://accardiweb.com/nofrio/.

Adamo, Vita. "An Interview with the Puppeteer Don Giovanni Filippo da Alcamo, Unpublished." Palermo: Antonio Pasqualino Museo Internazionale delle Marionette, Undated.

Alberti, Carmelo. *Il Teatro dei Pupi e lo Spettacolo Popolare Siciliano.* Milan: Mursia, 1977.

Argento, Giuseppe, Vincenzo Argento, Giacomo Cuticchio, Nino Cuticchio, Sir Antonino Mancuso, and Pino Mancuso. *Morte dei Paladini* (Palermo: Antonio Pasqualino Museo Internazionale delle Marionette , 1980): Audiotape.

Bakhtin, Mikhail. "Problems of Dostoevsky's Poetics." In *Theory and History of Literature*, Vol. . Translated by Caryl Emerson. Minneapolis: University of Minnesota Press, 1984.

Banfield, Edward C. *The Moral Basis of a Backward Society.* Glencoe, Illinois: Free Press, 1958.

Basile, David. "Agricultural Sicily." *Economic Geography* 17, no. 2 (April 1941): pp. 109-120.

Blok, Anton. *The Mafia of a Sicilian Village, 1860-1960: A Study of Violent Peasant Entrepreneurs.* Prospect Heights, Illinois: Waveland Press, 1974.

Bodel, Jean. *La Chanson des Saisnes.* Edited by Francisque Michel. Paris: J. Techner, 1839.

Brault, Gerard J. "Introduction." *The Song of Roland.* University Park: Pennsylvania State University Press, 1978.

Brinton, Crane. *The Anatomy of Revolution.* New York: Vintage Books, 1965.

Brooke, Robert, and Charlotte Hogg. "Open to Change: Ethos, Identification, and Critical Ethnography in Composition Studies." In *Ethnography Unbound: From Theory Shock to Critical Praxis*, edited by Stephen Gilbert Brown and Sidney I. Dobrin. Albany: State University of New York Press, 2004, pp. 115-129.

Buonanno, Michael. "The Genius of Palermo." In *The World Observed: Reflections on the Fieldwork Process*, edited by Bruce Jackson and Edward Ives. Champaign/Urbana: University of Illinois Press, 1997: pp. 84-99.

———. "The Palermitan Epic: Dialogism and the Inscription of Social Relations." *Journal of American Folklore* 103, no. 409 (July-September 1990): pp. 324-333.

Cammarata, Felice. "Gli Eroi Carolingi in Terra di Sicilia." In *Storia dei Paladini di Francia*, by Giusto Lodico. Palermo: Mazzone, 1970: pp. 5-22.

Celano, don Peppino. *Morte di Re Pepino* (Palermo: Antonio Pasqualino Museo Internazionale delle Marionette, Undated): Audiotape.

Cohn, Norman. *The Pursuit of the Millenium: Revolutionary Millenarians and Mystic Anarchists of the Middle Ages.*

Bibliography

New York, Oxford: Oxford University Press, 1961.

Cooperativa Teatrale Nuove Proposte. *Salvatore Giuliano*. Enna, Sicily: Playbill, 1986.

Croce, Marcella. *Pupi, Caretti, Contastorie: L'epica Cavalleresca nelle Tradizioni Popolari Siciliane*. Palermo: Diario Flacovia, 1999.

Cuticchio, Carmelo, and Giacomo Cuticchio. *Prime Imprese di Orlandino* (Palermo. Antonio Pasqualino Museo Internazionale delle Marionette, 1987): Audiotape.

Cuticchio, Girolamo and Sons. *Morte di Re Pepino* (Palermo: Antonio Pasqualino Museo Internazionale delle Marionette, 1985): Audiotape.

———. *Rinaldo Rubba la Bella Clarice* (Palermo: Antonio Pasqualino Museo Internazionale delle Marionette, 1987): Audiotape.

Cuticchio, Mimmo. *Storia e Testimonianze di una Famiglia di Pupari*. Palermo: Stass, 1978.

Cuticchio, Nino, and Rosa Cuticchio. *Battaglia di Orlando e Agricane* (Palermo: Antonio Pasqualino Museo Internazionale delle Marionette, 1987): Audiotape.

Danesi, Marcel. *A Basic Course in Anthropological Linguistics*. Toronto: Canadian Scholars Press, 2004.

Derrida, Jaques. "The Law of Genre." Translated by Avital Ronell. *Critical Inquiry: On Narrative* 7, no. 1 (Autumn 1980), pp. 55–81.

Di Lampedusa, Giuseppe. *The Leopard*. Translated by Archibald Colquhoun. London: Pantheon Books, 1960.

Dolci, Danilo. *Sicilian Lives*. Translated by Justin Vitiello. New York, Pantheon Books, 1981.

Douthat, Ross. "The Better Pope." *New York Times* Op-Ed, April 12, 2010: p. A25.

———. "A Time for Contrition." *New York Times* Op-Ed, March 28, 2010: p. A21.

Duggan, Joseph J. *The Song of Roland: Formulaic Style and Poetic Craft*. Berkeley: California University Press, 1973.

Einhard the Frank. *Life of Charlemagne*. Translated by Lewis Thorpe. Harmonsworth, Middlesex, England: Penguin, 1969.

Finley, M. I., Denis Mack Smith, and Christopher Duggan. *A History of Sicily*. New York: Viking, 1986.

Giuliano, Giuseppe Sciortino. *La Vera Storia di Salvatore Giuliano* (Web site): http://www.sicilian.net/salvatoregiuliano/itturiddu.php.

Gordon, Dexter. *Identity, Rhetoric, Ideology, and Nineteenth-Century Black Nationalism*. Carbondale: Southern Illinois University Press, 2003.

Gramsci, Antonio. *Selections from the Prison Notebooks*. Translated by Quintin Hoare and Geoffrey Nowell Smith. New York: International Publishers, 1972.

Hammer, Joshua. "In Sicily, Defying the Mafia." *Smithsonian*, October 2010: Online.

Hobsbawm, Eric. *Primitive Rebels: Studies in Archaic Forms of Social Movement in the 19th and 20th Centuries*. Manchester, UK: Manchester University Press, 1971.

Holmes, Urban Tigner. *A History of Old French Literature: The Origins to 1300*. New York: F. S. Crofts, 1937.

Howard, Robert Glen. "A Theory of Vernacular Rhetoric: The Case of the 'Sinner's Prayer' Online." *Folklore* 116, no. 2 (August 2005): pp. 175–191.

Jones, Henry Festing. *Diversions in Sicily*. London: Alston Rivers, 1909.

Koenigsberger, Helmut. *The Government of Sicily under Phillip II of Spain: A Study in the Practice of Empire*. London: Staples Press, 1951.

Le Gentil, Pierre. *The Chanson de Roland*. Cambridge, Massachusetts: Harvard University Press, 1969.

Linares, Vincenzo. *I racconti popolari*. Palermo: Luigi Pedone Lauriel, 1886.

Lodico, Giusto. *Storia dei Paladini di Francia*. Edited by Felice Cammarata. Trapani, Sicily: Celebes Editore, 1971.

Loewe, Ronald. "Euphemism, Parody, Insult, and Innuendo: Rhetoric and Ethnic Identity at the Mexican Periphery." *Journal of American Folklore* 120, no. 477 (Summer 2007): pp. 284–307.

Bibliography

Magliocco, Sabina. *The Two Madonnas: The Politics of Festival in a Sardinian Community*. New York: Peter Lang, 1993.

Mangione, Jerre. *Mount Allegro: A Memoir of Italian American Life*. Syracuse, New York: Syracuse University Press, 1981.

———, and Ben Morreale. *La Storia: Five Centuries of the Italian American Experience*. New York: Harper Perennial, 1992.

Matthew, Donald. *The Norman Kingdom of Sicily*. Cambridge: Cambridge University Press, 1992.

McCormick, John, Alfonso Cipolla, and Alessandro Napoli. *The Italian Puppet Theater: A History*. Jefferson, North Carolina: McFarland and Company, 2010.

Meli, Natale. *Primo Quaderno die Reali di Francia di Giusto Lodico* (Palermo: Antonio Pasqualino Museo Internazionale delle Marionette, Undated): Notebook.

Ono, Kent, and John Sloop. "The Critique of Vernacular Discourse." *Communication Monographs* 62, no. 1 (March 1995): pp. 19–46.

Oring, Elliott. "Legendry and the Rhetoric of Truth." *Journal of American Folklore* 121, no. 480 (Spring 2008): pp. 127–166.

Pasqualino, Antonio. *Del Testo alla Rappresentazione: Le Prime Imprese di Carlo Magno*. Palermo: Laboratorio Antropologico Universitario, 1986.

———. "Marionettes and Glove Puppets: Two Theatrical Systems in Southern Italy." *Semiotica* 47, nos. 1–4 (1983): pp. 219–280.

———. *L'Opera dei Pupi*. Palermo: Sellerio, 1977.

———. "Transformations of Chivalrous Literature in the Subject Matter of the Sicilian Marionette Theater." In *Varia Folklorica*, edited by Alan Dundes. The Hague, Paris: Mouton, 1978, pp. 183–200.

Pitrè, Giuseppe. *Fiabe e Leggende Popolari Siciliane*. Palermo: Luigi Pendone Lauriel, 1888.

———. *Novelle e Racconti Popolari Siciliani*, Vol. 1 In *Biblioteca delle Tradizioni Popolari Siciliane*, Vol. 4. Palermo: Luigi Pedone Lauriel, 1875.

———. "Le tradizioni cavalleresche popolari in Sicilia." *Romania* 13 (1884): pp. 315–398.

———. *Usi e Costumi, Credenze e Pregiudizi del Popolo Siciliano*. In *Biblioteca delle Tradizioni Popolari Siciliane*, Vol. 16. Bologna: Forni, 1969.

———. *Il Vespro Siciliano: Delle Tradizioni Popolari della Sicilia*. Palermo: Edizioni "Il Vespro," 1979.

Puzo, Mario. *The Sicilian*. New York: Random House, 1984.

Quatriglio, Giuseppe. *A Thousand Years in Sicily: From the Arabs to the Bourbons*. 2nd ed. Translated by Justin Vitiello. Brooklyn, New York: Legas, 1997.

Rajna, Pio. *Le Fonti dell'Orlando Furioso*. Florence: G. C. Sansoni, 1900.

Runciman, Steven. *The Sicilian Vespers*. Baltimore: Penguin, 1960.

Sciascia, Leonardo, and Rosario La Duca. *Palermo Felicissima*. Palermo: Edizioni il Punto, 1974.

Serrill, Michael, Erik Amfitheatrof, and Judith Harris. "Italy Slicing up the Beast." *Time* 27, no. 8 (February 24, 1986): pp. 147–152.

Shannon, Jonathan. "Performing al-Andalus, Remembering al-Andalus: Mediterranean Soundings from Mashriq to Maghrib." *Journal of American Folklore* 120, no. 477 (Summer 2007): pp. 308–334.

Simeti, Mary Taylor. *On Persephone's Island: A Sicilian Journal*. San Francisco: North Point Press, 1986.

Smith, Denis Mack. *A History of Sicily: Medieval Sicily 800–1713*. London: Chatto and Windus, 1968.

Tannen, Deborah. "I Can't Even Open my Mouth." In *Annual Editions: Anthropology 4/5*, edited by Elvio Angeloni. Guilford, Connecticut: McGraw-Hill/Dushkin, 2003, pp. 38–46.

———. "Interactional Sociolinguistics as a Resource for Intercultural Pragmatics." *Journal of Intercultural Pragmatics* 2, no. 2 (July 2005): pp. 205–208.

Tedlock, Dennis. *The Spoken Word and the Work of Interpretation*. Philadelphia: University of Pennsylvania Press, 1983.

Tilly, Charles. "Foreword." In *The Mafia of*

Bibliography

a Sicilian Village, 1860–1960, by Anton Blok. Prospect Heights, Illinois: Waveland Press, 1974): pp. xiii-xxiv.

Uccello, Antonino. *Carcere e Mafia nei Canti Popolari Siciliani*. Palermo: Edizioni Libri Siciliani, 1965.

_____. "Copioni di Briganti nel Repertorio dell'Opra." *Bollettino: Centro di Studi Filologici e Linguistici Siciliani* 10 (1965): pp. 354–370.

Zipes, Jack, and Joseph Russo. *The Collected Sicilian Folk and Fairy Tales of Giuseppe Pitrè*. New York and London: Routledge, 2009.

Index

abduction *see* themes
affiliation 85, 87, 89, 91–92, 94–95, 11–112, 124–125, 156, 158, 163, 172, 211n4, 211n6
affirmation *see* rhetoric of identity
Agrican 47, 49, 85, 108, 110, 112–121, 124–125, 211n4, 218
Alda the Beautiful 12, 48, 95–96, 99, 119, 139
allegory *see* legend
allocution *see* tones
amoral familism 153–155, 181–182
anaphora *see* tropes
ancestors *see* genii
angel 16, 40, 48, 57, 107–108, 117, 119–120, 145–146, 149–151; angel of the apocalypse 191; archangel 132
Angelica 12, 47, 49, 112–121, 139, 173, 211n3
Angevin Sicily 33–36, 33–36, 82–83, 167, 209n27
announcement *see* themes
antonomasia *see* tropes
apocalypse 10, 16, 111, 119–120, 124–125, 129, 132–133, 139–140, 191
apology *see* speech acts
apostrophe *see* tropes
apparition *see* themes
Arab Sicily 5–6, 7, 28–30, 32–33, 36, 40, 44, 50, 110–111, 126, 129, 167
Ariosto, Ludovico 70, 107, 135, 135–136, 195
aristocracy 5, 10, 14–15, 20, 22, 25, 30, 35, 36, 38, 46, 52, 65, 68–69, 79, 80, 82–83, 92, 97, 124, 152, 155–158, 163–172, 174, 181, 189–190, 193–196
armor 56, 63, 64, 65, 66, 74, 146, 151
Artemis 192
Arthur, King *see* Arthurian Cycle
Arthurian Cycle 2–3, 8, 49, 52, , 98, 99, 119, 124–125, 128–129, 140, 164–165, 211–212n2
Astolphe (Astolfo) 49, 143–144, 147, 150, 203–204
audience *see* themes

bandit (banditry) 10, 14–17, 20, 22, 51, 92, 95, 99–102, 103–106, 108, 112, 124, 133, 134, 150, 151–152, 158, 169–170, 172–173, 179– 180, 181, 182, 185–189, 190, 191, 194, 196, 211n3; courtly bandit 95, 99–103
bandits' lives 5, 9, 10, 14–17, 48, 67, 70, 86, 95, 100, 102, 103–106, 107, 124, 135, 173, 179–180, 185–189, 194, 195, 196; knight-become-bandit 108, 152, 173, 189, 193; *The Life and Death of Antonio DiBlasi* 103–106; *The Life and Death of Salvatore Giuliano* 185–189
banishment 10, 14, 15, 48, 49, 72, 74, 101, 106, 144, 163
baptism 16, 107, 108, 116–117, 121–122, 142–145, 154, 198–203
battle *see* themes
The Battle of Roland and Agrican 112–121
Bayard 49, 145, 146, 151
Beati Paoli *see* city legend
The Beautiful Annichia see fairy tales
benediction *see* speech acts
Berta (Charlemagne's sister; Roland's mother) 48, 72–81, 133, 144, 212n1
Berta de la Gran Piè (Charlemagne's mother) 48, 54–55, 133, 137–139
biblical heroes *see* Christian myth
Bishop Turpin 10, 130, 147, 143, 148–149
Bourbon Sicily 6, 24, 38–40, 41
bravado *see* tones
brawl *see* themes
Buiaforte 147–148, 151–152, 196
Byzantine Sicily 6, 29–30, 36, 208n26

cantastoria (epic singer) 52, 118, 135, 136
Cape Roland (Capo d'Orlando) 4, 134
Carolingian Cycle 3–4, 7–12, 25, 27, 46–51, 52, 54, 67–68, 70–71, 87, 122, 128–139, 140, 165, 191–193, 209n4, 211–212n2; malleability of 139–140; Palermitanization of 8–11, 25, 27, 46–48, 49–51, 67, 70–71, 87, 124–125, 139–140, 153, 191–193
Carolingian Dynasty 49–50, 122, 124, 128, 132–133, 166–167
Catechism *see* speech acts
challenge ("know that") *see* speech acts
Chanson de Roland *see* Song of Roland

Bibliography

Charlemagne 3, 4, 8, 10, 12, 14, 15, 16, 47, 48–49, 50, 52, 54, 55–68, 71, 72, 74, 77, 82, 87, 95, 96, 99, 100, 101, 108, 110, 111, 112, 114, 115, 121, 122, 124, 128, 129–134, 137, 141–143, 145–147, 149, 150, 189, 191, 196, 199–205, 209n2, 210n5, 212n1
chivalric romance see epic
Christ 12, 15–16, 90, 105–106, 107, 116, 117, 119, 120, 132, 146, 165, 176, 191, 192–193, 196, 215n9
Christian knight 49, 69, 112–117, 121, 125, 134, 146, 149, 151
Christian myth 5, 9, 48, 67, 111, 129, 159, 191–192; biblical heroes 16, 105, 106, 111, 191–192
"Christian soil" 55, 62, 109–112, 125, 126–127
Christianity 2–3, 10, 11, 16–19, 22, 28–33, 36, 49, 55, 58, 62, 67, 69, 90, 95, 109–117, 121, 122, 125–127, 129, 131–133, 134, 140, 142–143, 145, 149, 150, 159, 166–167, 191, 192, 199, 208n26
Church of the Holy Spirit see The Sicilian Vespers
city legend: Beati Paoli 22–23, 167, 170, 173–181, 189, 190, 196; Genius of Palermo 21, 23–25, 81, 88, 91, 191, 196, 217; Sicilian Vespers 33–35
Clarice 49, 95–103, 118–119, 125, 139, 145, 150
class 5, 9, 11, 15, 24, 36, 39, 41, 46, 53, 68–69, 71, 78, 80, 85, 89, 92, 95, 97, 106–107, 152, 153, 155–158, 163, 165–171, 172, 176, 181, 189, 192, 193, 194–196, 214n14; see also aristocracy; clergy; Mafia; the people
clergy (clerical class, clerics) 5, 10, 14, 15, 17, 20, 92, 124, 152, 155–156, 165–171, 172, 181, 192, 193, 194–196; see also priest
Clermont, House of 54, 134–135
Cola Pesce 3
Commedia dell'Arte 14, 66–69
contastoria (storyteller) 52, 65, 122, 135–137, 139–140
copione see notebook
corporate structure see culture
Corrado 21–23, 172–181
Costanza 21–23, 172–181
council see themes
courtly bandit see bandit
cowardice (accusation of) see speech acts
creed see speech acts
Cross Eyes (Occhi Storti; Roland's nickname) 12, 71, 119, 152, 173
cryptonym see tropes
cultural text see culture
culture 8, 89–90, 92–94, 194, 207n3, 209n42; corporate structure 94; cultural text 91; enculturation 194; "grouping up" 95; wiki 94

Cupid 98, 99
Cyclops 1

damsel 14, 97–98, 102, 118
David, King 16, 105–106, 119–121, 191, 192, 196, 215n9
Death of King Pepin 55–67
Death of the Paladins 141–152, 199–205
destrier see Bayard and Vegliantin
devil 111, 147
dialogism 16, 17–20, 79, 83–87, 103, 156, 159, 163–164, 193–194
DiBlasi, Antonio see bandits' lives
diction see voice
dispatch see themes
dragon 73, 77–78, 80, 86, 113, 119–120
Durandal 48, 86, 113–114, 142, 148

economy see Palermo
encounter see themes
enculturation see culture
entrance see themes
epic (chivalric romance) 5, 7–17, 20, 25, 30, 46–48, 52, 55, 64, 66–67, 70, 77–81, 82, 83–87, 92, 93, 94–95, 101, 102, 105, 106–108, 110–111, 112, 118, 119, 120, 121, 124, 125, 127, 129, 133–135, 137, 140, 152, 156, 158–159, 163–165, 166, 170, 185–186, 190–196, 213n2
exit see themes

Faerie 164
fairy tales 5, 9, 48, 52, 55, 80, 119, 156–164, 165, 193, 213n2, 213n13; The Beautiful Annichia 156–158; The Talking Belly 159–164
farce (Vastasate) 5, 9, 10, 14, 16, 48, 54, 66–71, 77–80, 95, 194–196, 213n11; see also Commedia dell'Arte
The First Adventures of Rolandin 72–82, 86–87
Florindo 97–99, 102, 106
folklore 3, 5, 10, 14–16, 27, 48, 50, 89–94, 111, 125–126, 128, 132–133, 136, 140, 165–166, 173
formulae (stock phrases) see tropes
Fusbert 49, 146, 151

Galerana 48, 95–96, 99–100, 212n1
Ganelon 10, 12, 14, 48, 49, 101–102, 131–132, 141–152, 189, 191, 209n2, 212n1
genealogy see genii
genii (ancestors) 49, 64, 122, 139
Genius of Palermo see city legend
Genre 5, 10, 14–16, 66–67, 70, 79–80, 106–108, 158–159, 164, 193–196, 215n14; see also multi-genericity
genres of discourse see tones

gestures 60–61, 63–64, 60, 66, 70–71, 95–96, 99–100, 113–114, 150, 184
giant 113–114, 119–120, 146
Giuliano, Salvatore 50–51, 186–189, 190, 214–215, 218; *see also* bandits' lives
glorification *see* themes
gnomic utterance *see* tropes
God (the Father) 22, 67–68, 108, 119–120, 129, 191–192
Greek Sicily 27–29
"grouping up" *see* culture

Hades 1–2
hermit 122, 144
heroes 1, 10, 16, 49–51, 52, 54, 71, 95, 118–119, 134, 139–140, 149, 164–165, 191–193, 214n14; biblical heroes *see* Christian myth
history *see* Palermo
History of the French Paladins 101, 137–139, 140–141
Hohenstaufen (Imperial) Sicily 3, 33–34, 36, 49–50, 126, 129, 166–168, 174, 208n27
Holy Roman Empire 49–50, 119–120, 128–129, 132–133
Holy Water *see* Baptism
homonym *see* tropes
honor *see* omertà
horn *see* oliphant
hyperbole *see* tropes

identification *see* affiliation
Iliad see Trojan Cycle
Immaculate Virgin 40, 173, 197; Immaculate Conception, Feast of the 5, 20–23, 27, 173, 197
intreccio 70
Iroquoian Folklore 164
Islam (Muslim) 2–3, 10, 17–18, 19, 28–33, 36, 69, 109–112, 125–127, 129, 131, 132–133, 166–167, 208n26, 211n2
Islamophobia 17–18, 69, 109–112, 125–127, 132–133, 139–140
Italian language *see* tones
Italian Sicily 6, 40–41, 166

Jesus *see* Christ
Judas 189, 191–192
justice 24, 76–77, 102, 163, 176–177, 179, 181
justification *see* speech acts

legend 1, 3, 4, 5, 8, 9, 12, 21–23, 23–25, 34–35, 48, 50, 90–91, 105, 129–132, 134, 139–140, 141, 164–165, 170, 172–181, 189, 191–193, 214n14; legend as allegory 12–14, 20, 105–106, 118–120, 159, 163–165, 190–193; legend as political critique 5, 15, 156, 165, 192–193, 213n2

The Life and Death of Antonio DiBlasi see bandits' lives
The Life and Death of Salvatore Giuliano see bandit's lives
Life of Charlemagne 129–130
Life of Constantine see saints' lives
litotes *see* tropes
liturgy *see* speech acts
Lodico, Giusto *see History of the French Paladins*

Mafia (Mafioso) 5, 10, 12, 14, 15, 17, 20, 46, 92, 94, 102, 118–119, 124, 152, 155–156, 165–171, 172–173, 181–182, 183–186, 188–190, 192, 193, 194–196
The Mafioso (Renaud's nickname) 12, 119, 152
Mahabharata 165
Maiance, House of 10, 14, 48–49, 54–55, 56–58, 65–66, 67, 133–134, 137–139, 142, 149–150, 190, 209n2, 212n1
Mainetto (Young Charlemagne's pseudonym) 58–59, 67, 133
marionette 10, 12, 59–60, 63–64, 66, 71, 207n2
marionette theater 4, 8, 10, 25, 27, 47, 52, 53, 59–67, 70, 154
Marsilius 10, 48–49, 110, 131, 141–149, 150–151, 212n1
masque (vastone) 14–17, 20, 22, 67–69, 70–71, 73–74, 77–87, 92, 95, 105, 124, 133, 150, 191, 193
Merlin *see* Arthurian Cycle
metaphor *see* tropes
metonymy *see* tropes
millenarianism *see* apocalypse
miracle *see* themes
Morgan la Fey *see* Arthurian Cycle
Mount Oliver (Monte Oliviero) 4, 134, 207n3
multi-genericity 14–17, 66–69, 70, 79–80, 106–108, 158–159, 193–196, 215n14
Muslim *see* Islam
myth *see* Christian myth

narrative 9–10, 15, 19, 24, 25, 47–48, 52, 53–54, 59, 66–67, 70, 77, 78, 79, 80, 83–84, 84–85, 94–95, 107–108, 139–140, 156, 158–159, 164–165, 173, 193–196, 214n14, 215n14
narrative repertoire *see* repertoire
nobility *see* aristocracy
noble diction *see* tones
Nofrio 14–15, 68–70, 73–75, 78–80, 84, 86–87, 213n11
Norman Sicily 2–4, 6–7, 8, 23, 27, 28–33, 36–38, 40–41, 47, 49–50, 110–111, 123–124, 126, 128–129, 165–167, 174, 208n27
notebook (*copione*) 103–104, 137, 138–139

223

oath *see* speech acts
obedience 11, 15–16, 112, 124, 139–140, 152, 172, 189–190, 196
Odysseus 1
oliphant 10, 15–16, 40, 111, 131–132, 146–148
Oliver 4, 70–71, 74–77, 80–81, 130–131, 140, 143–144, 146–148, 207n3
omertà (code of silence, honor) 12, 100–102, 105, 152, 181, 182, 189

Paladins 3–4, 8, 11, 49, 50, 106–107, 111, 128–129, 131–133
Palermitanization *see* Carolingian Cycle
Palermo 5–25; economy 41–46; 52, 127, 191, 207n3; history 5–6, 27–41; 49–50, 82–83, 110–111, 152, 155, 165–166, 168, 170, 185, 190–191; social order 5, 16, 20, 24–25, 27, 41–46, 67, 87, 93–94, 95, 118–119, 124–125, 139, 152, 153–156, 165–171, 172, 181–182, 185–186, 190–191, 192–196
Papacy 33–34, 48, 49–50, 109, 122, 123–124, 126, 166–168
paralipsis *see* tropes
parallelism *see* tropes
paraphrasis *see* tropes
Paris 48–49, 55, 57, 60–61, 65, 72, 82, 112, 114, 134
peers *see* Paladins
penitence *see* speech acts
the people (*popolo*; *popolino*) 5, 14, 15, 16, 20, 22, 24, 25, 36, 38, 41–44, 46, 52, 53, 54, 67–69, 71, 78, 79, 80, 82–83, 92, 97, 106–107, 133, 152, 153, 155–158, 163–164, 165–171, 172, 181–182, 186, 189–190, 193–196
Pepin, King 48, 54–61, 64–65, 122, 133, 137–139
Persephone 1–2
Phoenician (Punic) Sicily 6, 27–28
play script *see* notebook
Polyphemos *see* Cyclops
pope *see* papacy
popular diction *see* tones
popular press 8, 94, 137, 138
porter *see* vastone
power 194–196
prayer *see* speech acts
priest 20, 39–40, 46, 92, 97, 99, 166, 172, 193–194, 213n2
prince 67–68, 78, 82, 83; *see also* aristocracy
Prospero 21–23, 172–181
protest *see* speech acts
pun *see* tropes
Punic Sicily *see* Phoenician Sicily
puppet *see* marionette
puppet theater *see* marionette theater
puppeteer 10, 12, 16–17, 48, 52–54, 59–66, 70, 71, 83–84, 92, 101, 103, 135–139, 141, 158–159, 179–180
puppetry *see* marionette theater

rebellion 10–11, 14–16, 22, 25, 30, 33–36, 38–40, 95, 105, 106–107, 112, 124, 129, 133–134, 139–140, 152
Renaud 3, 10–12, 14–17, 20, 22, 25, 47–50, 52, 71, 82, 87, 95–103, 105–108, 117–120, 125, 128, 133–139, 141, 144–146, 149–152, 173, 189–193, 196
Renaud Abducts the Beautiful Clarice 95–103
repertoire 14, 47–48, 52–53, 66–67, 70, 128, 133–136, 140, 156, 158–159, 164, 214n14
retribution *see* vendetta
revolt *see* rebellion
rhetoric 16, 64, 83–87, 88–95, 99–100, 109–112, 124–127, 156, 185, 193–195, 213n2; *see also* speech acts; tones; tropes
rhetoric of identity 10, 20, 87, 88–95, 111, 163, 193; affirmation 90, 91
righteous indignation *see* tones
riot *see* rebellion
Roland 2–3, 10–11, 14–17, 20, 25, 47–50, 52, 55, 85–87, 111–121, 125, 128–140, 141–152, 173, 180, 189–193, 196; *see also* Rolandin
Rolandin (diminutive of Roland) 20, 48–49, 52, 70–82, 85–87, 133, 211n9
Roman Sicily 6–7, 21–22, 24–25, 27–29, 49–50
Roncevaux 10, 15–16, 49, 70–71, 80, 95, 122, 129–132, 133–134, 137, 141–152, 190, 196, 199–205
Rosalia, Saint *see* saints' lives
ruling class *see* aristocracy

saint 7, 14–17, 22, 86, 92, 95, 102, 105, 108, 112, 121–124, 132–134, 150, 152, 158, 173, 189–190, 193–195
saints' lives 5, 9–10, 14, 16, 48, 67, 70, 107, 121–124, 196; Constantine 122; Rosalia 122–124
Saracen (Saracen knight) 10–11, 14, 15, 16, 33, 47, 49, 55, 60–62, 66, 68–69, 79, 96, 110, 111, 120–121, 125, 130–134, 139–140, 141–149, 151–152, 191, 196
Saragossa 48–49, 66, 130–131, 134, 141–143, 212n1
sarcasm *see* tones
Saturn 24–25
script *see* notebook
shepherd 12, 41–42, 44, 48, 57–58, 67–68, 72–73, 77–78, 82, 86–87, 97–99, 155, 169
Sicilian dialect *see* tones
Sicilian Vespers *see* city legend
Sicily 1–4, 8, 17–18, 27–43, 49–50, 83, 103,

110–111, 120, 122–124, 125–126, 128–129, 152, 155, 165–171, 182–183; *see also* Palermo
singer *see* cantastoria
social order *see* Palermo
soldier 14, 34, 46, 49, 62–63, 76–77, 104–105, 119, 120, 142, 183–185, 196
soliloquy *see* speech acts
The Song of Roland 130–132
Spanish Sicily 35–36, 40, 174–175, 208–209n27
speech acts 19, 20, 80, 85, 88, 89, 93, 100, 101, 193; accusation (of cowardice) 10, 53, 56, 75, 80, 81, 97, 98, 99, 113, 116, 149; apology 100; benediction 121; boast 15, 20, 66, 86, 99, 100, 101, 117, 118; Catechism 67; challenge ("know that") 15, 20, 59, 75, 85, 115, 116; creed 116–117, 121; insinuation 150; justification 100, 125; lament (complaint) 19–20, 57, 72, 75–76, 144–145; liturgy 67, 121; oath 79, 101, 117, 119, 120–121; penitence 121; prayer 14, 20, 121; protest 75, 118; soliloquy 84; submission 150; supplication 14, 86, 118, 121; threat 17, 79, 89, 101, 102, 190, 211n3; vocative 84, 118, 150
speech patterns *see* tones
storyteller *see* contastoria
stychomachia *see* tropes
sub-themes *see* themes
supplication *see* speech acts
sword *see* Durandal; Fusbert
synecdoche *see* tropes
synonymy *see* tropes

The Talking Belly see fairy tales
theft *see* themes
themes 14, 16–17, 64, 66–67, 70, 79, 193–194, 207n7; abduction 17, 95, 99, 100, 118; announcement 62–63, 70, 77, 79; apparition 16, 107–108, 124; audience 62–63, 77, 79; battle 16, 64, 65–66, 70, 79, 80, 135–136, 209n3; brawl 16, 79–80; council 16, 59, 60–65, 66, 70, 77, 79, 84, 99–100, 110, 131, 137–139, 149–150; dispatch 62–63, 70, 77, 79; encounter 16, 79; entrance 16, 79; exit 16, 79; glorification 16, 107–108, 124; miracle 16, 107–108, 124; theft 17, 95
Three Matters 128–129, 211n2
tones (speech patterns; genres of speech) 20, 83–89, 93, 100, 118, 121, 150–151, 193–194; allocution (hortatory address) 84, 149–150; bravado 101; familiar diction (tu) 17, 20, 71, 78, 79, 80, 82, 85, 95, 121; ferocity 94, 100, 101, 102, 151, 190, 211n3; imperative 100, 101, 118, 151; irony 86, 89, 100, 151; Italian (or noble) diction 17, 20, 71, 78, 82, 85–86, 183; polite diction (voi) 17, 20, 71, 78, 80, 82, 85, 121; righteous indignation 101; sarcasm 17, 20, 89, 101, 151, 185; Sicilian (or popular) diction 17, 20, 69, 71, 78, 79, 82, 85–86, 87
traitor 10, 14, 48, 49, 54, 66, 116, 132, 134, 147, 149–150, 189–190
Trojan Cycle 128–129, 165, 192, 211n2
tropes (figures of speech) 20, 80, 83, 84–85, 86–87, 88, 89, 90, 91, 92–93, 101, 121, 193; anaphora 20, 79, 118; antonomasia 88; apostrophe 15, 20, 84, 86, 88; cryptonym 88; formulae (stock phrases) 66, 83, 85, 86, 121, 211n4; gnomic utterance 163–164; hyperbole 15, 20, 88, 100; litotes 88; metaphor 84, 88, 92; metonymy 88; paralipsis 81, 84, 85; parallelism 101, 118; paraphrasis 121; pun 15, 20, 69, 84–85, 159; stychomachia 54; synecdoche 88; synonymy 101, 118
tu *see* tones
Tunisia (and Tunisians) 17–20, 28–30, 109–110

Vastasate *see* farce
vastone *see* masque
Vegliantin 117, 147–148
vendetta 10–11, 22–23, 35, 48–49, 55, 57, 102, 104, 114, 131–132, 152, 172, 177, 180–182, 184, 187, 189–190, 195–196
vengeance *see* vendetta
Venus 97–98
Virgin Mary *see* Immaculate Virgin
Virticchio 14–15, 68–70, 73–75, 77–80, 84, 86–87
vocative *see* speech acts
voi *see* tones
voice (diction) 10, 14–16, 20, 48, 60, 77, 79–80, 83–87, 91, 93, 94, 100–103, 118–119, 121, 124–125, 149–151, 163–164, 180, 185, 193–194, 195, 211n3; *see also* speech acts; tones; tropes

web of signification 25, 91, 93, 189
wiki *see* culture

www.ingramcontent.com/pod-product-compliance
Lightning Source LLC
Chambersburg PA
CBHW032050300426
44116CB00007B/679